Course **3**
Part B

Contemporary Mathematics in Context

A Unified Approach

CORE-PLUS MATHEMATICS PROJECT

Course 3 Part B

Contemporary Mathematics in Context
A Unified Approach

Arthur F. Coxford
James T. Fey
Christian R. Hirsch
Harold L. Schoen
Gail Burrill
Eric W. Hart
Ann E. Watkins
with
Mary Jo Messenger
Beth Ritsema

Glencoe McGraw-Hill

New York, New York   Columbus, Ohio   Woodland Hills, California   Peoria, Illinois

Glencoe/McGraw-Hill

*A Division of The **McGraw·Hill** Companies*

This project was supported, in part, by the National Science Foundation.
The opinions expressed are those of the authors and not necessarily those of the Foundation.

Send all inquiries to:
Glencoe/McGraw-Hill
8787 Orion Place
Columbus, OH 43240-4027

ISBN 1-57039-575-6 (Part A)
ISBN 1-57039-579-9 (Part B)   Core-Plus Course 3 SE Part B

Printed in the United States of America.

4 5 6 7 8 9 10 11 12   058   06 05 04 03 02 01

Core-Plus Mathematics Project

Project Director
Christian R. Hirsch
Western Michigan University

Project Co-Directors
Arthur F. Coxford
University of Michigan

James T. Fey
University of Maryland

Harold L. Schoen
University of Iowa

Senior Curriculum Developers
Gail Burrill
University of Wisconsin-Madison

Eric W. Hart
Western Michigan University

Ann E. Watkins
California State University, Northridge

Professional Development Coordinator
Beth Ritsema
Western Michigan University

Evaluation Coordinator
Steven W. Ziebarth
Western Michigan University

Advisory Board
Diane Briars
Pittsburgh Public Schools

Jeremy Kilpatrick
University of Georgia

Kenneth Ruthven
University of Cambridge

David A. Smith
Duke University

Edna Vasquez
Detroit Renaissance High School

Curriculum Development Consultants
Alverna Champion
Grand Valley State University

Cherie Cornick
Wayne County Alliance for Mathematics and Science

Edgar Edwards
(Formerly) Virginia State Department of Education

Richard Scheaffer
University of Florida

Martha Siegel
Towson University

Edward Silver
University of Pittsburgh

Lee Stiff
North Carolina State University

Collaborating Teachers
Emma Ames
Oakland Mills High School, Maryland

Cheryl Bach
Sitka High School, Alaska

Mary Jo Messenger
Howard County Public Schools, Maryland

Valerie Mills
Ann Arbor Public Schools, Michigan

Jacqueline Stewart
Okemos High School, Michigan

Michael Verkaik
Holland Christian High School, Michigan

Marcia Weinhold
Kalamazoo Area Mathematics and Science Center, Michigan

Graduate Assistants
Kelly Finn
University of Iowa

Judy Flowers
University of Michigan

Johnette Masson
University of Iowa

Chris Rasmussen
University of Maryland

Bettie Truitt
University of Iowa

Roberto Villarubi
University of Maryland

Rebecca Walker
Western Michigan University

Technical Coordinator
Wendy Weaver
Western Michigan University

Production and Support Staff
James Laser
Kelly MacLean
Michelle Magers
Cheryl Peters
Jennifer Rosenboom
Kathryn Wright
Western Michigan University

Software Developers
Jim Flanders
Colorado Springs, Colorado

Eric Kamischke
Interlochen, Michigan

Core-Plus Mathematics Project Field-Test Sites

Special thanks are extended to these teachers and their students who participated in the testing and evaluation of Course 3.

Ann Arbor Huron High School
Ann Arbor, Michigan
Ginger Gajar
Brenda Garr

Ann Arbor Pioneer High School
Ann Arbor, Michigan
Jim Brink
Tammy Schirmer

Arthur Hill High School
Saginaw, Michigan
Virginia Abbott

Battle Creek Central High School
Battle Creek, Michigan
Teresa Ballard
Steven Ohs

Bedford High School
Temperance, Michigan
Ellen Bacon
David J. DeGrace

Bloomfield Hills Andover High School
Bloomfield Hills, Michigan
Jane Briskey
Homer Hassenzahl
Cathy King
Linda Robinson
Mike Shelley
Roger Siwajek

Brookwood High School
Snellville, Georgia
Ginny Hanley
Marie Knox

Caledonia High School
Caledonia, Michigan
Deborah Bates
Jenny Diekevers
Kim Drefcenski
Larry Timmer
Gerard Wagner

Centaurus High School
Lafayette, Colorado
Gail Reichert

Clio High School
Clio, Michigan
Bruce Hanson
Lee Sheridan

Davison High School
Davison, Michigan
Evelyn Ailing
John Bale
Dan Tomczak

Dexter High School
Dexter, Michigan
Kris Chatas

Ellet High School
Akron, Ohio
Marcia Csipke
Jim Fillmore

Firestone High School
Akron, Ohio
Barbara Crucs

Flint Northern High School
Flint, Michigan
Al Wojtowicz

Goodrich High School
Goodrich, Michigan
John Doerr
Barbara Ravas
Bonnie Stojek

Grand Blanc High School
Grand Blanc, Michigan
Charles Carmody
Maria Uhler-Chargo

Grass Lake Junior/Senior High School
Grass Lake, Michigan
Brad Coffey
Larry Poertner

Gull Lake High School
Richland, Michigan
   Dorothy Louden

Kalamazoo Central High School
Kalamazoo, Michigan
   Gloria Foster
   Amy Schwentor

Kelloggsville Public Schools
Wyoming, Michigan
   Nancy Hoorn
   Steve Ramsey
   John Ritzler

Knott County Central High School
Hindman, Kentucky
   P. Denise Gibson
   Cynthia Tackett

Midland Valley High School
Langley, South Carolina
   Ron Bell
   Janice Lee

North Lamar High School
Paris, Texas
   Tommy Eads
   Barbara Eatherly

Okemos High School
Okemos, Michigan
   Lisa Crites
   Jacqueline Stewart

Portage Northern High School
Portage, Michigan
   Pete Jarrad
   Scott Moore
   Jerry Swoboda

Prairie High School
Cedar Rapids, Iowa
   Dave LaGrange
   Judy Slezak

San Pasqual High School
Escondido, California
   Damon Blackman
   Ron Peet

Sitka High School
Sitka, Alaska
   Cheryl Bach
   Mikolas Bekeris
   Dan Langbauer
   Tom Smircich

Sturgis High School
Sturgis, Michigan
   Kathy Parkhurst
   Jo Ann Roe

Sweetwater High School
National City, California
   Bill Bokesch

Tecumseh High School
Tecumseh, Michigan
   Jennifer Keffer
   Elizabeth Lentz
   Carl Novak

Traverse City High School
Traverse City, Michigan
   Diana Lyon-Schumacher
   Ken May
   Diane Moore

Vallivue High School
Caldwell, Idaho
   Scott Coulter
   Kathy Harris

Ypsilanti High School
Ypsilanti, Michigan
   Keith Kellman
   Mark McClure
   Valerie Mills

Overview of Course 3

Part A

Unit 1 ▶ Multiple-Variable Models

Multiple-Variable Models develops student ability to construct and reason with linked quantitative variables and relations involving several variables and several constraints.

Topics include formulas relating several variables by a single equation, systems of equations with several dependent variables or constraints, patterns of change in one or more variables in response to changes in others, solution of systems of equations and inequalities, and linear programming.

Lesson 1 *Linked Variables*
Lesson 2 *Algebra, Geometry, and Trigonometry*
Lesson 3 *Linked Equations*
Lesson 4 *Linear Programming*
Lesson 5 *Looking Back*

Unit 3 ▶ Symbol Sense and Algebraic Reasoning

Symbol Sense and Algebraic Reasoning develops student ability to represent and draw inferences about algebraic relations and functions using symbolic expressions and manipulations.

Topics include use of polynomial, exponential, and rational expressions to model relations among quantitative variables and field properties of real numbers and their application to expression of algebraic relations in equivalent forms and to solution of equations and inequalities by methods including factoring and the quadratic formula.

Lesson 1 *Algebra and Functions*
Lesson 2 *Algebraic Operations: Part 1*
Lesson 3 *Algebraic Operations: Part 2*
Lesson 4 *Reasoning to Solve Equations and Inequalities*
Lesson 5 *Proof through Algebraic Reasoning*
Lesson 6 *Looking Back*

Unit 2 ▶ Modeling Public Opinion

Modeling Public Opinion develops student understanding of how public opinion can be measured. The situations analyzed include elections (in which there are more than two choices) and sample surveys, including political polling.

Topics include preferential voting, election analysis methods, Arrow's Theorem, fairness in social decision making, surveys, sampling, sampling distributions, relationship between a sample and a population, confidence intervals, margin of error, and critical analysis of elections and surveys.

Lesson 1 *Voting Models*
Lesson 2 *Surveys and Samples*
Lesson 3 *Sampling Distributions: From Population to Sample*
Lesson 4 *Confidence Intervals: From Sample to Population*
Lesson 5 *Looking Back*

Unit 4 ▶ Shapes and Geometric Reasoning

Shapes and Geometric Reasoning introduces students to formal reasoning and deduction in geometric settings.

Topics include inductive and deductive reasoning, counterexamples, the role of assumptions in proof, conclusions concerning supplementary and vertical angles and the angles formed by parallel lines and transversals, conditions insuring similarity and congruence of triangles and their application to quadrilaterals and other shapes, and necessary and sufficient conditions for parallelograms.

Lesson 1 *Reasoned Arguments*
Lesson 2 *Reasoning about Similar and Congruent Triangles*
Lesson 3 *Parallelograms: Necessary and Sufficient Conditions*
Lesson 4 *Looking Back*

Overview of Course 3

Part B

Unit 5 ▷ Patterns in Variation

Patterns in Variation extends student understanding of the measurement of variation, develops student ability to use the normal distribution as a model of variation, and introduces students to the probability and statistical inference involved in the control charts used in industry for statistical process control.

Topics include standard deviation and its properties, normal distribution and its relation to standard deviation, statistical process control, control charts, control limits, mutually exclusive events, and the Addition Rule of probability.

Lesson 1 *Measuring Variation with the Standard Deviation*
Lesson 2 *The Normal Distribution*
Lesson 3 *Statistical Process Control*
Lesson 4 *Looking Back*

Unit 6 ▷ Families of Functions

Families of Functions reviews and extends student ability to recognize different function patterns in numerical and graphical data and to interpret and construct appropriate symbolic representations modeling those data patterns.

Topics include review of linear, polynomial, exponential, rational, and periodic functions (including effects of parameters on numeric and graphic patterns) and construction of function rules for function tables and graphs that are transformations of basic types (translation, reflection, stretch).

Lesson 1 *Function Models Revisited*
Lesson 2 *Customizing Models 1: Reflections and Vertical Transformations*
Lesson 3 *Customizing Models 2: Horizontal Transformations*
Lesson 4 *Looking Back*

Unit 7 ▷ Discrete Models of Change

Discrete Models of Change extends student ability to represent, analyze, and solve problems in situations involving sequential and recursive change.

Topics include iteration and recursion as tools to model and analyze sequential change in real-world contexts; arithmetic, geometric, and other sequences; arithmetic and geometric series; finite differences; linear and nonlinear recurrence relations; and function iteration, including graphical iteration and fixed points.

Lesson 1 *Modeling Sequential Change Using Recursion*
Lesson 2 *A Discrete View of Function Models*
Lesson 3 *Iterating Functions*
Lesson 4 *Looking Back*

Capstone ▷ Looking Back at Course 3

Making the Best of It: Optimal Forms and Strategies is a thematic, two-week, project-oriented activity that enables students to pull together and apply the important mathematical concepts and methods developed throughout the course.

Contents

Preface

The first three courses in the *Contemporary Mathematics in Context* series provide a common core of broadly useful mathematics for all students. They were developed to prepare students for success in college, in careers, and in daily life in contemporary society. The series builds upon the theme of *mathematics as sense-making*. Through investigations of real-life contexts, students develop a rich understanding of important mathematics that makes sense to them and which, in turn, enables them to make sense out of new situations and problems.

Each course in the *Contemporary Mathematics in Context* curriculum shares the following mathematical and instructional features.

■ *Multiple Connected Strands* Each year the curriculum features four strands of mathematics, unified by fundamental themes, by common topics, and by habits of mind or ways of thinking. Developing mathematics each year along multiple strands helps students develop diverse mathematical insights and nurtures their differing strengths and talents.

■ *Mathematical Modeling* The curriculum emphasizes mathematical modeling and modeling concepts, including data collection, representation, interpretation, prediction, and simulation. The modeling perspective permits students to experience mathematics as a means of making sense of data and problems that arise in diverse contexts within and across cultures.

■ *Access* The curriculum is designed so that core topics are accessible to a wide range of students.

Differences in student performance and interest can be accommodated by the depth and level of abstraction to which common topics are pursued, by the nature and degree of difficulty of applications, and by opportunities for student choice on homework tasks and projects.

■ *Technology* Numerical, graphics, and programming and link capabilities, such as those found on many graphics calculators, are assumed and capitalized on. This use of technology permits the curriculum and instruction to emphasize multiple representations (numerical, graphical, and symbolic) and to focus on goals in which mathematical thinking and problem solving are central.

■ *Active Learning* Instruction and assessment practices are designed to promote mathematical thinking through the use of engaging problem situations. Both collaborative groups and individual work are used as students explore, conjecture, verify, apply, evaluate, and communicate mathematical ideas.

Unified Mathematics

Each course of *Contemporary Mathematics in Context* features important mathematics drawn from four "strands."

The Algebra and Functions strand develops student ability to recognize, represent, and solve problems involving relations among quantitative variables. Central to the development is the use of functions as mathematical models. The key algebraic models in the curriculum are linear, exponential, power, and periodic functions, as well as combinations of these various types. Attention is also given to modeling with systems of equations, both linear and nonlinear, and to symbolic reasoning.

The primary goal of the Geometry and Trigonometry strand is to develop visual thinking and the ability to construct, reason with, interpret, and apply mathematical models of patterns in visual and physical contexts. Specific activities include describing patterns with regard to shape, size, and location; representing patterns with drawings or coordinates; predicting changes and invariants in shapes and patterns; and organizing geometric facts and relationships through deductive reasoning.

The primary role of the Statistics and Probability strand is to develop student ability to analyze data intelligently, to recognize and measure variation, and to understand the patterns that underlie probabilistic situations. Graphical methods of data analysis, simulations, sampling, and experience with the collection and interpretation of real data are featured.

The Discrete Mathematics strand develops student ability to model and solve problems involving sequential change, decision-making in finite settings, and relationships among a finite number of elements. Topics include matrices, vertex-edge graphs, recursion, voting methods, and systematic counting methods (combinatorics). Key themes are existence (Is there a solution?), optimization (What is the best solution?), and algorithmic problem-solving (Can you efficiently construct a solution?).

These four strands are connected within units by fundamental ideas, such as symmetry, matrices, recursion, functions, and data analysis and curve-fitting. The strands also are connected across units by mathematical habits of mind, such as visual thinking, recursive thinking, searching for and describing patterns, making and checking conjectures, reasoning with multiple representations, inventing mathematics, and providing convincing arguments. The strands are unified further by the fundamental themes of data, representation, shape, and change. Important mathematical ideas are continually revisited through this attention to connections within and across strands, enabling students to develop a robust understanding of mathematics.

Active Learning and Teaching

The manner in which mathematical ideas are developed can be as important as the mathematics to which students are introduced. *Contemporary Mathematics in Context* features multi-day lessons centered on big ideas. Lessons are organized around a four-phase cycle of classroom activities, described on the following page, designed to engage students in investigating and making sense of problem situations, in constructing important mathematical concepts and methods, and in communicating, both orally and in writing, their thinking and the results of their efforts. Most classroom activities are designed to be completed by students working together collaboratively in heterogeneous groupings of two to four students.

The launch phase promotes class discussion of a situation and of related questions to think about, setting the context for the student work to follow. In the second or explore phase, students investigate more focused problems and questions related to the launch situation. This investigative work is followed by a class discussion in which students summarize mathematical ideas developed in their groups, providing an opportunity to construct a shared understanding of important concepts, methods, and approaches. Finally, students are given a task to complete on their own, assessing their initial understanding of the concepts and methods.

Each lesson also includes tasks to engage students in Modeling with, Organizing, Reflecting on, and Extending their mathematical understanding. These MORE tasks are central to the learning goals of each lesson and are intended primarily for individual work outside of class. Selection of tasks for use with a class should be based on student performance and the availability of time and technology. Students can exercise some choice of tasks to pursue, and at times they can be given the opportunity to pose their own problems and questions to investigate.

Multiple Approaches to Assessment

Assessing what students know and are able to do is an integral part of *Contemporary Mathematics in Context*. Initially, as students pursue the investigations that make up the curriculum, the teacher is able to informally assess student performance in terms of process, content, disposition, and other factors. At the end of each investigation, the "Checkpoint" and accompanying class discussion provide an opportunity for the teacher to assess the levels of understanding that the various groups of students have reached. Finally, the "On Your Own" problem situation and the tasks in the MORE sets provide further opportunities to assess the level of understanding of each individual student. Quizzes, in-class exams, take-home assessment activities, and extended projects are included in the teacher resource materials.

Acknowledgments

Development and evaluation of the student text materials, teacher materials, assessments, and calculator software for *Contemporary Mathematics in Context* were funded through a grant from the National Science Foundation to the Core-Plus Mathematics Project (CPMP). We are indebted to Midge Cozzens, Director of the NSF Division of Elementary, Secondary, and Informal Education, and to our program officers James Sandefur, Eric Robinson, and John Bradley for their support, understanding, and input.

In addition to the NSF grant, a series of grants from the Dwight D. Eisenhower Higher Education Professional Development Program has helped to provide professional development support for Michigan teachers involved in the testing of each year of the curriculum.

Computing tools are fundamental to the use of *Contemporary Mathematics in Context*. Appreciation is expressed to Texas Instruments and, in particular, Dave Santucci for collaborating with us by providing classroom sets of graphing calculators to field-test schools.

As seen on page v, CPMP has been a collaborative effort that has drawn on the talents and energies of teams of mathematics educators at several institutions. This diversity of experiences and ideas has been a particular strength of the project. Special thanks is owed to the support staff at these institutions, particularly at Western Michigan University.

From the outset, our work has been guided by the advice of an international advisory board consisting of Diane Briars (Pittsburgh Public Schools), Jeremy Kilpatrick (University of Georgia), Kenneth Ruthven (University of Cambridge), David A. Smith (Duke University), and Edna Vasquez (Detroit Renaissance High School). Preliminary versions of the curriculum materials also benefited from careful reviews by the following mathematicians and mathematics educators: Alverna Champion (Grand Valley State University), Cherie Cornick (Wayne County Alliance for Mathematics and Science), Edgar Edwards (formerly of the Virginia State Department of Education), Richard Scheaffer (University of Florida), Martha Siegel (Towson University), Edward Silver (University of Pittsburgh), and Lee Stiff (North Carolina State University).

Our gratitude is expressed to the teachers and students at our 35 evaluation sites listed on pages vi and vii. Their experiences using pilot- and field-test versions of *Contemporary Mathematics in Context* provided constructive feedback and improvements. We learned a lot together about making mathematics meaningful and accessible to a wide range of students.

A very special thank you is extended to Barbara Janson for her interest and encouragement in publishing a core mathematical sciences curriculum that breaks new ground in terms of content, instructional practices, and student assessment. Finally, we want to acknowledge Eric Karnowski for his thoughtful and careful editorial work and express our appreciation to the staff of Everyday Learning who contributed to the publication of this program.

To the Student

Contemporary Mathematics in Context, Course 3 builds on the mathematical concepts, methods, and habits of mind developed in Courses 1 and 2. With this text, you will continue to learn mathematics by doing mathematics, not by studying "worked out" examples. You will investigate important mathematical ideas and ways of thinking as you try to understand and make sense of realistic situations. Because real-world situations and problems often involve data, shape, change, or chance, you will learn fundamental concepts and methods from several strands of mathematics. In particular, you will develop an understanding of broadly useful ideas from algebra and functions, from statistics and probability, from geometry and trigonometry, and from discrete mathematics. You also will see connections among these strands—how they weave together to form the fabric of mathematics.

Because real-world situations and problems are often open-ended, you will find that there may be more than one correct approach and more than one correct solution. Therefore, you will frequently be asked to explain your ideas. You also will increasingly be asked to provide more general arguments or proofs for mathematical statements. This text will provide help and practice in reasoning and communicating clearly about mathematics.

Because solving real-world problems often involves teamwork, you will continue to often work collaboratively with a partner or in small groups as you investigate realistic and interesting situations. As in Courses 1 and 2, you will find that two or four students working collaboratively on a problem can often accomplish more than any one of you would working individually. Because technology is commonly used in solving real-world problems, you will continue to use a graphing calculator or computer as a tool to help you understand and make sense of situations and problems you encounter.

As in Courses 1 and 2, you're going to learn a lot of useful mathematics—and it's going to make sense to you. You're going to strengthen your skills in working cooperatively and communicating with others as well. You're also going to strengthen your skills in using technology tools intelligently and effectively. You'll have plenty of opportunities to be creative, too, so let your imagination lead you and enjoy.

Patterns in Variation

Measuring Variation with the Standard Deviation

Manufacturing involves processes that vary. When Boeing builds a jet airplane, steps in the production process include design, buying raw materials and some parts, manufacturing other parts, assembling the parts, and testing the result. If different machines are used to make the same type of part, the sizes of the produced parts could be slightly different. Even parts made by the same machine will vary slightly in their dimensions.

Think About This Situation

Variation is inherent in the manufacturing of products, ranging from computer chips to jumbo jets.

a Name some specific problems that could occur with an airplane if the manufacturing process produces parts that vary too much in size.

b How could a company detect and minimize variation in the manufacturing of products?

c What ways do you know for measuring variability?

d How does a box plot help you visualize variability? How does a histogram help? How does a stem-and-leaf plot help?

In this unit, you will investigate how some basic statistical methods can improve the production process and the quality of a service or product. Using statistical signals to improve quality is called **statistical process control**, **quality control**, or **quality improvement**. These methods can be effectively applied to any area in which there is variation in the process—essentially every area of human endeavor!

INVESTIGATION 1 ► Computing and Interpreting the Standard Deviation

In earlier courses, you learned about three measures that describe the variation in a set of data: the range, the interquartile range (IQR), and the mean absolute deviation (MAD). Another measure used to describe the variation in a set of data is the *standard deviation*. In this lesson, you will learn how to compute the standard deviation, and you will explore some of its uses and properties.

1. Suppose your class is working on a project making school award certificates. You have decided to outline the edge of a design on the certificates with a continuous piece of thin gold braid.

Certificate of Distinction

This certificate is awarded to

_____

to recognize achievement in

_____

on this day, _____ .

   a. What variability would exist in the process of preparing the strips of braid?

   b. Without comparing measurements to those of other students, find the perimeter (in millimeters) of the outline on the sample certificate above. Record your perimeter measurement.

   c. As a class, make a line plot of the perimeters recorded by the members of your class. Describe the distribution.

2. Recall that the interquartile range (IQR) of a distribution is a measure of how much the middle half of the values vary. It is a measure of variation often associated with the median.

   a. Find the median, the quartiles (Q_1 and Q_3), and the IQR of the class set of perimeter measurements. Mark these on your line plot.

   b. What does the interquartile range tell you about how much the measurements vary?

   c. You may recall that an *outlier* is a data value x such that $x > Q_3 + 1.5(\text{IQR})$ or $x < Q_1 - 1.5(\text{IQR})$. Are there any outliers according to this $1.5(\text{IQR})$ rule? If so, describe their location on your line plot.

3. In your previous work, when the mean was used to describe the center of a distribution, you used the mean absolute deviation (MAD) as a measure of variation. It is the average distance of the data values from the mean.

a. Compute the MAD for the perimeter measurements from your group only. Use the formula

$$\text{MAD} = \frac{\sum |x - \bar{x}|}{n}$$

where the values of x are your measurements, $\bar{x}$ is the mean of your measurements, and n is the number of values.

b. What does the MAD tell you about the variation in the measurements of the perimeter?

c. Why is absolute value used in the formula for the MAD?

4. The **standard deviation** is another measure of how much the values vary about the mean. It is found by first computing the average of the *squares* of the differences between each data point and the mean, and then finding the square root of that average.

a. In your group, discuss how you would compute the standard deviation of the perimeter measurements made by your group. How might you organize your work?

b. Individually, compute the standard deviation. Compare your answers and resolve any differences.

c. Compare the MAD of the measurements of your group to the standard deviation of the measurements of your group. Are they the same or different? Is the same conclusion true for other groups' measurements?

d. Compare the process for computing the standard deviation to the process for computing the mean absolute deviation. In what ways are they alike? In what ways are they different?

e. Write a symbolic rule for computing the standard deviation (SD) of a set of n data values.

5. Now exchange perimeter measurements with another group.

a. Compute the standard deviation of the measurements of that group.

b. Is the other group's standard deviation larger or smaller than your group's standard deviation? How might you explain this in terms of the data?

6. Think about the process of finding the standard deviation.

a. What is accomplished by squaring the differences from the mean?

b. What is accomplished by dividing by n?

c. Why do you need to take the square root?

d. What unit of measurement should be attached to the standard deviation of the measurements of the perimeters? Why?

e. What formulas have you seen that involve a sum of squared differences?

7. Graphics calculators and statistical computer software will calculate the standard deviation of data that have been entered into a list.

a. Use your calculator or software to find the mean and the standard deviation (usually denoted σ on the menu) of the perimeter measurements for your entire class. Compare these numbers to your line plot from Activity 1 Part c. Does the mean appear to be the balance point of the distribution? Does the standard deviation appear to represent a distance from the mean that is typical for the data values?

b. Is the standard deviation of the class larger or smaller than the standard deviation of your group? What characteristic of the data made that the case? Is the same conclusion true for all groups?

Now use the idea of standard deviation to explore the variability in hand spans among your classmates.

8. Each member of your group should measure his or her hand span: Spread your right hand as wide as possible, place it on a ruler, and measure the distance from the end of your thumb across to the end of your little finger.

a. Find the mean and standard deviation of the hand spans of the students in your group.

b. Report your group's mean and standard deviation to your teacher.

c. As a class, examine the means and standard deviations from the groups in your class. Consider the specific people in each group, and try to match each set of statistics with the correct group.

d. Now compute the mean and standard deviation of the hand spans of all class members. Are the mean and standard deviation larger or smaller than your group's mean and standard deviation? What characteristics of the data explain these results? Is the same conclusion true for all groups?

9. Consider the heights of the people in the following two groups:

■ The members of the Chicago Bulls basketball team

■ The people in Chicago named Smith

a. Which group would you expect to have the larger mean height? Which group would you expect to have the larger standard deviation? Explain your reasoning.

b. Sketch or describe what you think histograms of these data would look like.

Look back at how you used the standard deviation to help you analyze measurement data.

a What does the standard deviation tell you about a distribution?

b Why can you think of the standard deviation of a set of data as a kind of average distance of the values from their mean?

c How is the standard deviation similar to, and different from, other measures of variation you have studied?

Be prepared to share your ideas with the entire class.

The standard deviation is the most widely used measure of variation in the practice and study of statistics. As you complete the remaining investigations in this unit, think about reasons why this is the case. You will be asked to give your reasons in the "Looking Back" lesson.

Portland, Oregon

On Your Own

Assess your understanding of the standard deviation as a measure of variation.

a. For each data set below, first find the mean and standard deviation *without* using the formulas. Then check your answers by actually computing these statistics using the formulas.

- 4, 4, 4, 4, 4, 4, 4
- 6, 6, 6, 10, 10, 10

b. The normal monthly precipitation (rain and snow) in inches for Portland,

Normal Monthly Precipitation

	Jan.	Feb.	Mar.	Apr.	May	June	July	Aug.	Sept.	Oct.	Nov.	Dec.
Portland, ME	3.5	3.3	3.7	4.1	3.6	3.4	3.1	2.9	3.1	3.9	5.2	4.6
Portland, OR	5.4	3.9	3.6	2.4	2.1	1.5	0.6	1.1	1.8	2.7	5.3	6.1

Source: *The World Almanac and Book of Facts 1997.* Mahwah, NJ: World Almanac, 1996.

Maine, and for Portland, Oregon, is given in the table below.

- From studying the data in the table, what comparisons can you make about the amount of precipitation for the two cities?
- Make a back-to-back stem-and-leaf plot of the precipitation in each of the cities. How do you think the mean monthly amounts of precipitation for the cities will compare? How will the standard deviations compare?
- Calculate the mean and standard deviation of the normal monthly precipitation for each city. How well did you estimate?

INVESTIGATION 2 ▸ Properties of the Standard Deviation

In other courses, you have examined the effect of transformations of data on the interquartile range and on the MAD. In this investigation, you will explore how transformations affect the standard deviation.

1. Working with your group, recall your previous work with data transformations.

   a. How does adding the same positive number to each value in a set of data affect the IQR? The MAD? Why does this make sense?

   b. If the standard deviation behaves like other measures of variation, how will the transformation in Part a affect it?

   c. How does multiplying each value in a data set by the same positive number affect the IQR? The MAD? Why does this make sense?

   d. If the standard deviation behaves like other measures of variation, how will the transformation in Part c affect it?

2. Ms. King polled her two senior mathematics classes to determine the hourly wage of students who had part-time jobs. The results are listed in the table below.

Student Wages

Student	Hourly Wage (in dollars)	Student	Hourly Wage (in dollars)
Neil	5.15	Mia	6.60
Bill	5.25	Tasha	6.60
Dimitri	5.30	Sarah	6.65
Jose	5.50	Vanita	6.70
Kerry	5.75	N'taka	6.70
Emerson	5.85	Olivia	6.75
Rashawnda	5.90	Katrina	6.80
Katie	5.90	Deeonna	6.90
Cleave	6.00	Jacob	7.00
Jan	6.10	Rusty	7.00
Kyle	6.25	Jennifer	7.25
Mike	6.25	Phuong	7.30
Toby	6.30	Corinna	7.45
Nafikah	6.40	John	7.50
Robert	6.40		

Here is a histogram of these data.

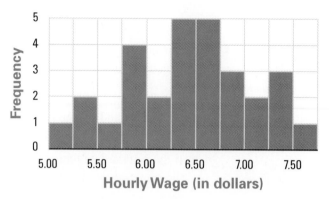

Hourly Wage (in dollars)

a. Estimate the average hourly wage of these students from the histogram. Compute the mean. How close was your estimate?

b. Estimate the standard deviation of the hourly wages. Compute the standard deviation. How close was your estimate?

3. Berry decided it was too much work to enter the decimal point in the wages each time in her calculator list, so she entered each wage without it.

a. What mathematical operation describes how Berry transformed the original data?

b. How will the histogram of her data be different from the one shown in Activity 2?

c. Predict the mean and standard deviation of her data. Check your predictions.

L1	L2	L3
500	-----	-----
525		
530		
550		
575		
▓▓▓		

L1 (6)=

4. Suppose each student in Ms. King's class gets a 4% raise.

a. What mathematical operation transforms the original data to reflect a 4% raise in hourly wages?

b. How will the histogram of the new hourly wages be different from the original one?

c. Predict the mean and standard deviation for the new wages of the students. Check your predictions.

5. Suppose that instead of a 4% raise, each student gets a raise of 25 cents per hour.

a. What mathematical operation transforms the original data to reflect an increase in hourly wages of 25 cents per hour?

b. How will the histogram of the new hourly wages be different from the original one?

c. How will the mean and standard deviation change? Explain why this is reasonable.

6. In this activity, you will examine symbolically the effect on the standard deviation of adding the same value c to each of the five values in a set of data,

$$x_1, x_2, x_3, x_4, x_5.$$

   a. Suppose the constant c is added to each of the values in the above set of data. What are the transformed values?

   b. Let $\bar{x}$ be the mean of the original values. Compute the mean of the transformed values.

   c. Compute the standard deviation of the transformed values.

   d. How does the standard deviation of the transformed values compare to the standard deviation of the original values?

   e. Write an if-then statement of what you proved in Parts a through d.

7. Now examine the effect of inserting a new value into the hourly wages data.

   a. Suppose Maurice was absent from the class the day of the wage poll. When he returned to school, his wage of $5.85 per hour was included in the data set. How do you think this additional value will affect the mean and standard deviation? Check your conjecture.

   b. Suppose that, instead, Maurice was a computer expert and had a programming job that paid $13.00 per hour. How do you think the mean and standard deviation of the hourly wage data will change? Compute the mean and standard deviation, and explain why the results are reasonable.

Checkpoint

You have seen that transforming or inserting a new value into a set of data affects summary statistics in predictable ways.

a If each value in a set of data is increased or decreased by the same amount, how does the mean change? How does the standard deviation change? Explain your reasoning.

b List summary statistics that do not change when the same positive number is added to, or subtracted from, each value in a set of data. What do these statistics have in common?

c If each value in a set of data is multiplied by the same amount, how does the mean change? How does the standard deviation change? Explain your reasoning.

d List summary statistics that are sensitive to outliers. List the ones that tend not to be affected by an outlier.

Be prepared to share with the class examples that illustrate your thinking.

In a community college class, all thirty-six students were working at jobs for which they were paid. The number of hours they worked per week is given below.

Community College Students' Employment								
5	5	5	6	10	11	12	12	12
13	14	15	15	16	16	16	17	17
17	17	18	19	19	20	20	20	20
20	20	23	25	25	25	27	28	40

a. Examine this histogram of these data. Describe the distribution.

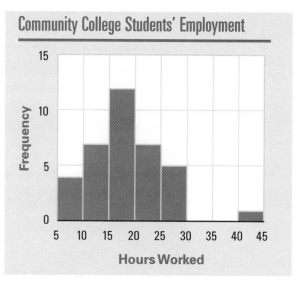

b. Find the mean and standard deviation. Locate the mean on a copy of the histogram. Locate the values one standard deviation above the mean and one standard deviation below the mean.

c. Saundra is the student who works 40 hours a week. She is thinking about reducing her work hours to 20 a week so she will have more time to study. What will happen to the mean and standard deviation if Saundra makes this change?

d. Describe two ways to find the mean and standard deviation of the number of hours worked *per semester* (15 weeks) by these students.

e. The instructor of the class expects students to do homework two hours every school night for a total of ten hours a week. If each student's homework hours are added to his or her work hours, how will the mean and standard deviation change?

MORE

Modeling • Organizing • Reflecting • Extending

Modeling

1. In an agricultural experiment, two different types of fertilizer were used on twelve orange trees each. The table below gives the number of kilograms of oranges produced per tree.

Kilograms of Oranges per Tree	
Fertilizer *A*	Fertilizer *B*
3	14
14	116
19	33
0	40
96	10
92	72
11	8
24	10
5	2
31	13
84	15
15	44

a. Make a back-to-back stem-and-leaf plot of the number of kilograms of oranges produced by trees with Fertilizer *A* and with Fertilizer *B*.

b. Use the stem-and-leaf plot to estimate the mean number of kilograms for each set of trees.

c. Which set do you think has the larger standard deviation? What clues suggest which set might have the larger standard deviation?

d. Compute the mean and standard deviation of each set. How close were your estimates in Parts b and c?

e. What are the mean and standard deviation of the number of *pounds* of oranges for Fertilizer *A*? For Fertilizer *B*? (There are about 2.2 pounds in a kilogram.)

2. The prices of used 1992 and 1993 Honda Civics advertised in a Sunday newspaper were $7,500, $8,900, $5,200, $6,000, $6,500, $8,000, and $8,995.

a. Compute the mean and standard deviation of the prices.

b. If the seven car owners all lower their prices by $500 for the next Sunday's edition of the paper, how will the mean and standard deviation of the prices change?

c. Suppose that there is a 5% sales tax on used cars. How will this affect the mean and standard deviation of the costs of these cars? How would these two statistics be affected if the buyer then also had to pay a $12.00 registration fee?

d. Suppose that another Honda Civic is listed for $4,900. How will this affect the mean and standard deviation of the listed prices?

201 Autos, Used

HONDA CIVIC, '93 – white, 68,000 miles, very clean. Only $7500. Call 555-5996.

HONDA CIVIC EX '92 – 50K, 5 spd., air, $8900 or best offer. 555-7641.

HONDA CIVIC SI '92 – hatch-back, 2 door, 5 spd., black, tint, runs excel, $5200. Call 555-1203.

HONDA CIVIC '92 – Loaded. Orchid. Moonroof. $6000. 555-0255.

HONDA CIVIC '92 – 2 dr. hatch. Green. Air. Only $6500. Call 555-5800.

HONDA CIVIC '93 – Loaded. Pwr sunroof, 5spd., 49K. $8000 obo. 555-8300.

HONDA CIVIC '93 – 43K mi, leather, sunroof, 4 dr, $8995. 555-2204.

3. Thirty-two students in a drafting class were asked to prepare a design to certain specifications, which included exact dimensions. A histogram of the perimeters of their designs is displayed below. The mean perimeter was 98.42 mm.

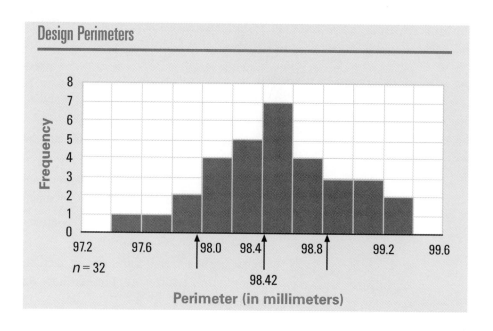

Design Perimeters

n = 32

98.42

Perimeter (in millimeters)

a. What might explain the variation in perimeters of the design?

b. The arrows mark the mean and the points one standard deviation above the mean and one standard deviation below the mean. Use the marked plot to estimate the standard deviation for the class's perimeters.

c. Estimate the percentage of the perimeters that are within one standard deviation of the mean.

d. Estimate the percentage of the perimeters that are within two standard deviations of the mean.

4. A large urban high school has 29 math classes. The number of students enrolled in each of the classes is displayed on the plot below. The outlier is a calculus class with only 7 students enrolled.

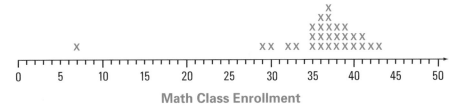

Math Class Enrollment

a. Jason computed the mean, both with and without the outlier. The two values were 35.97 and 37.00. Which value was computed with the outlier, and which was computed without the outlier?

b. Jason also computed the standard deviation, both with and without the outlier. The two values were 3.31 and 6.45. Which value was computed with the outlier, and which was computed without the outlier?

c. How many standard deviations below the mean is the enrollment in the calculus class when it is included in computing the mean and standard deviation? How many standard deviations below the mean is the enrollment in the calculus class when it is not included in the calculations?

d. If five students drop out of each class, what will be the new mean and standard deviation if the calculus class is included in the computations?

Organizing

1. Match each of the following histograms of test scores in three classes, *A*, *B*, and *C*, to the best description of class performance.

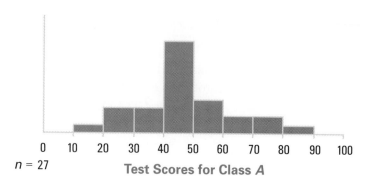

n = 27   **Test Scores for Class *A***

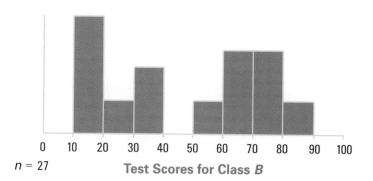

n = 27   **Test Scores for Class *B***

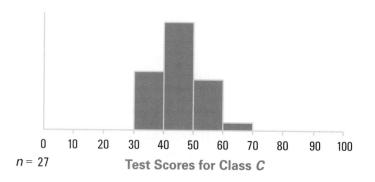

n = 27   **Test Scores for Class *C***

a. The mean of the test scores is 46, and the standard deviation is 26.

b. The mean of the test scores is 46, and the standard deviation is 8.

c. The mean of the test scores is 46, and the standard deviation is 16.

2. Give an example of two data sets that each have the same number of values, the same mean, and the same range, but one data set has a standard deviation that is at least twice as big as the standard deviation of the other data set. Use at least eight data values.

3. In this task, you will examine symbolically the effect on the standard deviation of multiplying each of the values in a set of five pieces of data,

$$x_1, x_2, x_3, x_4, x_5,$$

by a positive number d.

   a. Suppose each of the five values in the set of data above is multiplied by the positive constant d. What are the transformed values?

   b. Let $\bar{x}$ be the mean of the original values. Compute the mean of the transformed values.

   c. Compute the standard deviation of the transformed values.

   d. How does the standard deviation of the transformed values compare to the standard deviation of the original values?

   e. Write an if-then statement of what you proved in Parts a through d.

4. Add one more number to the set {10, 20, 22, 32, 36} so the set has a standard deviation that is as small as possible. Explain your method.

Reflecting

1. How is the standard deviation formula like the distance formula?

2. Why is there more than one measure of center? More than one measure of variation?

3. How do you think the "standard deviation" got its name?

4. Think about the meaning of a standard deviation.

   a. Describe two situations in which it would be important that the data values have a standard deviation as small as possible.

   b. Describe a situation in which you would like to be more than two standard deviations above the mean of all people. Describe a situation in which you would like to be more than two standard deviations below the mean of all people.

5. Under what conditions will the standard deviation of a data set be equal to 0? Explain your reasoning.

Extending

1. Runners in the Boston Marathon compete in divisions determined by age and gender. In a recent marathon, the mean time for the 18- to 39-year-old women's division was 225.31 minutes with a standard deviation of 26.64 minutes, and the mean time for the 50- to 59-year-old women's division was 242.58 minutes with a standard deviation of 21.78 minutes. In that marathon, a 57-year-old woman finished the race in 4:09:08 (hours:minutes:seconds), and a 34-year-old woman finished the race in 4:00:15.

   a. How many standard deviations above the mean for her division was each runner? Explain your reasoning.

   b. Write a formula that gives the number of standard deviations above the mean for a time of x minutes by a woman in the 50- to 59-year-old division.

   c. Does your formula from Part c also work for times below the mean? If not, adjust your formula.

   d. Write a formula that gives the number of standard deviations above or below the mean for a time of x minutes by a woman in the 18- to 39-year-old division.

2. A set of data consists of the numbers 2, 2, 2, 4, 7, 8, and 10. Here, the sample size, n, is 7, and the individual values that should be substituted for x in the following formulas are 2, 2, 2, 4, 7, 8, and 10.

   a. One at a time, substitute each measure of center (the mean, median, and mode) for C in the formula below. Which measure of center gives the smallest value?

$$\sqrt{\frac{\Sigma(x - C)^2}{n}}$$

   b. One at a time, substitute each measure of center (the mean, median, and mode) for C in the formula below. Which measure of center gives the smallest value?

$$\frac{\Sigma |x - C|}{n}$$

c. One at a time, substitute each measure of center (the mean, median, and mode) for C in the word formula below. What does this formula count? Which measure of center makes this count as small as possible?

> Start with a sum of 0.
>
> Look at each value of x.
>
> Add 0 to the sum if $x = C$.
>
> Add 1 to the sum if $x \neq C$.

d. Look over your answers to Parts a, b, and c. Which measures of center are paired with which measures of variation?

3. Compare the mean absolute deviation, standard deviation, and half the range.

a. One of these measures is always smaller than or equal to the other two. One of the others is always larger than or equal to the other two. One is always in the middle. Which is which?

b. Describe a situation in which all three measures of variation will be equal.

4. In this task, you will investigate one reason why the standard deviation is considered to be so important. The number of raisins in three boxes of Brand A raisins was counted, as was the number of raisins in three boxes of Brand B. The results are shown in the table below. Suppose you select one of the Brand A boxes and one of the Brand B boxes at random.

Raisin Box Contents	
Brand *A*	Brand *B*
20	20
25	40
30	90

a. List all nine of the possible pairs that you could get.

b. Compute the nine possible total numbers of raisins that you could get.

c. Compute the standard deviation of the total number of raisins.

d. Square this standard deviation. The square of the standard deviation is called the **variance**.

e. Compute the variance of the three boxes of Brand A. Compute the variance of the three boxes of Brand B. Add these two variances.

f. What can you conclude?

g. Can you add the mean of Brand A to the mean of Brand B to get the mean of the total?

h. Can you add the mean absolute deviation of Brand A to the mean absolute deviation of Brand B to get the mean absolute deviation of the total?

The Normal Distribution

Lesson 2

In a science class, you may have weighed something by balancing it on a scale against a standard weight. To be sure the standard weight is reasonably accurate, its manufacturer can have it weighed at the National Bureau of Standards in Washington, D.C. The accuracy of the weighing procedure at the National Bureau of Standards is itself checked about once a week by weighing a known 10-gram weight, NB 10. The histogram below is based on 100 consecutive measurements of the weight of NB 10 using the same apparatus and procedure. Shown is the distribution of weighings, in micrograms *below* 10 grams. (A microgram is a millionth of a gram.) Examine this histogram and the two that follow for common features.

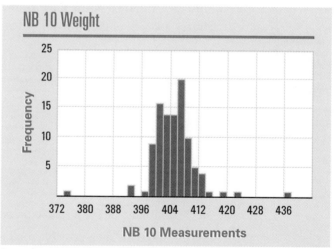

Source: Freedman, David, et al. *Statistics*, 3rd edition. New York: W. W. Norton & Company, 1998.

At the right is a picture of a device called a *quincunx*. Small balls are dropped into the device and fall through several levels of pins, which cause the balls to bounce left or right at each level. The balls are collected in columns at the bottom.

This third histogram shows the political points of view of a sample of 1,271 voters in the United States in 1976. The voters were asked a series of questions to determine their political philosophy and then rated on a scale from liberal to conservative.

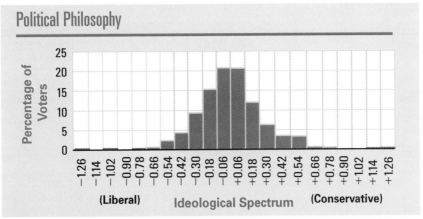

Source: Romer, Thomas, and Howard Rosenthal. 1984. Voting models and empirical evidence. *American Scientist*, 72: 465-473.

Think About This Situation

Compare the histogram above and the two on the previous page.

a What do the three distributions have in common? What other distributions have you seen in this unit or in other units that have approximately the same overall shape?

b What other sets of data might have this same shape?

c How might understanding this shape be helpful in studying variation?

INVESTIGATION 1 Characteristics of the Normal Distribution

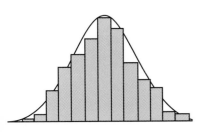

Many naturally occurring characteristics, such as human heights or the lengths or weights of supposedly identical objects produced by machines, are approximately **normally distributed**. Their histograms are "bell-shaped," with the data clustered symmetrically about the mean and tapering off gradually on both ends.

In this lesson, you will explore how the standard deviation is related to normal distributions. In Lesson 3, you will see how this relationship is used in industry to study the variability in a quality control process. In these lessons, as in the "Modeling Public Opinion" unit, distinguishing between a population and a sample taken from that population is important. The symbol for the mean of a population is μ, the lower case Greek letter "mu." As in the case of $\bar{x}$, the mean of a sample, it is calculated by dividing the sum of the data values by n, the number of values.

There are two types of standard deviation on many calculators and statistical software: σ (lower case Greek letter "sigma") and s. Like μ, the standard deviation σ is used for a population; that is, compute σ when you have all the values from a particular population or you have a theoretical distribution. The standard deviation s is used for a sample; that is, compute s when you have only some of the values from the population. The formulas for σ and s differ in only one small way. When computing σ, you divide by n. When computing s, you divide by $(n-1)$. (A technical argument shows that dividing by $n-1$ makes s^2, for the sample, a better estimate of σ^2, for the population from which the sample was drawn.) You will gain some experience interpreting and calculating the sample standard deviation s in the activities that follow.

The first three activities provide data about weights of nickels, heights of women in a college course, and the times for a solute to dissolve. Your teacher will assign one of the three activities to your group. Study your distribution and think about its characteristics. Be prepared to share and compare your group's results with the rest of the class.

1. **Weights of Nickels** The data below and the accompanying histogram give the weights, to the nearest hundredth of a gram, of a sample of 100 new nickels. The mean weight is 4.9941 grams and the standard deviation s is approximately 0.0551 gram.

Nickel Weights (in grams)

4.87	4.92	4.95	4.97	4.98	5.00	5.01	5.03	5.04	5.07
4.87	4.92	4.95	4.97	4.98	5.00	5.01	5.03	5.04	5.07
4.88	4.93	4.95	4.97	4.99	5.00	5.01	5.03	5.04	5.07
4.89	4.93	4.95	4.97	4.99	5.00	5.02	5.03	5.05	5.08
4.90	4.93	4.95	4.97	4.99	5.00	5.02	5.03	5.05	5.08
4.90	4.93	4.96	4.97	4.99	5.01	5.02	5.03	5.05	5.09
4.91	4.94	4.96	4.98	4.99	5.01	5.02	5.03	5.06	5.09
4.91	4.94	4.96	4.98	4.99	5.01	5.02	5.04	5.06	5.10
4.92	4.94	4.96	4.98	5.00	5.01	5.02	5.04	5.06	5.11
4.92	4.94	4.96	4.98	5.00	5.01	5.02	5.04	5.06	5.11

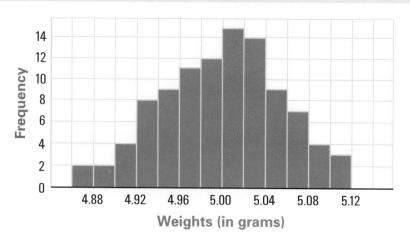

a. How do the mean weight and the median weight compare?

b. On a copy of the histogram, mark points along the horizontal axis that correspond to the mean, one standard deviation above the mean, one standard deviation below the mean, two standard deviations above the mean, two standard deviations below the mean, three standard deviations above the mean, and three standard deviations below the mean.

c. What percentage of the data are within one standard deviation of the mean? Within two standard deviations? Within three standard deviations?

d. Suppose you weigh a randomly chosen nickel from this collection. Find the probability its weight would be within two standard deviations of the mean.

2. **Heights of Female Students** The table and histogram below give the heights of 123 women in a statistics class at Penn State University in the 1970s. The mean height of the women in this sample is approximately 64.626 inches, and the standard deviation s is approximately 2.606 inches.

Female Students' Heights

Height (inches)	Frequency	Height (inches)	Frequency
59	2	66	15
60	5	67	9
61	7	68	6
62	10	69	6
63	16	70	3
64	22	71	1
65	20	72	1

Source: Joiner, Brian L. 1975. Living histograms. *International Statistical Review* 3: 339–340.

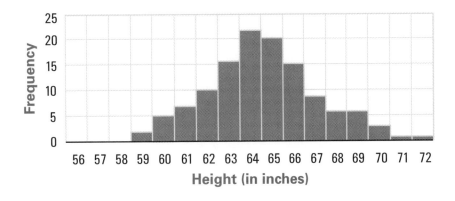

a. How do the mean and the median of the women's heights compare?

b. On a copy of the histogram, mark points along the horizontal axis that correspond to the mean, one standard deviation above the mean, one standard deviation below the mean, two standard deviations above the mean, two standard deviations below the mean, three standard deviations above the mean, and three standard deviations below the mean.

c. What percentage of the data are within one standard deviation of the mean? Within two standard deviations? Within three standard deviations?

d. Suppose you pick a female student from the class at random. Find the probability that her height would be within two standard deviations of the mean.

3. **Dissolution Times** For a chemistry experiment, students measured the time for a solute to dissolve. The experiment was repeated 50 times. The results are shown in the following chart and histogram. The mean time for the 50 experiments is 11.8 seconds, and the standard deviation s is approximately 3.32 seconds.

Dissolution Time (in seconds)

12	10	10	12	17	10	13	11	12	17
10	6	5	16	8	8	15	7	11	10
14	14	9	14	19	4	16	9	12	19
12	13	11	14	13	12	9	11	14	15
8	8	11	13	10	12	13	12	12	17

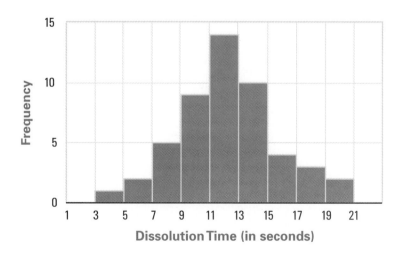

a. How do the mean and the median of the times compare?

b. On a copy of the histogram, mark points along the horizontal axis that correspond to the mean, one standard deviation above the mean, one standard deviation below the mean, two standard deviations above the mean, two standard deviations below the mean, three standard deviations above the mean, and three standard deviations below the mean.

c. What percentage of the data are within one standard deviation of the mean? Within two standard deviations? Within three standard deviations?

d. Suppose you repeat this experiment. Estimate the probability that the time for the solute to dissolve will be within two standard deviations of the mean.

Checkpoint

After groups have reported their findings to the class, consider the following questions about the shapes of the distributions and their characteristics.

a How are the distributions alike? How are they different?

b How are the mean and median related in each of the distributions?

c In each case, about what percentage of the values are within one standard deviation of the mean? Within two standard deviations? Within three standard deviations?

Be prepared to explain your ideas to the whole class.

On Your Own

If the set of data is the entire population you are interested in studying, you use σ, the population standard deviation. If you are looking at the set of data as a sample from a larger population of data, you use s. (See page 364.)

a. For a given set of data, which is larger: σ or s? Explain your reasoning.

b. Suppose you are computing the standard deviation, and the sum of the squared differences is 1,500. Assume there are 15 values and find σ and s. Assume there are 100 values and find σ and s. What do you conclude?

All normal distributions have the same overall shape, differing only in mean μ and standard deviation σ. Some look tall and skinny; others look more spread out. All normal distributions, however, have certain characteristics in common. They are symmetric about the mean; 68% of the data values lie within one standard deviation of the mean; 95% of the data values lie within two standard deviations of the mean; and 99.7% of the data values lie within three standard deviations of the mean. The distributions in Activities 1 through 3 were *approximately normal*. Each was a sample taken from a larger population that is more nearly normal.

4. The normal distribution shown here has mean μ of 125 and standard deviation σ of 8.

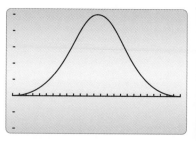

  a. On three copies of this distribution, mark points along the horizontal axis that correspond to the mean, one standard deviation above and below the mean, two standard deviations above and below the mean, and three standard deviations above and below the mean.

  b. On one copy of the distribution, shade and label the region under the curve that represents 68% of the data values.

  c. On another copy of the distribution, shade and label the region that represents 95% of the data values.

  d. On the third copy of the distribution, shade and label the region that corresponds to 99.7% of the data values.

  e. Compare your graphs to those of other groups. Resolve any differences.

5. Suppose that the distribution of the weights of newly minted nickels is a normal distribution with mean μ of 5 grams and standard deviation σ of 0.10 gram.

  a. Draw a sketch of this distribution and label the points on the horizontal axis that correspond to the mean, one standard deviation above and below the mean, two standard deviations above and below the mean, and three standard deviations above and below the mean.

  b. What can you conclude about the middle 68% of the weights of these newly minted nickels? About the middle 95% of the weights? About the middle 99.7% of the weights?

  c. Explain or illustrate your answers in Part b in terms of your sketch.

6. Think about the overall shape of a normal distribution as you answer the following questions. Then draw sketches illustrating your answers.

  a. What percentage of the values in a normal distribution lie above the mean?

  b. What percentage of the values in a normal distribution lie more than two standard deviations away from the mean?

  c. What percentage of the values in a normal distribution lie more than two standard deviations above the mean?

  d. What percentage of the values in a normal distribution lie more than one standard deviation away from the mean?

7. Three very large sets of data have approximately normal distributions, each with a mean of 10. Sketches of the overall shapes of the distributions are shown below. The scale on the horizontal axis is the same in each case. The standard deviation of the distribution in Figure A is 2. Estimate the standard deviations of the distributions in Figures B and C.

Figure A

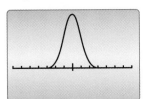

Figure B

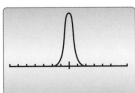

Figure C

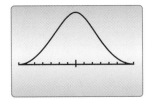

8. The weights of babies of a given age and gender are approximately normally distributed. This fact allows a doctor or nurse to use a baby's weight to find the weight percentile to which the child belongs. The table below gives information about the weights of six-month-old and twelve-month-old baby boys.

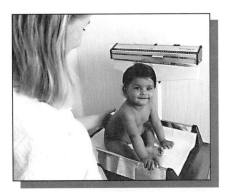

Weights of Baby Boys

	Weight at Six Months (in pounds)	Weight at Twelve Months (in pounds)
Mean μ	17.25	22.50
Standard Deviation σ	2.0	2.2

Source: Tannenbaum, Peter, and Robert Arnold. *Excursions in Modern Mathematics*. Englewood Cliffs, New Jersey: Prentice Hall. 1992.

a. On separate sets of axes with the same scales, draw sketches that represent the distribution of weights for six-month-old boys and the distribution of weights for twelve-month-old boys. How do the distributions differ?

b. About what percentage of twelve-month-old boys weigh more than 26.9 pounds?

c. About what percentage of six-month-old boys weigh between 15.25 pounds and 19.25 pounds?

d. A twelve-month-old boy who weighs 24.7 pounds is at what percentile for weight?

e. A six-month-old boy who weighs 21.25 pounds is at what percentile?

9. The producers of a movie did a survey of the ages of the people attending one screening of the movie. The data are shown here in the table and histogram.

Saturday Night at the Movies	
Age	Frequency
12	2
13	26
14	38
15	32
16	22
17	10
18	8
19	8
20	6
21	4
22	1
23	3
27	2
32	2
40	1

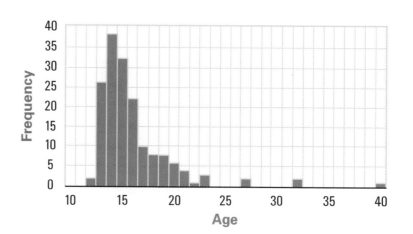

a. Compute the mean and standard deviation for these data. Find a way to do this without entering each of the individual ages (for example, entering the age "14" thirty-eight times) into a calculator or computer software.

b. What percentage of values fall within one standard deviation of the mean? Within two standard deviations of the mean? Within three standard deviations of the mean?

c. Compare the percentages from Part b to those from a normal distribution. Explain your findings in terms of the shapes of the two distributions.

d. What kind of a movie do you think was playing?

In this investigation, you examined connections between the overall shape of a distribution and its mean and standard deviation.

ⓐ Describe and illustrate with sketches some of the characteristics of a normal distribution.

ⓑ Estimate the mean and the standard deviation of this normal distribution. Explain how you found your estimate. The scale on the horizontal axis is 5 units per tick mark.

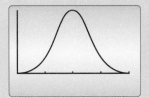

Be prepared to explain your ideas to the entire class.

▶On Your Own

Scores on the verbal section of the SAT I are approximately normally distributed with mean μ of 500 and standard deviation σ of 100.

a. What percentage of students score between 400 and 600 on the verbal section of the SAT I?

b. What percentage of students score over 600 on the verbal section of the SAT I?

c. What percentage of students score less than 600 on the verbal section of the SAT I?

INVESTIGATION ▶2 Standardizing Scores

In a previous course, you learned how to describe the location of a value in a distribution by giving its *percentile*, that is, the percentage of values that are smaller than the one given. In this investigation, you will explore how to use the standard deviation to describe the location of a value in a distribution that is normal, or approximately so.

1. Examine the chart below, which gives approximate information about the heights of young Americans aged 18 to 24. Each distribution is approximately normal.

Heights of American Young Adults

	Men	Women
Mean μ	68.5"	65.5"
Standard Deviation σ	2.7"	2.5"

a. Sketch the two distributions. Include a scale on the horizontal axis.

b. What can you conclude about the following?

- The percentage of young adult American women who are within one standard deviation of the average in height

  The percentage of young adult American men who are within one standard deviation of the average in height

- The percentage of young adult American women who are within two standard deviations of the average in height

  The percentage of young adult American men who are within two standard deviations of the average in height

c. On what assumptions are your conclusions in Part b based?

d. Alex is 3 standard deviations above average in height. How tall is she?

e. Miguel is 2.1 standard deviations below average in height. How tall is he?

f. Marcus is 74" tall. How many standard deviations above average height is he?

g. Jackie is 62" tall. How many standard deviations below average height is she?

h. Mary is 68" tall. Steve is 71" tall. Who is relatively taller for her or his gender, Mary or Steve? Explain your reasoning.

The **standardized value** or **z-score** is the number of standard deviations a given value lies from the mean. For example, in Activity 1 Part d, since Alex is 3 standard deviations *above* average in height, the *z*-score for her height is 3. Similarly, in Activity 1 Part e, since Miguel is 2.1 standard deviations *below* average in height, the *z*-score for his height is –2.1.

2. Look more generally at how standardized values are computed.

a. Compute the standardized values for Marcus's height and for Jackie's height.

b. Write a formula for computing the standardized value z of a data point if you know the value of the data point x, the mean of the population μ, and the standard deviation of the population σ.

3. Now consider how standardizing scores can help you make comparisons.

a. Find the standardized value for the height of a young woman who is 5' tall.

b. Find the standardized value for the height of a young man who is 5'2" tall.

c. Is the young woman in Part a or the young man in Part b shorter, relative to his or her own gender?

The following table gives the proportion of values in a normal distribution that are less than the given standardized value z.

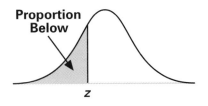

Proportion Below

z

Proportion of Values Below Standardized Value

z	Proportion Below	z	Proportion Below	z	Proportion Below
−3.5	0.0002	−1.1	0.1357	1.3	0.9032
−3.4	0.0003	−1.0	0.1587	1.4	0.9192
−3.3	0.0005	−0.9	0.1841	1.5	0.9332
−3.2	0.0007	−0.8	0.2119	1.6	0.9452
−3.1	0.0010	−0.7	0.2420	1.7	0.9554
−3.0	0.0013	−0.6	0.2743	1.8	0.9641
−2.9	0.0019	−0.5	0.3085	1.9	0.9713
−2.8	0.0026	−0.4	0.3446	2.0	0.9772
−2.7	0.0035	−0.3	0.3821	2.1	0.9821
−2.6	0.0047	−0.2	0.4207	2.2	0.9861
−2.5	0.0062	−0.1	0.4602	2.3	0.9893
−2.4	0.0082	0.0	0.5000	2.4	0.9918
−2.3	0.0107	0.1	0.5398	2.5	0.9938
−2.2	0.0139	0.2	0.5793	2.6	0.9953
−2.1	0.0179	0.3	0.6179	2.7	0.9965
−2.0	0.0228	0.4	0.6554	2.8	0.9974
−1.9	0.0287	0.5	0.6915	2.9	0.9981
−1.8	0.0359	0.6	0.7257	3.0	0.9987
−1.7	0.0446	0.7	0.7580	3.1	0.9990
−1.6	0.0548	0.8	0.7881	3.2	0.9993
−1.5	0.0668	0.9	0.8159	3.3	0.9995
−1.4	0.0808	1.0	0.8413	3.4	0.9997
−1.3	0.0968	1.1	0.8643	3.5	0.9998
−1.2	0.1151	1.2	0.8849		

4. As you complete this activity, think about the relation between the table entries and the graph of a normal distribution.

  a. If a value from a normal distribution is 2 standard deviations below the mean, what percentage of the values are below it? Above it? Draw sketches illustrating your answers.

  b. If a value from a normal distribution is 1.3 standard deviations above the mean, what percentage of the values are below it? Above it? Illustrate your answers with sketches.

  c. Based on the table, what percentage of values are within one standard deviation of the mean? Within two standard deviations of the mean? Within three standard deviations of the mean? What do you notice?

5. Now practice converting between heights and percentiles for Americans aged 18 to 24.

  a. Marcus is 74" tall. What is Marcus's percentile for height? (That is, what percentage of young men are shorter than Marcus?)

  b. Jackie is 62" tall. What is Jackie's percentile for height?

  c. Abby is 68" tall. What percentage of young women are between Jackie (Part b) and Abby in height?

  d. Cesar is at the 20th percentile in height. What is his height?

6. There are different scales for Intelligence Quotients (IQs). Scores on the Wechsler Intelligence Scale for Children are (within each age group) approximately normally distributed with a mean of 100 and standard deviation of 15.

  a. Draw a sketch of the distribution of these scores, with a marked scale on the horizontal axis.

  b. What percentage of children of a given age group have IQs above 150?

  c. What IQ score would be at the 50th percentile?

  d. Javier's IQ was at the 75th percentile. What was his IQ score on this test?

Checkpoint

Think about the meaning and use of standardized values.

ⓐ What is the purpose of standardizing scores?

ⓑ Kua earned a grade of 50 on a normally distributed test with a mean of 45 and a standard deviation of 10. On another normally distributed test with a mean of 70 and a standard deviation of 15, she earned a 78. On which of the two tests did she do better, relative to the others who took the tests? Explain your reasoning.

ⓒ How would your reasoning for Part b change if the distributions weren't normal?

Be prepared to explain your thinking to the entire class.

The standard deviation is the measure of variability most often paired with the mean, particularly for investigating measurement data. By standardizing values, you can use the table on page 373 for *any* normal distribution. If the distribution is not normal, the percentages given in the table do not necessarily hold.

▶ **On Your Own**

Mensa is an organization for people who score very high on certain tests. You can become a member by scoring at or above the 98th percentile on an IQ test or, for example, the math section of the SAT.

a. It was reported that Brooke Shields, the actress, scored 608 on the math section of the SAT. When she took the SAT, the scores were approximately normally distributed with an average on the math section of about 462 and a standard deviation of 100. How many standard deviations above average was her score?

b. What was Brooke's percentile on the math section of the SAT?

c. Can Brooke get into Mensa on the basis of this test?

The clinical definition of mental retardation includes several levels of severity. People who score between two and three deviations below average on the Stanford-Binet intelligence test are generally considered to have mild mental retardation. The IQ scores on the Stanford-Binet intelligence test are approximately normal with a mean of 100 and a standard deviation of 15.

d. Suppose Jim has an IQ of 75. Would Jim be considered to have mild mental retardation?

e. What percentage of people have an IQ higher than Jim's?

MORE
Modeling • Organizing • Reflecting • Extending

Modeling

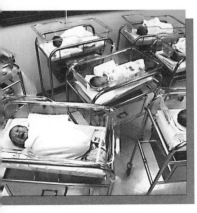

1. The length of a human pregnancy is often said to be 9 months. Actually, the length of pregnancy from conception to natural birth varies according to a distribution that is approximately normal with mean 266 days and standard deviation 16 days.

a. Draw a sketch of the distribution of pregnancy lengths. Include a scale on the horizontal axis.

b. What percentage of pregnancies last less than 250 days?

c. What percentage of pregnancies are longer than 298 days?

d. To be in the shortest 2.5% of pregnancies, what is the longest that a pregnancy can last?

e. What is the median length of pregnancy?

2. In April 1995, scores on the mathematics section of the SAT were "recentered" so that they are approximately normally distributed with mean 500 and standard deviation 100. Scores on the mathematics part of the ACT are approximately normally distributed with mean 18 and standard deviation 6.

a. Sketch graphs of the distribution of scores on each test. Include a scale on the horizontal axis.

b. What percentage of the SAT scores lie between 400 and 600? Between what two ACT scores would this same percentage of scores lie?

c. What percentage of SAT scores lie above 600?

d. Find the percentile of a person who gets an SAT score of 450.

e. One of the colleges to which Ellen is applying accepts either SAT or ACT mathematics scores. Ellen scored 680 on the mathematics part of the SAT and 27 on the mathematics section of the ACT. Should she submit her SAT or ACT mathematics score to this college? Explain your reasoning.

3. Many body dimensions of adult males and females in the United States are approximately normally distributed. Approximate means and standard deviations for two such measurements are given in the table below.

Adult Height and Shoulder Width

		Male	Female
Height (in.)	Mean	68.8	63.6
	Standard Deviation	2.65	2.5
Shoulder Width (in.)	Mean	17.7	16.0
	Standard Deviation	0.85	0.85

a. What percentage of American women are taller than the average height for American men?

b. What percentage of adult males will be uncomfortable in an airplane seat designed for people with shoulder width less than 18.5 inches? What percentage of adult females will be uncomfortable?

c. If you sampled 100,000 American males, approximately how many would you expect to be taller than 6'5"?

d. What percentage of women have a shoulder width of less than 15.5 inches? Of more than 15.5 inches?

e. What percentage of men have a shoulder width between 16 and 18 inches?

4. Karl Pearson and Alice Lee collected the heights of 1,052 mothers. Their data are summarized in the table below. A mother who was exactly 53 inches tall, for example, would be in the 53–54 inches row.

Heights of Mothers			
Height (in.)	Number of Mothers	Height (in.)	Number of Mothers
52–53	1	62–63	183
53–54	1	63–64	163
54–55	1	64–65	115
55–56	2	65–66	78
56–57	7	66–67	41
57–58	18	67–68	16
58–59	34	68–69	7
59–60	80	69–70	5
60–61	135	70–71	2
61–62	163		

Source: Pearson, Karl and Alice Lee. 1903. On the laws of inheritance in man. *Biometrika*: 364.

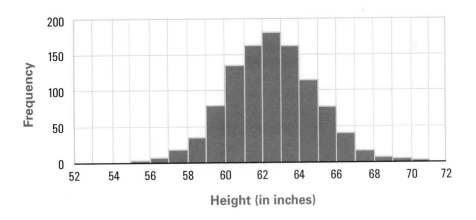

a. Is this distribution of heights approximately normal? Why or why not?

b. Collect the heights of 30 mothers. How does the distribution of your sample compare to the distribution generated in 1903?

c. What hypothesis might you make? Design a plan you could use to test your hypothesis.

Organizing

1. Make a rough sketch of the overall shape of each distribution below. Indicate an appropriate scale on the horizontal axes. Explain why you believe the distribution has the shape you sketched.

   a. The ages of everyone who died in the United States last year

   b. The weights of all adult men in the United States

   c. The prices of all pairs of blue jeans sold in the United States last week

2. In this task, "standard deviation" refers to the population standard deviation σ.

   a. For each condition below, try to find a set of 10 numbers which fit it.

   - All of the numbers are less than one standard deviation from the mean.
   - All of the numbers are exactly one standard deviation from the mean.
   - All of the numbers are more than one standard deviation from the mean.

   b. Try to find a set of numbers so that none of them are more than two standard deviations from the mean.

   c. Try to find a set of numbers so that half of the values are more than two standard deviations from the mean.

   d. What is the largest percentage of values that you were able to find in Part c that are more than two standard deviations from the mean? Compare your results to those of other students completing this task.

3. Is it true that in all symmetric distributions, exactly 68% of the values are within one standard deviation of the mean? Give an example to illustrate your answer.

4. Examine how a normal distribution and the distribution of its standardized values are related.

   a. Suppose a normal distribution has a mean of 100 and a standard deviation of 15. Now suppose every value in the distribution is converted to a standardized value. What is true about the mean of the standardized values? What is true about the standard deviation of the standardized values?

   b. Describe geometrically how a normal distribution and the distribution of its standardized values are related.

Reflecting

1. Make a list of all of the types of distributions you have studied, including those from previous courses, and illustrate each with a sketch. Then look back at the shapes of the distributions you constructed in the "Modeling Public Opinion" unit. What types of distributions did you find?

2. What variables studied in your other school subjects might have distributions that are approximately normal?

3. ACT and SAT scores have a normal distribution. Scores on classroom tests are sometimes assumed to have a normal distribution.

   a. What do teachers mean when they say they "grade on a curve"?

   b. Explain how a teacher might use a normal distribution to "grade on a curve."

   c. Do you think this is a fair way to grade? Why or why not?

4. Why is the standard deviation important in science?

Extending

1. One formula for the correlation coefficient is

$$r = \frac{1}{n-1} \sum \left(\frac{x - \overline{x}}{s_x}\right) \left(\frac{y - \overline{y}}{s_y}\right).$$

   Here, n is the sample size, $\overline{x}$ is the mean of the values of x, $\overline{y}$ is the mean of the values of y, s_x is the standard deviation of the values of x, and s_y is the standard deviation of the values of y.

   a. Use this formula to find the correlation between x and y for the following data.

x	y
1	1
2	2
3	6

   b. Explain the meaning of the correlation coefficient in the context of standardized scores.

2. Discuss whether the situations below are consistent with what you know about normal distributions and IQ tests. What could account for any inconsistencies you see?

   a. The Los Angeles Unified School District is one of the largest K–12 districts in the country, with between 500,000 and 600,000 children. In this district, there are special magnet schools for "highly gifted" children. The only way for a child in this district to be classified as highly gifted is to score 145 or above on an IQ test given by a school psychologist. Recently at the Portola Highly Gifted Magnet School, one of two such middle schools in Los Angeles, there were 61 students in the ninth grade class.

   b. One way for a child to be identified as gifted in California is to have an IQ of 130 or above. El Camino Real High School in Los Angeles has a total enrollment of 2,830 students, of whom 410 are identified as gifted.

3. This task is best done with statistical software on a computer. The points scored by the winning and losing teams in the NCAA men's championship basketball games for the years 1939–1996 are given in the following table.

1939 NCAA Championship

NCAA Men's Basketball Championships

Year	Champion	Score	Year	Champion	Score
1939	Oregon	46–33	1968	UCLA	78–55
1940	Indiana	60–42	1969	UCLA	92–72
1941	Wisconsin	39–34	1970	UCLA	80–69
1942	Stanford	53–38	1971	UCLA	68–62
1943	Wyoming	46–34	1972	UCLA	81–76
1944	Utah	42–40	1973	UCLA	87–66
1945	Oklahoma State	49–45	1974	North Carolina State	76–64
1946	Oklahoma State	43–40	1975	UCLA	92–85
1947	Holy Cross	58–47	1976	Indiana	86–68
1948	Kentucky	58–42	1977	Marquette	67–59
1949	Kentucky	46–36	1978	Kentucky	94–88
1950	CCNY	71–68	1979	Michigan State	75–64
1951	Kentucky	68–58	1980	Louisville	59–54
1952	Kansas	80–63	1981	Indiana	63–50
1953	Indiana	69–68	1982	North Carolina	63–62
1954	LaSalle	92–76	1983	North Carolina State	54–52
1955	San Francisco	77–63	1984	Georgetown	84–75
1956	San Francisco	83–71	1985	Villanova	66–64
1957	North Carolina	54–53	1986	Louisville	72–69
1958	Kentucky	84–72	1987	Indiana	74–73
1959	California	71–70	1988	Kansas	83–79
1960	Ohio State	75–55	1989	Michigan	80–79
1961	Cincinnati	70–65	1990	UNLV	103–73
1962	Cincinnati	71–59	1991	Duke	72–65
1963	Loyola (Illinois)	60–58	1992	Duke	71–51
1964	UCLA	98–83	1993	North Carolina	77–71
1965	UCLA	91–80	1994	Arkansas	76–72
1966	UTEP	72–65	1995	UCLA	89–78
1967	UCLA	79–64	1996	Kentucky	76–67

Idea from Don Bentley, Pomona College. Source: *The World Almanac and Book of Facts 1997*. Mahwah, NJ: World Almanac, 1996.

a. Are the points scored by the winning team approximately normally distributed?

b. Assuming a normal distribution, estimate the probability that the winner of the next championship game will score more than 100 points. Estimate the probability that the winner will score fewer than 80 points.

c. Often, plots over time reveal additional interesting trends. Plot the points scored by the winning teams over time. Draw horizontal lines at the mean, at two standard deviations above the mean, and at two standard deviations below the mean. Comment on any patterns or trends you observe.

The table below gives the scores for the NCAA Division I women's basketball championships for the years 1982–1996.

1982 NCAA Women's Championship

NCAA Division I Women's Basketball Championships

Year	Champion	Score	Year	Champion	Score
1982	Louisiana Tech	76–62	1990	Stanford	88–81
1983	Southern California	69–67	1991	Tennessee	70–67
1984	Southern California	72–61	1992	Stanford	78–62
1985	Old Dominion	70–65	1993	Texas Tech	84–82
1986	Texas	97–81	1994	North Carolina	60–59
1987	Stanford	67–44	1995	Connecticut	70–64
1988	Louisiana Tech	56–54	1996	Tennessee	83–65
1989	Tennessee	76–60			

Source: *The World Almanac and Book of Facts 1997.* Mahwah, NJ: World Almanac, 1996.

d. Do the scores for the winning teams appear to be approximately normal?

e. How does the distribution of the women's winning scores compare to the distribution of the men's winning scores?

4. Following is the equation of a curve that describes a normal distribution:

$$f(x) = \frac{1}{\sigma\sqrt{2\pi}} e^{-\frac{1}{2}\left(\frac{x-\mu}{\sigma}\right)^2}$$

In this formula, μ is the mean of the distribution, σ is the standard deviation, and the number e is approximately equal to 2.71828.

a. On your calculator, graph the normal curve that has a mean of 0 and a standard deviation of 1.

b. What is the total area under the normal curve and above the x-axis?

c. Describe what happens to the distribution if you change the mean. Describe what happens if you change the standard deviation.

d. There is a "bend," or **point of inflection**, in the curve where the graph changes from curved up to curved down. Estimate the point where the "bend" seems to occur. What relation does this point have to the mean and standard deviation?

5. Ozone is one of the pollutants in smog. Ozone is toxic to most living organisms and often causes eye irritations and breathing problems. In most cities, the amount of ozone in the air is carefully monitored. The following data are the daily high readings for the month of June 1994 at a station in Bayside, Wisconsin. The readings are for the number of parts per million (ppm). The mean was 0.0678 ppm and the standard deviation was 0.02879 ppm.

Highest Daily Ozone Reading (in ppm) at Bayside

0.042	0.044	0.062	0.082	0.104	0.070	0.057	0.039	0.052	0.066
0.060	0.082	0.099	0.162	0.109	0.134	0.049	0.071	0.055	0.062
0.057	0.059	0.047	0.052	0.050	0.029	0.063	0.046	0.072	0.058

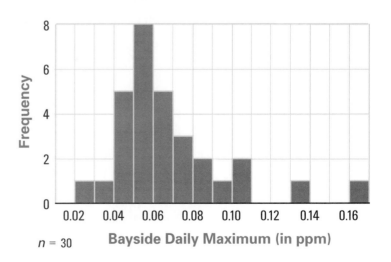

$n = 30$

a. How many standard deviations above the mean was the highest reading?

A plot over time of the daily high readings at Bayside is given below. These readings are taken hourly, unless equipment or weather conditions interfere.

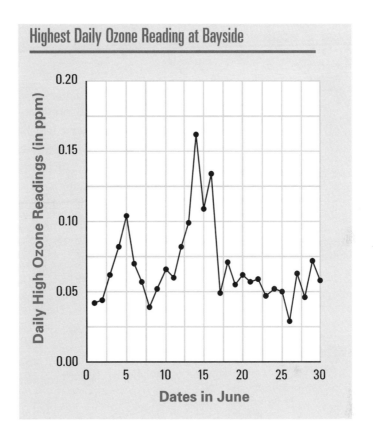

b. On a copy of this plot, draw a horizontal line that represents the mean of the daily high readings. How do the readings vary around the mean?

c. Draw horizontal lines two standard deviations above the mean and two standard deviations below the mean. How many values are outside this band?

d. Are these values outliers (1.5 IQR beyond the quartiles)? Are there other outliers? Is this reasonable?

Statistical Process Control

A major West Coast metal producer received the following complaint from a customer. The customer said that the metal they had recently received had an impurity in it. (The impurity was a trace element in the metal that affected how the metal performed.) Since this particular impurity hadn't been a problem in the past, the metal producer hadn't been monitoring it. The metal producer looked up the records on metal shipped recently to that customer. The percentage of the impurity in the metal for each week's shipment is given in the table below.

Metal Impurity

Week Ending	Percentage	Week Ending	Percentage	Week Ending	Percentage
4/7	0.000533	5/26	0.000721	7/14	0.002192
4/14	0.000472	6/2	0.000331	7/21	0.002205
4/21	0.000426	6/9	0.000537	7/28	0.002372
4/28	0.000481	6/16	0.000458	8/4	0.001866
5/5	0.000351	6/23	0.000420	8/11	0.002691
5/12	0.000471	6/30	0.000500	8/18	0.002721
5/19	0.000661	7/7	0.001976	8/25	0.002887

Source: From "Metal Impurity" by Lynda Finn. Copyright © Oriel Incorporated (formerly Joiner Associates), 1993. All rights reserved. Reprinted with permission.

The metal producer graphed the data on a plot over time (called a **run chart** when used for an industrial process). The run chart is shown below.

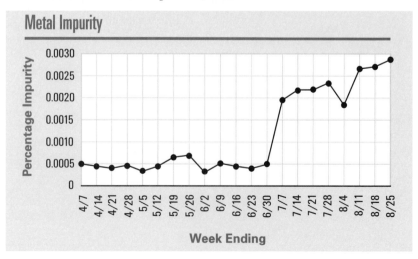

The metal producer checked with its supplier and found that the supplier had substituted a different raw material, which contained the impurity, in place of its regular raw material. The metal producer now routinely plots impurity levels of all types of impurities so that the customer will never again be the first to know!

Think About This Situation

Think about this example of metal impurity.

a When do you think the metal producer first started using the lower quality raw material?

b The percentage of impurity varies even for raw material that comes from the same source. How could you estimate the variation in the percentage impurity in shipments from any supplier?

c Companies want to stop production as soon as possible after a process goes **out of control**. In the case of the metal producer, it was obvious when that happened. Often, a process goes out of control much more gradually. What should a company look for in a run chart to indicate its process might have gone out of control? Try to list several tests or rules that would signal that the process may have gone out of control.

INVESTIGATION 1 Out-of-Control Signals

In this investigation, you will examine what the run charts of out-of-control processes look like. You will then explore some of the tests employed by industry to signal that a process may have gone out of control.

1. A process of filling milk containers is supposed to give a mean of 64 ounces and a standard deviation of 0.2 ounces. The four run charts on the next page come from four different machines. For each machine, 30 milk containers were filled and the number of ounces of milk measured. Two of the four machines are out of control.

   a. Which two machines appear to be out of control?

   b. On which of these machines did the mean change?

   c. On which of these machines did the standard deviation change?

Machine 1

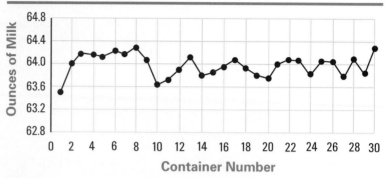

Machine 2

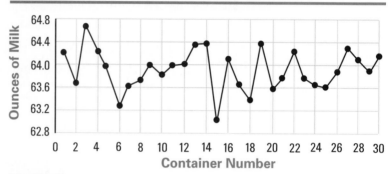

Machine 3

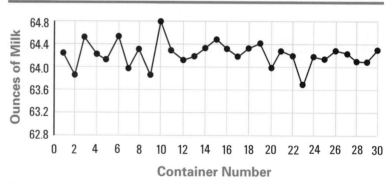

Machine 4

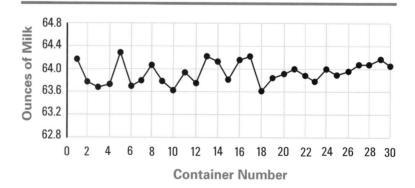

In Activity 1, you saw two ways that an out-of-control machine might behave. Since the people who monitor machines want to stop the machine as soon as possible after it has gone out of control, they have signs and patterns they look for in run charts.

2. Reexamine the data from the West Coast metal producer, reproduced below.

Metal Impurity

Week Ending	Percentage	Week Ending	Percentage	Week Ending	Percentage
4/7	0.000533	5/26	0.000721	7/14	0.002192
4/14	0.000472	6/2	0.000331	7/21	0.002205
4/21	0.000426	6/9	0.000537	7/28	0.002372
4/28	0.000481	6/16	0.000458	8/4	0.001866
5/5	0.000351	6/23	0.000420	8/11	0.002691
5/12	0.000471	6/30	0.000500	8/18	0.002721
5/19	0.000661	7/7	0.001976	8/25	0.002887

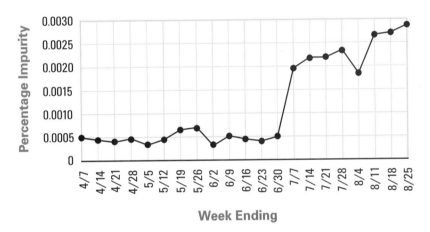

a. In the first 13 weeks of metal production, the percentage of the impurity was under control. That is, the percentage of the impurity varied a little but was of a level acceptable to the customer. Make a plot that displays the variability in these 13 percentages, and estimate the mean and standard deviation. Compare your estimates to calculated values.

b. Now look at the percentage of impurity for the 14th week, which ended July 7. How many standard deviations from the mean computed in Part a is this percentage?

c. Assume that when the level of impurity is under control, the percentages of impurity are normally distributed with the mean and standard deviation you calculated in Part a. If the level of impurity is under control, what is the probability of getting a percentage as high or higher than the one for July 7?

One test, often used, is to declare a process out of control when a single value is more than three standard deviations from the mean. This test assumes that the individual values are approximately normally distributed.

3. In a normal distribution, what is the probability that a single value will be more than three standard deviations away from the mean?

4. Each of the run charts below and on the next page was made from a process that was supposed to be normally distributed with a mean of 5 and a standard deviation of 1. The charts were made by the statistical software *Minitab*.

Chart 1

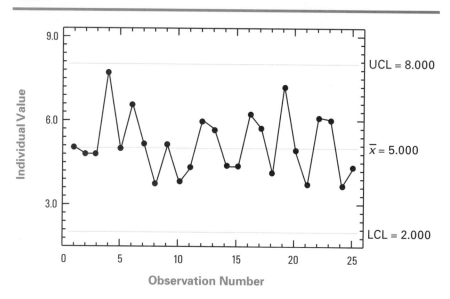

Chart 2

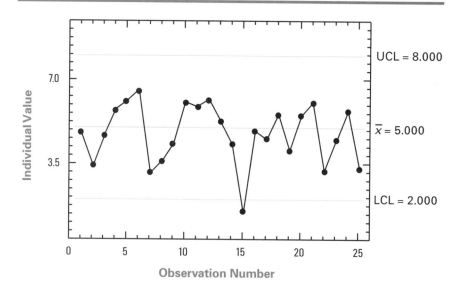

Chart 3

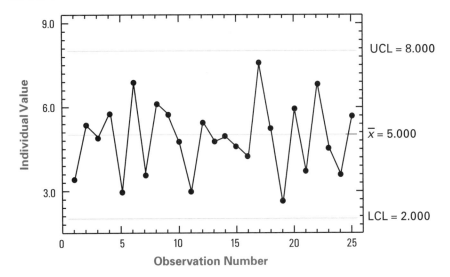

a. UCL means "upper control limit" and LCL means "lower control limit." How were these limits computed?

b. On which chart is there a point where the process should be suspected to be out of control, using the test of three standard deviations or more from the mean?

5. The process documented on the run chart below is supposed to be normally distributed with a mean of 5 and a standard deviation of 1. The small "2" below the final point, where the process was stopped, indicates that the process may have gone out of control. Why do you think *Minitab* has declared the process out of control?

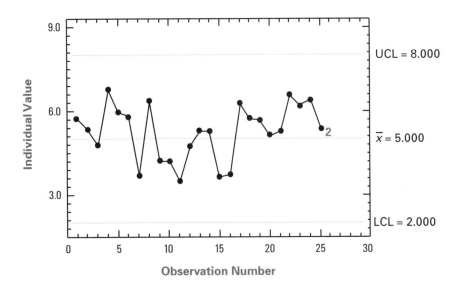

On the chart "Illustrations of Tests," reproduced below, are eight tests used by industry to signal that a process may have changed. This chart is from Western Electric's *Statistical Quality Control Handbook*. The zones are marked off in standard deviations. For example, if a value falls in Zone A, it is more than two, but less than three standard deviations from the mean $\bar{x}$. The small x marks the value at which the process is first declared out of control. Each of these tests assumes that the individual values come from a normal distribution.

Illustration of Tests

Test 1. One observation beyond either Zone A. (Two examples are shown.)

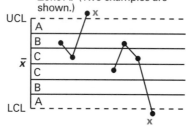

Test 2. Nine observations in a row on one half of the chart.

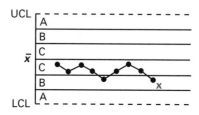

Test 3. Six observations in a row steadily increasing or decreasing. (Two examples are shown.)

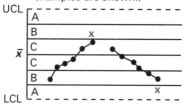

Test 4. Fourteen observations in a row alternating up or down.

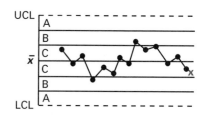

Test 5. Two out of three observations in a row on one half of the chart and in Zone A or beyond. (Three examples are shown.)

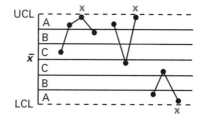

Test 6. Four out of five observations in a row on one half of the chart and in Zone B or beyond. (Two examples are shown.)

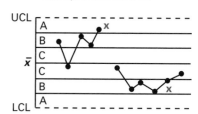

Test 7. Fifteen observations in a row within the two C zones.

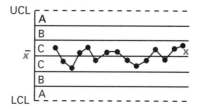

Test 8. Eight observations in a row with none in either Zone C.

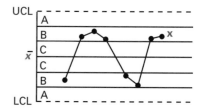

Source: Western Electric. *Statistical Quality Control Handbook*. Chicago: American Telephone and Telegraph Company, 1956.

6. Match each of the eight tests to the best description below.

    a. The observations are gradually getting larger (or smaller).

    b. One observation is very far from the mean.

    c. Two of three observations are unusually high (or low).

    d. Four of five observations are all somewhat high (or low).

    e. The mean seems to have decreased (or increased).

    f. The standard deviation seems to have decreased.

    g. The standard deviation seems to have increased.

    h. The process shows a nonrandom pattern that should be explained.

7. Look back at how these tests relate to your previous work in this investigation.

    a. What is the number of the test that signals when a single value is more than three standard deviations from the mean?

    b. Which test signaled the point marked "2" in Activity 5 (page 389)?

8. For each of the run charts below and on the next page, there is an x at the point when the process first was declared to be out of control. Give the number of the test used to decide that the process was out of control.

    a.

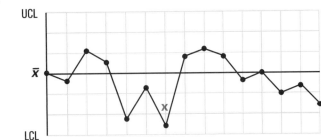

    b.

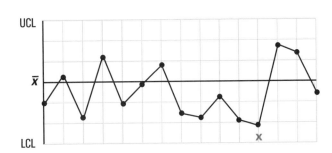

    c.

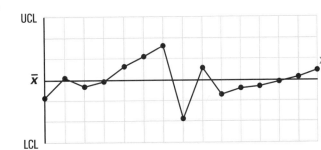

d.

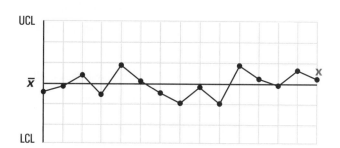

9. Here is a run chart for a process that is supposed to have a mean of 28 and a standard deviation of 2.

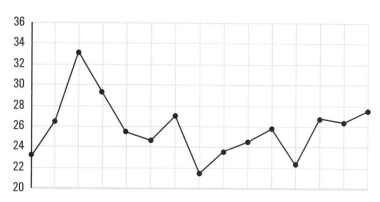

    a. On a copy of the chart, identify and label the horizontal lines dividing the zones.

    b. When did the process first go out of control? By which test?

    c. Has the mean or the standard deviation changed?

Checkpoint

In this investigation, you have examined eight tests used by industry to signal that a process may have gone out of control.

a Describe each of these tests in your own words.

b Name three tests that will detect a change in the mean of a process.

c Which tests will detect a change in the standard deviation of a process?

d Suppose you are monitoring a process that is in control. What is the probability that Test 1 will signal on the very next value that the process is out of control?

Be prepared to share your descriptions and thinking with the class.

The run charts that you have been examining are sometimes called Shewhart control charts. Dr. Walter A. Shewhart invented these charts during the late 1920s and early 1930s while he worked for Bell Laboratories. These charts provide a quick, visual check if a process has changed or gone "out of control." When there is change in an industrial process, the machine operator wants to know why and may have to adjust the machine.

On Your Own

Carefully examine each of the following run charts.

a. For this run chart, there is an asterisk (*) below the observation at which the statistical software warned that the process may have gone out of control. Give the number of the test used.

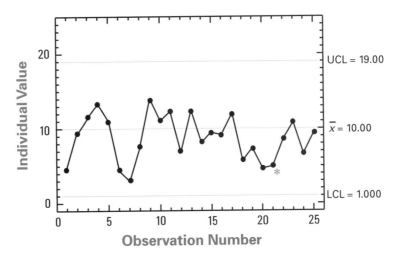

b. The process graphed on the run chart below is supposed to have a mean of 8 ounces and a standard deviation of 1 ounce. Find the point at which the process should first be declared out of control. Give the number of the test used.

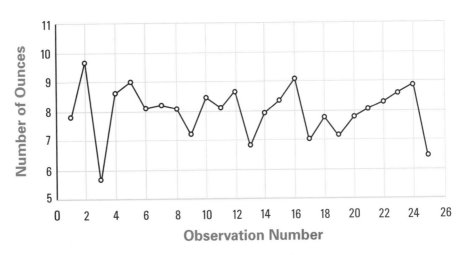

INVESTIGATION 2 Getting Things under Control

You are now familiar with several tests commonly used by industry to signal that a process may have gone out of control. Once you have determined that a process is out of control, you are faced with determining the best way to get things back under control. Consider a process such as throwing darts or bowling.

1. In bowling, most bowlers put a slight spin on the ball when they roll it down the lane. This causes the ball to curve eventually, rather than always following a straight line, which actually makes it easier to make a strike (knock down all ten pins). By hitting a "pocket" between the lead pin and one of the two pins on either side, the ball and any pins knocked down are more likely to knock down other pins as well. Because of the curve, bowlers usually aim not for the pins themselves but for one of a series of arrows on the lane floor.

Whenever a bowler uses a lane for the first time and aims toward the usual arrow, it's difficult to tell just where the ball will hit the pins. Lane conditions, such as how slick the floor is, can cause slight changes in what the bowler might expect from previous experience. One way a bowler can increase his or her accuracy is to observe where the ball hits the pins and adjust where to roll the ball in relation to the arrows.

The bowler has several possibilities for deciding how to adjust his or her roll:

- Roll once, decide which arrow to aim for, and then always aim at that arrow.

- After every roll, readjust which arrow to aim for, based on the last roll.

- Roll a number of times, observe the results, and then decide which arrow to aim for.

a. Which strategy do you think is the best? Explain your choice.

Suppose a bowler's spin always causes the ball to curve to the left. The best pocket to hit for such a spin is the pocket to the right of the lead pin, so the ball continues toward the center of the pins after it first hits. This bowler aims for the second arrow from the right and gets the pattern at the right for where the ball hits the pins.

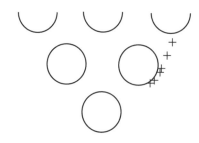

b. Suppose the bowler chooses the third strategy above to adjust his or her aim. Describe how the bowler can decide what adjustments to make.

2. Now refer back to the milk-container-filling process at the beginning of Investigation 1 (page 385).

   a. Suppose that an operator is trying to adjust the machine that fills milk containers so that there is an average of 64 ounces per container. The operator measures the volume of milk in each container as it is filled. If the container has less than 64 ounces in it, the operator increases the amount of milk that goes into the next container. If the container has more than 64 ounces in it, the operator decreases the amount of milk that goes into the next container. Can you suggest a better strategy for the operator?

   b. Based on your strategy, what action would you suggest the operator take if the next container has 64.5 ounces in it?

Checkpoint

There is a natural variation in most processes. Knowing when to adjust, in which direction to adjust, and how much to adjust are important considerations in quality control.

   a In what situations have you noticed that it is best to watch the process for a while before taking action?

   b In what situations have you noticed that it is best to make adjustments immediately?

   Be prepared to explain your examples to the class.

▶ **On Your Own**

Mrs. Carter is a new bus driver. Her bus is scheduled to arrive at school at 7:46 A.M. On Monday morning, the bus arrives at 7:44 A.M. Mrs. Carter suggests that she pick up all the students two minutes later on Tuesday. What would you say to her?

Modeling

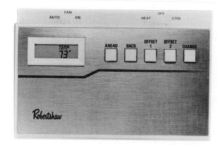

1. The thermostat in the Silvermans' apartment is set at 70° Fahrenheit. Mr. Silverman checks the temperature in the apartment every day at noon. The table and plot below give his observations over the last 25 days. At noon today, the temperature in his apartment was 63°. Should Mr. Silverman call building maintenance? Explain why or why not, in terms of statistical process control methods.

Temperature Observations

Day	Temp in °F	Day	Temp in °F
1	72	14	67
2	71	15	72
3	67	16	73
4	72	17	71
5	72	18	70
6	71	19	70
7	73	20	67
8	72	21	69
9	69	22	68
10	70	23	72
11	68	24	71
12	65	25	70
13	68		

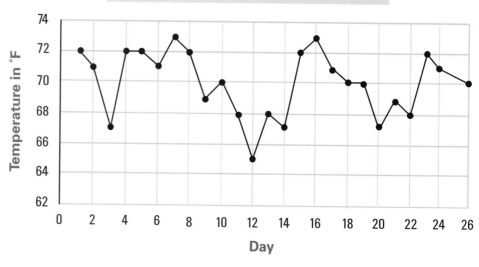

2. The plot below gives the gas mileage for a car for 20 consecutive tanks of gas. During this time, the owner drove the car only to work and back. Do you think that at any point the car got a tune-up, which generally improves gas mileage? If so, when and why do you think so? If not, why not?

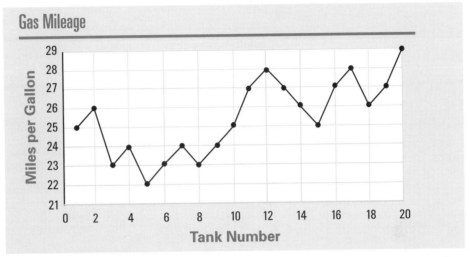

Gas Mileage

3. A person is running a machine that makes nails. The nails are supposed to have a mean length of 2 inches. But, as in all processes, the nails don't come out *exactly* 2 inches long each time. The machine is supposed to be set so the distribution of the lengths of the nails is normal and the standard deviation of the lengths of the nails is 0.03 inch.

   a. Sketch the distribution of the lengths of the nails when the machine is under control. Mark the mean and one, two, and three standard deviations from the mean on the horizontal axis.

   b. If the machine is set correctly, what percentage of the nails will be more than 2.06 inches long? Less than 1.94 inches long?

   c. What percentage of the nails will be more than 2.09 inches long? Less than 1.91 inches long?

   d. Suppose the machinist turns on the machine one morning after it has been cleaned and finds these lengths for the first ten nails: 2.01, 2.08, 1.97, 1.99, 1.92, 2.00, 2.03, 1.99, 1.97, and 1.95. Explain what your advice would be and why.

4. Think of a process for which you can collect data that you think will be approximately normally distributed and for which you can make at least 35 observations. For example, you might count the number of raisins in small boxes or the number of drops of water that will fit on a penny. To estimate the mean and standard deviation of your process, make 10 observations of the process when you have reason to believe that it is behaving in a typical manner. Compute the mean and standard deviation from those 10 observations. Make a run chart of the next 25 observations. Did the process go out of control according to any of the eight tests? If so, do you have an explanation?

Organizing

1. Suppose you are operating a machine that fills cereal boxes. The boxes are supposed to contain 16 ounces. The machine fills the boxes so that the distribution of weights is normal and the standard deviation is 0.2 ounce. You can adjust the mean.

Cleaning a cereal machine

   a. If you set the machine so that the mean is 16 ounces, what percentage of customers will get a box of cereal that weighs less than 16 ounces?

   b. Explain where you would set the mean and why.

   c. Suppose you are buying a new box-filling machine. All else being equal, should you buy one with a standard deviation of 0.2 ounce or 0.4 ounce? Explain your reasoning.

2. If a process is in control and data collected from the process are approximately normally distributed, what is the probability that the next reading on a control chart lies outside the control limits?

3. A paper clip machine makes 4,000,000 paper clips each month. The machinist measures every 10,000th paper clip to be sure the machine is still set correctly. When the machine is set correctly, the measurements follow a normal distribution. The machinist uses *only* Test 1 (one value more than three standard deviations from the mean). Suppose the machine remains set correctly for a month. How many times would you expect the operator to stop production anyway?

4. Make a run chart with at least 25 observations on it that have an obvious pattern but for which none of the eight tests signal that the process may have gone out of control. Invent a test that would give an out-of-control signal for your run chart. Copy your chart and explanation of your test onto a larger piece of paper that can be displayed in your classroom.

Reflecting

1. What types of data can be displayed on a run chart?

2. A machinist is making video game tokens that are supposed to be a certain diameter.

   a. What might cause the mean diameter to change?

   b. What might cause the standard deviation of the diameter to change while the mean stays the same?

3. Find out what businesspeople mean when they use the word "micromanage." In what way is adjusting a process too often like micromanaging?

4. Why might a company want to detect a decrease in variation in the manufacturing of a product or in the processing of a service?

5. Suppose you had to select four of the tests to use for a process of filling milk containers so that the mean is 8 ounces. Explain which four tests you would choose.

Extending

1. The eight tests assume that observations come from a distribution that is approximately normal. For individual observations, this is not always the case. For example, suppose the Random Digit Company has a machine that produces random digits from the set {0, 1, 2, 3, 4, 5, 6, 7, 8, 9}.

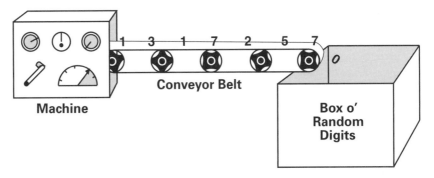

   a. Suppose the machine produces one random digit.

   ▪ Make a graph of the probability distribution of all possible outcomes.

   ▪ What is the mean of the distribution?

   ▪ What is the standard deviation of the distribution?

   b. Are there any tests by which the process could never be classified "out of control"? Explain.

   Since the distribution isn't approximately normal, the Random Digit Company shouldn't use the eight tests. In Parts c through f, you will explore what the Random Digit Company might do so it *can* use the tests.

   c. Using a table of random digits or your calculator, select 5 digits at random and find their sum.

   d. Noah repeated Part c 1,400 times on his computer. That is, his computer selected 5 digits at random and found the sum. The computer repeated this process until it had 1,400 sums. What is the smallest sum Noah could have gotten? The largest?

e. The histogram below shows the 1,400 sums that Noah got. About how many times did he get a sum of 10? Of 21?

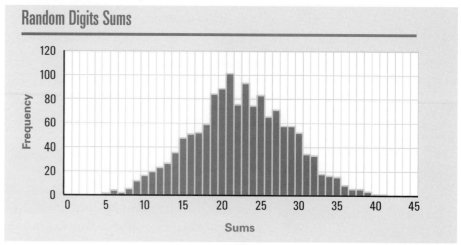

f. How could the Random Digit Company use sums to meet the normality assumption of the eight tests?

2. In Lesson 3 of the "Modeling Public Opinion" unit, you used simulation to construct sampling distributions. A sampling distribution for the situation of flipping a coin 20 times and counting the number of heads appears at the right. This sampling distribution of 2,500 trials was constructed using computer software.

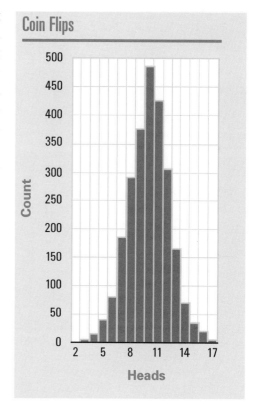

a. Describe how to construct this sampling distribution using a table of random digits. Perform one trial of the simulation.

b. What is the shape of the sampling distribution shown?

c. For your trial of the simulation in Part a, code each head as a 1 and each tail as a 0. That is, suppose your simulation began H, T, T, H, H, H. You would code this as 1, 0, 0, 1, 1, 1. What is the sum of the digits from your trial?

d. Suppose you perform many trials, code the results, and make a histogram of the sums. What would this histogram look like?

e. How is this task like Extending Task 1? What statement can you make about the distribution of sums?

3. When we say we want to get things under control, sometimes we mean making things better. In that case, we need statistical techniques other than the eight tests. The graph below gives the highest recorded ozone reading in parts per million for each year from 1955 through 1993 in downtown Los Angeles. (Ozone is a component of smog.)

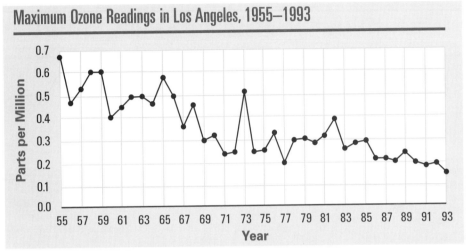

Maximum Ozone Readings in Los Angeles, 1955–1993

Source: Southern California Air Quality Management District. *www.aqmd.gov*

a. This graph shows several interesting trends. Describe what is happening to the highest recorded ozone levels in Los Angeles during the period from 1955 to 1993. Do you know any possible explanations for this trend?

b. Estimate the slope of the regression line. Describe, in words, what this slope means in terms of ozone levels.

c. Estimate the parts per million for ozone in the year 2000.

d. In 1955, the worst year, the maximum ozone level was 0.68 part per million (ppm). What proportion of the air was ozone? What percentage?

e. Estimate the median of the highest ozone readings for Los Angeles for the 39 years from 1955 to 1993.

f. For how many years immediately following and including 1955 was the maximum ozone level above the median? For how many years immediately before and including 1993 was the maximum ozone level below the median?

g. If eleven numbers are selected at random from a large set of numbers, what is the probability that they are all below the median?

h. What do you conclude from observing where the points lie in relation to the median?

4. In the case of Los Angeles (Extending Task 3), it is easy to see that the ozone problem is getting better because there are so many years of data and the trend is so strong. In some cases, it's not so easy to tell. For example, records of ozone have been kept in Lancaster, California, only since 1970. Lancaster is a rapidly growing community in the desert north of the mountains that rim Los Angeles. The plot below shows maximum ozone levels in Lancaster.

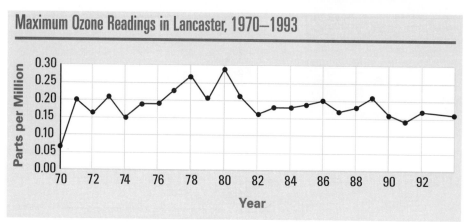

Maximum Ozone Readings in Lancaster, 1970–1993

Source: Southern California Air Quality Management District. *www.agmd.gov*

a. Describe what you see in the plot above.

b. Estimate the median of these maximum ozone levels.

c. How do the values in the last few years in Lancaster compare to the median for the entire 24 years? Was any other long consecutive set of readings either all above or all below the median?

d. If four numbers are selected at random from a large set of numbers, what is the probability that they are all below the median of the set?

e. If seven numbers are selected at random from a large set of numbers, what is the probability that they are all above the median of the set?

f. From your results in Parts d and e, what can you conclude about the ozone levels in Lancaster?

g. Why is the median used as the measure of center in the Los Angeles (Extending Task 3) and Lancaster ozone problems?

INVESTIGATION 3 False Alarms

Even a process that is under control exhibits variation. Consequently, the eight tests on page 390 occasionally will give an out-of-control signal, called a **false alarm**, for a process that is under control. For example, if you watch a process that is in control long enough, eventually one observation will be beyond one of the A zones. Eventually six observations in a row will be steadily increasing, and so on. The tests have been designed so that false alarms occur very rarely. If you have been monitoring a process that is under control, the probability of a false alarm on the next set of observations is very small.

1. Assuming that the observations of a process are normally distributed, fill in the "Percentage of Values" entries on a copy of the chart and graph below. You can then refer to the chart when working on the remaining activities.

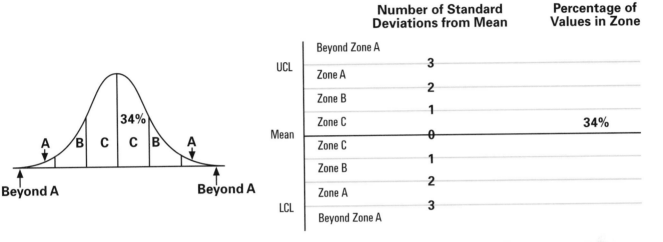

2. Suppose a machine is filling cartons of ice cream and is under control. The operator uses only Test 1 to signal that the weight of the ice cream may have gone out of control. What is the probability of a false alarm on the very next carton of ice cream being filled? Place your result in the appropriate row of a copy of the table below. Keep your table; you will fill out the other rows in subsequent activities.

False Alarms

Test		Probability of a False Alarm on the Next Set of Observations of a Process under Control
1	One observation beyond either Zone A	
2	Nine observations in a row on one half of the chart	
3	Six observations in a row steadily increasing or decreasing	
4	Fourteen observations in a row alternating up and down	
5	Two out of three observations in a row on one half of the chart and in Zone A or beyond	
6	Four out of five observations in a row on one half of the chart and in Zone B or beyond	
7	Fifteen observations in a row within the two C zones	
8	Eight observations in a row with none in either Zone C	

3. Now suppose the ice cream machine operator is using only Test 7. The machine continues to stay in control.

a. What is the probability that a single observation will fall either within Zone C in the top half of the chart or within Zone C in the bottom half of the chart?

b. What is the probability that the observations from each of the next 15 cartons filled will all fall within either of the two C zones? Explain how you calculated this.

c. What is the probability that the ice cream machine operator will get a false alarm from the next 15 cartons being filled? Place your result in the appropriate row of your copy of the table, rounding to the nearest ten-thousandth.

4. Now suppose the ice cream machine operator is using only Test 2. The machine continues to stay in control.

a. What is the probability that the next nine observations are all in the bottom half of the chart?

b. What is the probability that the next nine observations are all in the top half of the chart?

c. What is the probability that the next nine observations are all in the top half of the chart *or* all in the bottom half of the chart?

d. What is the probability that the operator will get a false alarm from the next nine cartons being filled? Place your result in the appropriate row of your copy of the table, rounding to the nearest ten-thousandth.

5. A ceramic plate machine makes 20,000 plates in a year. It is under control. If the operator uses Test 1 only and measures every hundredth plate, what is the probability the operator will get through the year without having to stop the machine?

Checkpoint

In this investigation, you examined the likelihood of a false alarm when using quality control tests.

a What is a false alarm? Why do false alarms occur occasionally if the process is under control?

b Suppose you are monitoring a manufacturing process that is under control. Describe how to find the probability that the next five observations will all be in Zone C in the top half of the chart.

Be prepared to explain your thinking and method to the class.

The eight tests were all devised so that, when you are monitoring a process that is in control, the probability of a false alarm on the next set of observations tested is about 0.005 or less. You will determine the probability of a false alarm for the remaining five tests in the next MORE section.

On Your Own

A machine operator is using the following rule as an out-of-control signal: six observations in a row in Zone B in the top half of the chart or six observations in a row in Zone B in the bottom half of the chart. Assume the machine is in control.

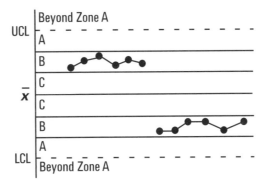

(Two examples are shown.)

a. What is the probability that the next six values are all in Zone B in the top half of the chart?

b. What is the probability that the next six values are all in Zone B in the bottom half of the chart?

c. What is the probability that the operator gets a false alarm from the next six values?

INVESTIGATION 4 The Addition Rule

In the previous investigation, you probably used the Multiplication Rule for independent events to estimate the probabilities of false alarms for processes under control. In completing the "On Your Own" task above, you may have used another rule for calculating a probability. In particular, to find the probability of a false alarm because six observations are in Zone B in the top half of the chart or six observations are in Zone B in the bottom half of the chart, you may have *added* the probabilities of the two events. In this investigation, you will explore more carefully when you can add probabilities to find the probability that one event happens or another event happens (or that both happen).

1. As a class, complete the following activity on clothing colors.

   a. Each member of your class should raise his or her hand when the appropriate category is called. (If your class wears uniforms, answer the question according to what you last wore before your uniform.) Record frequencies on a copy of the table below on the blackboard or overhead projector.

   ### Current Clothing Colors

Principal Color of Pants or Skirt That You Are Wearing Today	Number of Students
Blue	
Black	
White	
Brown or Beige	
Gray	
Green	
Other	

   b. Some students have pants or skirts of many different colors, while other students prefer one or two colors and so have all of their pants or skirts in just those colors. Fill in the following chart. Students should raise their hands for each category for which they own pants or skirts of that color. For example, a student who has all pants in the colors blue and white would raise his or her hand for those two colors.

   ### General Clothing Colors

Principal Color of Pants or Skirts That You Own	Number of Students
Blue	
Black	
White	
Brown or Beige	
Gray	
Green	
Other	

   Consider these two questions about the information you gathered.

   ■ What is the probability that a randomly selected student from your class is wearing a skirt or pants that are black or white?

   ■ What is the probability that a randomly selected student from your class owns pants or skirts that are black or white?

c. Which question from Part b can be answered using just the data in the tables?

d. Why can't the other question be answered using just the information in the tables?

e. Find the answer to that question by asking students directly.

2. The table below gives the percentage of high school graduates who have taken selected science courses in high school. The information was gathered from high school transcripts.

Science Course Enrollment

Science Course	Percentage of Graduates
Biology	93.5
Chemistry	56.0
Physics	24.4

Source: National Center for Education Statistics. *The Condition of Education 1997.* Washington, D.C.: U.S. Dept. of Education, 1997.

Use the data in the table to answer, if possible, each of the following questions. If a question cannot be answered, explain why not.

a. What is the probability that a randomly selected graduate has taken chemistry?

b. What is the probability that a randomly selected graduate has taken physics?

c. What is the probability that a randomly selected graduate has taken chemistry or physics?

d. What is the probability that a randomly selected graduate has taken chemistry or biology?

e. What is the probability that a randomly selected graduate has taken chemistry and biology?

3. Companies must not only manufacture products, they must also market them. One study asked 299 randomly selected people in a large city to complete a personality questionnaire and then classified each person as a *cautious conservative,* a *middle-of-the-roader,* or a *confident explorer.* Each person was also asked how he or she felt about small cars. The number of people in each category is shown in the table below.

Small Car Survey

		Personality Type			
		Cautious Conservative	Middle-of-the-Roader	Confident Explorer	Total
Opinion	Favorable	79	58	49	186
	Neutral	10	8	9	27
	Unfavorable	10	34	42	86
	Total	99	100	100	299

Source: Jacobson, Eugene, and Jerome Kossoff. "Self-percept and Consumer Attitudes Toward Small Cars," in *Consumer Behavior in Theory and in Action.* Steuart Henderson Britt (Ed.). New York: Wiley, 1970.

a. Estimate the probability that a randomly selected person in the city is a cautious conservative.

b. Estimate the probability that a randomly selected person in the city is a middle-of-the-roader.

c. Estimate the probability that a randomly selected person in the city will be favorable to small cars.

d. Estimate the probability that a person in the city will be a cautious conservative or a middle-of-the-roader.

e. Can you find the answer to Part d using your probability estimates from just Parts a and b? Why or why not?

f. Estimate the probability that a person in the city is a cautious conservative or has a favorable opinion of small cars.

g. Can you find the answer to Part f by just adding two probabilities? Why or why not?

Two events are said to be **mutually exclusive** if it is impossible for both of them to occur on the same trial.

4. In your group, discuss which of the following pairs of events are mutually exclusive. Be sure everyone understands the reasoning behind your conclusions.

   a. Being a cautious conservative or being a confident explorer

   b. Being a confident explorer or having a neutral opinion of small cars

   c. Chemistry on a high school transcript or physics on a high school transcript

   d. A student owning white pants or skirts or a student owning black pants or skirts

   e. A student wearing white pants or a white skirt today or a student wearing black pants or a black skirt today

   f. Rolling a sum of 7 with a pair of dice or rolling doubles with a pair of dice

   g. Rolling a sum of 8 with a pair of dice or rolling doubles with a pair of dice

5. For each situation below, explain why the two events are mutually exclusive, and then determine the probability.

   a. If you pick one value at random from a normal distribution, what is the probability that it will be more than two standard deviations above the mean or more than two standard deviations below the mean?

   b. If you pick one value at random from a normal distribution, what is the probability that it will be below the mean or more than two standard deviations above the mean?

6. Suppose two events A and B are mutually exclusive. Write a symbolic rule for computing $P(A$ or $B)$. This rule is called the **Addition Rule** for mutually exclusive events.

7. Now consider probabilistic situations in which there are more than two events.

   a. If you roll a pair of dice three times, what is the probability that you will get doubles on all three rolls?

   b. If you flip a coin four times, what is the probability that you will get heads on all four flips?

   c. If you pick five values at random from a normal distribution, what is the probability that all five values will be above the mean or all will be below the mean?

   d. If you pick four values at random from a normal distribution, what is the probability that all four values will be more than two standard deviations above the mean?

   e. If you pick five values at random from a normal distribution, what is the probability that all five values will be more than one standard deviation above the mean or all will be more than one standard deviation below the mean?

   f. If you pick six values at random from a normal distribution, what is the probability that all six values will be below the mean?

8. In the Monopoly® game, a player who gets sent to jail gets three turns to roll doubles. If one of the three rolls is doubles, the player gets out of jail. If none of the three rolls is doubles, the player has to pay $50 and gets out of jail. Gina has been sent to jail. She wants to know the probability that she will get out of jail without having to pay $50.

She computes this way:

P(doubles) = P(doubles on 1st roll, doubles on 2nd roll, or doubles on 3rd roll)

$$= P(\text{doubles on 1st roll}) + P(\text{doubles on 2nd}) + P(\text{doubles on 3rd})$$

$$= \frac{1}{6} + \frac{1}{6} + \frac{1}{6}$$

$$= \frac{3}{6}$$

$$= \frac{1}{2}$$

a. Use Gina's method to compute the probability of rolling doubles in seven rolls of the dice. Is her method correct?

b. What would you say to Gina about her reasoning?

c. What is the probability of rolling doubles at least once in three tries?

Checkpoint

In this investigation, you explored conditions for which it is appropriate to add probabilities and reexamined conditions for multiplying probabilities.

a If you select two values at random from a normal distribution, what is the probability that they both are more than two standard deviations above the mean or that they both are more than two standard deviations below the mean? How did you use the rules of probability in finding your answer?

b In general, under what conditions would you add probabilities? Multiply probabilities?

c Give an original example of two mutually exclusive events. Give an original example of two independent events.

Be prepared to share and explain your responses to the entire class.

On Your Own

a. Which of the following pairs of events are mutually exclusive? Explain your reasoning.

- Rolling a pair of dice and getting a sum of 6
  Rolling a pair of dice and getting one die with a 6 on it

- Flipping a coin 7 times and getting at least 3 heads
  Flipping a coin 7 times and getting at least 5 heads

b. Janet, a 60% free-throw shooter, finds herself in a two-shot foul situation. What is the probability that she will score only one point? What assumptions did you make?

MORE
Modeling • Organizing • Reflecting • Extending

Modeling

1. In Investigation 3, page 403, you explored the probabilities of false alarms in the context of a machine filling cartons of ice cream, with the process under control. Suppose now that the operator is using only Test 8 on page 390.

   a. What is the probability that the next observation isn't in either Zone C?

   b. What is the probability that none of the next eight observations are in either Zone C?

   c. What is the probability that the operator will get a false alarm from the next eight cartons being filled? Place your result in the appropriate row of your copy of the table from Investigation 3. Round your answer to the nearest ten-thousandth.

2. Suppose that the ice cream machine in Investigation 3, page 403, is under control and the operator is using only Test 4. In this task, you will use simulation to estimate the probability of a false alarm with the next fourteen observations.

   a. First, describe a simulation to estimate the probability that if the digits 1, 2, 3, 4, and 5 are listed in a random order, they will alternate larger, smaller, larger, smaller, larger (for example: 5, 1, 3, 2, 4) or they will alternate smaller, larger, smaller, larger, smaller (for example: 4, 5, 2, 3, 1).

   b. Perform your simulation 20 times. What is your estimate of the probability that the digits will alternate?

   c. Make or obtain a listing of all possible sequences of {1, 2, 3, 4, 5}. What is the theoretical probability that if these digits are listed at random, they will alternate?

d. Design and carry out a simulation to estimate the probability that if the digits 1 through 14 are listed in a random order, they will alternate. Place your result on the appropriate row of your copy of the table from Investigation 3, rounding to the nearest ten-thousandth.

3. Suppose that the ice cream machine in Investigation 3, page 403, is under control and the operator is using only Test 5. You will now find the probability of a false alarm with the next three observations.

a. What is the probability that an observation will fall in Zone A at the top of the chart or beyond?

b. There are four ways that at least two of the next three observations can be in Zone A at the top of the chart or beyond. Three ways are described here:

■ The first observation is in Zone A or beyond; so are the second and third.

■ The first observation is not in Zone A or beyond; the second and third are.

■ The first observation is in Zone A or beyond; the second is not; the third is.

What is the fourth way?

c. Find the probability of each of the four ways in Part b. Are these four ways mutually exclusive?

d. What is the probability that at least two of the next three observations will be in Zone A at the top of the chart or beyond?

e. What is the probability that at least two of the next three observations will be in Zone A at the *bottom* of the chart or beyond?

f. Are the events described in Parts d and e mutually exclusive?

g. What is the probability that the ice cream machine operator will get a false alarm from the next three cartons being filled? Place your result in your copy of the table from Investigation 3. Round your answer to the nearest ten-thousandth.

4. Suppose that the ice cream machine in Investigation 3, page 403, is under control and the operator is using only Test 6. Find the probability of a false alarm from the next five observations. Place your result in your copy of the table from Investigation 3, rounding to the nearest ten-thousandth.

Organizing

1. In Course 2, you learned that the expected waiting time for a success in a waiting-time distribution is $\frac{1}{p}$, if p is the probability of a success on any one trial.

a. Suppose a machine operator is using only Test 1. If the process is under control, what is the expected number of items tested until a false alarm is given by Test 1? This is called the **average run length** or **ARL**.

b. If a machine operator uses both Test 1 and Test 2, is the ARL longer or shorter than if he or she uses just Test 1? Explain.

2. Give an example of two tests from the "Illustration of Tests" chart, page 390, that are *not* independent. That is, if a set of observations triggers a warning from one of the tests, it is more likely or less likely to trigger a warning by the other. Explain why you selected these two tests.

3. The probability of a false alarm using Test 8 is much smaller than the probability of a false alarm using any of the other tests. Describe how you could change Test 8 in order to make the probability of a false alarm closer to those of the other tests.

4. Imagine rolling a pair of tetrahedral dice.

   a. Make a chart showing all possible outcomes for the sum when you roll a pair of tetrahedral dice.

   b. What is the probability that if you roll a pair of tetrahedral dice, you get a sum of 5 or doubles? Are these two events mutually exclusive?

Reflecting

1. A false alarm occurs when a machine is in control and a test warns that it may not be.

   a. What could you call a situation for which the machine isn't in control and no test has given a warning?

   b. The following chart has four empty cells. Two of the cells should contain the words "correct decision." Another cell should contain the words "false alarm." The fourth cell should contain your answer from Part a. Write these words in the correct cells on a copy of the chart.

	Result of Test	
Condition of Machine	Gives Alarm	Doesn't Give Alarm
In Control		
Not in Control		

2. Why is it best if a machine operator does not use all eight tests but rather picks out just a few to use?

3. If you pick six values at random from a distribution with unknown shape, what is the probability that all six values are more than the median? Can you answer this question for the mean? Explain.

4. If a person started flipping a coin and got heads on each flip, how many heads would it take before you were confident that the person had a two-headed coin? What is the probability that a person who begins to flip a fair coin will get this many heads in a row just by chance?

5. What is the difference between independent events and mutually exclusive events?

Extending

1. Invent another out-of-control signal that is different from the eight tests you have studied. That is, design another test that signals when the observations don't seem to be following a random pattern in their variation around the mean. If you can, compute the probability of a false alarm in a set of observations of appropriate size.

2. The Ford Motor Company lists these four signals on its control charts:

   ■ Any point outside of the control limits (more than three standard deviations from the mean)

   ■ Seven points in a row that are all above or all below the central line

   ■ Seven points in a row that are either increasing or decreasing

   ■ Any other obviously nonrandom pattern

   Source: Ford Motor Company, *Continuing Process Control and Process Capability Improvement.* December, 1987.

   Assume that a manufacturing process is in control.

   a. Which of these tests is exactly the same as one of the tests on page 390, taken from the Western Electric handbook?

   b. If you are using only Ford's first test, what is the probability of a false alarm on the next observation?

   c. What is the probability of a false alarm on the next seven observations, if you are using only Ford's second test?

   d. Is Ford's second test more or less likely to produce a false alarm than the corresponding test from the Western Electric handbook? Explain.

   e. Is Ford's third test more or less likely to produce a false alarm than the corresponding test from the Western Electric handbook? Explain.

3. Suppose that the ice cream machine in Investigation 3, page 403, is under control and the operator is using only Test 3 from the chart on page 390. To find the probability of a false alarm, you can use the idea of permutations or ordered arrangements.

   a. In how many different orders can the digits 1, 2, and 3 be listed?

   b. In how many different orders can the digits 1, 2, 3, and 4 be listed?

   c. Compute 4! and 3! using the factorial function (!) on a calculator. Compare the calculator values of 4! and 3! to your answers in Parts a and b.

   d. Use the factorial function to compute the number of different orders in which the digits 1, 2, 3, 4, 5, and 6 can be listed.

   e. If the digits 1, 2, 3, 4, 5, and 6 are listed in a random order, what is the probability that they are in order from smallest to largest?

   f. If the digits 1, 2, 3, 4, 5, and 6 are listed in a random order, what is the probability that they are in order from largest to smallest?

   g. Are the two events described in Part e and Part f mutually exclusive? If any six numbers are listed at random, what is the probability that they are in order from largest to smallest or in order from smallest to largest?

   h. What is the probability that the ice cream machine operator will get a false alarm using only Test 3 with the next six cartons filled? Place your result in the appropriate row of your copy of the table from Investigation 3. Round your answer to the nearest ten-thousandth.

4. Refer back to your work for Activity 3 of Investigation 4 (page 408).

   a. Describe how to find the probability that event A or event B occurs if A and B are not mutually exclusive.

   b. Write a symbolic rule for $P(A \text{ or } B)$ in the case that A and B are not mutually exclusive.

   c. Pose and solve a probability problem involving two events that are not mutually exclusive.

Lesson 4

Looking Back

In this unit, you have learned about quality control and some of the statistical ideas that are important in a quality control process. The essential element in analyzing and controlling a process is to understand and quantify the variation. Many different factors can contribute to the variation, such as the time of day, the temperature, the machine, the operator, and the raw materials. If you can measure the output and variability in numerical terms, you can establish patterns and criteria that will enable you to see when a process is "out of control." This is a signal to investigate what factors may have changed.

You studied three basic tools in this unit: the standard deviation as a way to measure the variation or spread in a distribution, the normal distribution as a useful model of the distribution of measurements, and the control chart as a way to determine when a measurement varies beyond what is expected. In the following situations, you will revisit these basic ideas.

1. A machine produces calculator buttons. When it is in control, the widths of the buttons are normally distributed with mean 8 mm and standard deviation 0.1 mm.

   a. Make a sketch of the distribution of the widths. Include a scale on the horizontal axis.

   b. The buttons work best if they are between 7.85 mm and 8.15 mm wide. What percentage of the buttons are between 7.85 mm and 8.15 mm wide?

   c. What are the mean and standard deviation of the widths, measured in centimeters? (There are 10 millimeters in a centimeter.)

   d. What widths would cause the process to be declared out of control by Test 1 on page 390?

   e. Which of the following pairs of events are mutually exclusive on the same observation?

   - The process is declared out of control by Test 1.
     The process is declared out of control by Test 2.

   - The process is declared out of control by Test 1.
     The process is declared out of control by Test 7.

   - The process is declared out of control by Test 7.
     The process is declared out of control by Test 4.

2. Suppose you kept track of the gas mileage for your car over a 25-week span. You recorded the data as follows:

Gas Mileage			
Week	**Miles per Gallon**	**Week**	**Miles per Gallon**
Feb 7	23	May 9	24
Feb 14	27	May 16	27
Feb 21	27	May 23	25
Feb 28	28	May 30	28
Mar 7	25	June 6	25
Mar 14	26	June 13	26
Mar 21	25	June 20	25
Mar 28	29.5	June 27	29
Apr 4	26	July 4	26
Apr 11	27	July 11	27
Apr 18	24	July 18	24
Apr 25	26	July 25	26
May 2	26		

a. Make a run chart for your gas mileage. What does it tell you about the consistency of your gas mileage?

b. Find the mean and standard deviation. Draw horizontal lines on the run chart representing the mean and one and two standard deviations from the mean. Was your mileage unusual for any week in that time period?

c. To use the eight out-of-control tests, the data must be approximately normally distributed. Does that appear to be the case here? Explain.

d. Would you say fuel consumption of your car is in control? If not, which test is violated?

e. Five weeks after July 25, you discovered that something seemed to be wrong with your car, affecting your gas mileage. Write down two different sets of mileage data for those five weeks that would indicate you had a problem. Explain the test you were using and how it would apply to your data. Use any test only once.

3. In each of the following run charts, the mean is 10 and the standard deviation is 1.

   a. On a copy of each chart, draw in the mean and the interval one, two, and three standard deviations away from the mean.

   b. If possible, locate the next point in each plot so the system is declared out of control by one of the tests. Indicate which test would apply. Use Test 1 no more than once.

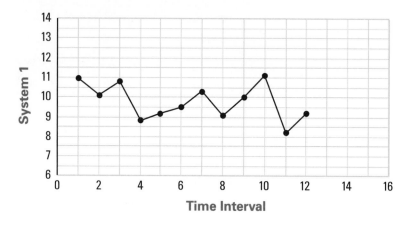

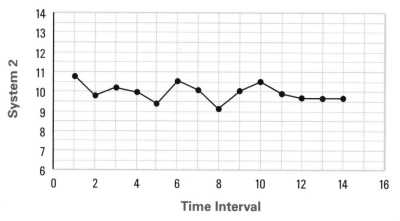

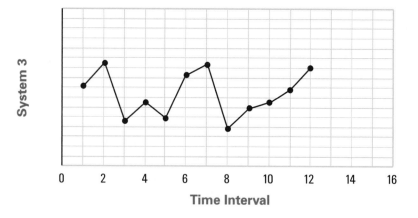

c. Assuming each system on the previous page is under control, what is the probability that the next observation will set off a false alarm? Show how you found your answers.

Checkpoint

Detecting variation in a process, service, or product is a key component of statistical process control methods.

a Why do you think the standard deviation is considered the most useful and important measure of variation?

b What are the characteristics of normal distributions?

c How are the mean, standard deviation, and normal distribution used in a quality control process?

d How are the probabilities of false alarms calculated?

e Give several examples for which it is appropriate to use the Addition Rule for mutually exclusive events. Give several examples for which it is appropriate to use the Multiplication Rule for independent events.

Be prepared to share your responses with the class.

Families of Functions

Unit 6

421

Function Models Revisited

One of the most important and controversial problems in earth and space science today is measuring, understanding, and predicting causes of global warming. There is concern that the average annual temperature of Earth appears to have been increasing over the past century. Many scientists believe the increase is probably caused by greenhouse gases that reduce the radiation of energy from Earth's surface into space. The graphs below show two key patterns of atmospheric change over time.

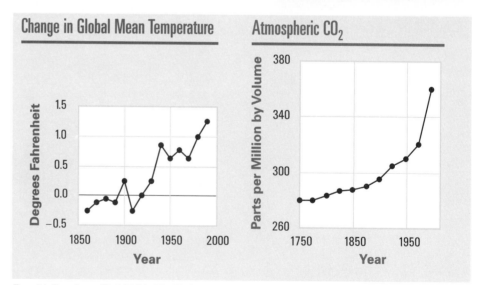

From "A Greenhouse Tool Kit" in *The Washington Post* 11/12/97. Copright © 1997, The Washington Post. Reprinted with permission.

The challenge for scientists is deciding how current trends in greenhouse gas amounts and world temperature change should be projected into the future. Different projections imply that different actions are needed, each with important consequences for industry, agriculture, and personal lifestyles.

Think about ways that future global warming could change Earth's atmosphere and your own life.

ⓐ Based on the data given in the graphs on the previous page, what strategy for projecting change in global temperature would make sense to you?

ⓑ What strategy for projecting change in atmospheric carbon dioxide makes most sense to you?

ⓒ If global temperature increases over the next 50 years, how do you think that change will affect our overall climate, agriculture, and personal lives?

In the first two courses of *Contemporary Mathematics in Context*, you investigated several important **families of functions** that are useful in describing and predicting patterns of change, some of which are similar to those you considered in the "Think About This Situation" above. The members of each family have closely related patterns in tables, graphs, and symbolic rules. In this unit, you will review the properties of each function family and investigate ways to modify the basic function rules to model more complex situations.

INVESTIGATION 1 ▶ Modeling Atmospheric Change

As different scientists have studied the historical records of temperature and carbon dioxide data, they've proposed different scenarios for the future of global warming. Each is based on certain assumptions about the best models for patterns of change.

1. Data giving Earth's surface temperatures are collected from several sources: over 10,000 land-based weather stations, weather balloons sent up regularly by several hundred of those stations, ships and fixed buoys in the ocean, and orbiting satellites. These data are combined to estimate Earth's annual average temperature, which is currently 60°F. The rate at which that average Earth temperature is changing is controversial. Many scientists believe it is rising, but estimates vary from about 0.05°F to 0.15°F per decade.

a. Write rules for function models that predict the annual average temperature x decades from now for three different rate-of-increase estimates: 0.05, 0.10, and 0.15 degree per decade. Draw sketches of the various models on the same coordinate system.

b. Write equations or inequalities whose solutions would answer the following questions in the cases of low (0.05° per decade) and high (0.15° per decade) rate-of-change estimates. In your group, discuss how the results could be determined using function tables and graphs and by manipulation of the symbolic expressions in each rule. Then individually answer the questions, in both the low-estimate and the high-estimate cases, using the method that seems most effective.

- What will the average Earth temperature be 50 years from now?

- When will the average Earth temperature reach 61°F?

- How long will the average Earth temperature remain below 62°F?

2. Perhaps the most well-known theory for global warming is that the increase of atmospheric carbon dioxide (CO_2), methane, nitrous oxide, and chlorofluorocarbon gases is responsible. Roughly 60% of the increase in these gases is from carbon dioxide. The mass of CO_2 in the atmosphere is commonly measured in billions of tons or *gigatons* (abbreviated Gt). Estimates in 1998 suggested that Earth's atmosphere contained about 750 Gt of CO_2, with another 3 Gt added each year. Atmospheric carbon dioxide is increasing because human activities send more CO_2 into the atmosphere than natural biological processes remove. For example, the burning of fossil fuels sends 5 to 6 Gt of CO_2 into Earth's atmosphere every year.

a. Write a function rule to estimate atmospheric CO_2 at any time x years after 1998.

b. Use the model from Part a to answer these questions:

- What level of atmospheric CO_2 can we expect in the year 2020?

- When can we expect atmospheric CO_2 to reach 800 Gt?

c. Suppose that when the atmospheric CO_2 reaches 800 Gt, we find a way to reduce human emissions and increase biological processes that extract CO_2 from the atmosphere.

- What rate of change would be required to bring atmospheric CO_2 back to 1998 levels in 20 years?

- What function would predict atmospheric CO_2 levels x years after the time at which corrective action began?

3. From the graph of atmospheric CO_2 reproduced at right, it looks as if, over the last 250 years, the rate of increase has not been constant. Suppose that the 1998 increase of 3 Gt per year is expressed as a percent and that future increases occur at that same percent rate.

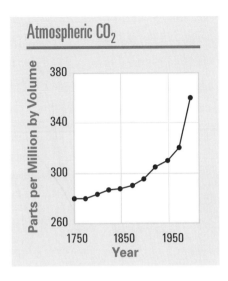

Atmospheric CO_2

a. What is the 1998 percent rate of increase?

b. Write a function rule to estimate atmospheric carbon dioxide x years after 1998, assuming growth from 750 Gt at a constant percent rate.

c. Compare estimates about the growth of atmospheric CO_2 over the next few decades using the model in Part b to your estimates using the model in Activity 2, which is based on different assumptions. Explain reasons why you believe one or the other model is better.

It has been estimated that in the 10,000 years since the end of the last ice age, the annual average temperature of Earth has increased by about 9°F and atmospheric carbon dioxide has increased by at least 50%. Scientists arrived at such estimates by analyzing material that has been trapped deep in very old glaciers and on the floors of lakes and oceans for thousands of years.

aciers sometimes hold clues to the past.

One of the interesting problems in such work is estimating the age of deposits that are uncovered by core drilling. A common technique is called *carbon dating*. Carbon occurs in all living matter in several different forms. The most common forms (carbon-12 and carbon-13) are chemically stable; the other form, carbon-14, is radioactive and decays at a rate of 1.2% per century. By measuring the proportion of carbon-14 in a scientific sample and comparing that figure to the proportion in living matter, it is possible to estimate the time when the matter in the sample stopped growing. Despite the very small amounts of carbon-14 involved (less than 0.000000001% of total carbon in living matter), modern instruments can make the required measurements.

4. Suppose that drilling into what was once a lake bottom produces a piece of wood which, according to its mass, would have contained 5 nanograms (5 billionths of a gram) of carbon-14 when the wood was alive. Use the fact that this radioactive carbon decays continuously at a rate of about 1.2% per century to analyze the sample.

a. How much of that carbon-14 would be expected to remain 1 century later? 2 centuries later? x centuries later?

b. Estimate the half-life of carbon-14.

c. What age estimate would make sense if the sample actually contained 3 nanograms of carbon-14? If it contained only 1 nanogram?

One of the ominous and spectacular predictions about global warming is that the melting of polar ice caps and expansion of ocean water will cause sea levels to rise and flood cities along all ocean shores. One estimate predicts a 1-meter rise in sea levels by the year 2100, a change that would flood large parts of low countries like the Netherlands and Bangladesh.

Estimates of such a rise in the sea level depend on measurements of glacier volumes and ocean surface areas. Earth is approximately a sphere, and oceans cover approximately 70% of Earth's surface. The Greenland and Antarctic ice sheets cover nearly 6 million square miles and contain nearly 7 million cubic miles of ice, but that water is only 2% of all water on the planet.

5. In making estimates of the size of Earth (and other spherical planets as well), it's useful to have formulas showing the circumference, surface area, and volume of a sphere as functions of the diameter or radius. Sometimes it's useful to modify those relationships to show the radius or diameter required to give specified circumference, surface area, or volume.

a. Which of the following function rules will give circumference as a function of radius r? Which will give area? Volume? What clues can you use to make the correct match, even if you don't remember the specific formulas?

   ■ $f(r) = 4\pi r^2$

   ■ $g(r) = \frac{4}{3}\pi r^3$

   ■ $h(r) = 2\pi r$

b. What patterns would you expect in graphs of the functions giving circumference, surface area, and volume of a sphere?

c. Earth is not a perfect sphere, but nearly so, with average radius of about 4,000 miles. What is the approximate surface area of Earth's oceans? What volume of water would be required to raise the level of those oceans by 3 feet? (Assume raising the level would not change the surface area of the ocean significantly.)

d. What rise in ocean levels would be caused by the total melting of the Greenland and Antarctic ice caps? (Again, assume the surface area of the oceans would not change.)

e. Earth is only the fifth largest of the planets in the solar system. The largest planet, Jupiter, has a radius roughly 11 times the radius of Earth. The radius of Mars is roughly half that of Earth. Based on these facts, how would you expect the circumference, surface area, and volume of Jupiter and of Mars to compare to the corresponding measures of Earth? Compare your answers and analysis methods to those of another group. Resolve any differences.

6. The gravitational force that holds all of us anchored to Earth's surface diminishes as one moves up into the atmosphere. In general, the gravitational force of attraction between two masses is directly proportional to the product of the masses and inversely proportional to the square of the distance between their centers.

   a. What does the above description of gravitational force suggest will happen as the distance between two planetary bodies increases? As one or both of the bodies increase in mass?

   b. Which of the following expressions matches the given information about the force between masses m_1 and m_2 located at a distance d apart?

   ■ $F = k(m_1 m_2 - d^2)$

   ■ $F = k\left(\dfrac{m_1 m_2}{d^2}\right)$

   ■ $F = k\left(\dfrac{m_1 m_2}{d^2}\right)^2$

   c. If the distance between two attracting masses is doubled, how will the gravitational force of attraction between those bodies change? What if the distance is tripled?

   d. How do your answers to Parts a through c help to explain the fact that most of Earth's atmospheric gases are concentrated close to Earth's surface?

Checkpoint

In this investigation, you modeled aspects and consequences of atmospheric change with various types of functions.

ⓐ Which of those situations (if any) involved the following families of functions?

   ■ Linear models

   ■ Exponential models

   ■ Power models

   ■ Quadratic models

ⓑ For each of the function families listed in Part a, what general patterns do you expect in the following?

   ■ Graphs

   ■ Tables of values

   ■ Symbolic rules

ⓒ What conditions or data patterns in problem situations provide clues about the appropriateness of using each of the function models in Part a?

Be prepared to share your ideas with the entire class.

On Your Own

Think back over previous units and courses and consider the variety of problem situations that you modeled with function rules. Which involved mathematical relations similar to those that you've just used to model patterns of change in global temperature, atmospheric CO_2, and decay of carbon-14? Which involved mathematical relations similar to those used to model patterns of Earth sea levels, planetary size, and gravity? Organize your responses by families of functions.

INVESTIGATION 2 Modeling Periodic Change

Increasing carbon dioxide in the atmosphere has been suggested as a leading cause for the recent observed increase in Earth temperatures. If such global warming continues, polar and glacial ice may melt and ocean waters may expand, causing the oceans to rise. However, not all changes in Earth's climate and geography are strictly increasing. Some important variables are **periodic**: They change in regular patterns that repeat over constant intervals of time.

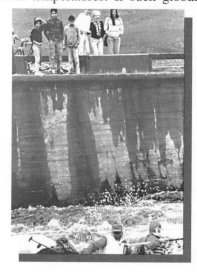

1. Suppose you lived near the Atlantic Ocean or a tidal bay and tracked the depth of the water on a retaining wall every three hours. If you began recording data at high tide of five feet, the data might yield a pattern like the one shown in the plot below.

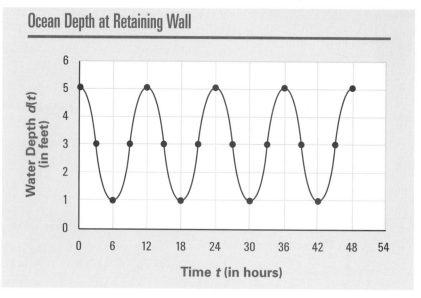

Ocean Depth at Retaining Wall

Water Depth $d(t)$ (in feet) vs. *Time t (in hours)*

a. Extend a copy of the graph on the previous page to show the predicted pattern of change for the previous 24 hours.

b. What is the period of this cyclical pattern?

c. Suppose melting of ice caps caused a four-inch rise in ocean levels. How would this change be reflected in the plot of water depths?

d. Which of the following rules models the water depth $d(t)$ in Part a as a function of time beginning at high tide? Assume radian measure for the input variable t.

- $d(t) = 2 \cos t$
- $d(t) = 2 \cos (t) + 3$
- $d(t) = 2 \cos \left(\frac{\pi}{6}t\right)$
- $d(t) = 2 \cos \left(\frac{\pi}{6}t\right) + 3$

e. Write a rule that models the water depth in Part c as a function of time beginning at high tide.

2. Suppose you began tracking the depth of the water on the retaining wall every three hours, beginning midway between low tide and high tide, as the tide is rising.

a. Make a graph of the expected pattern of change in water depth over the first 48 hours.

b. How is your graph similar to and different from the graph of $y = \sin t$?

c. Write a rule using the sine function that models the water depth in this situation.

d. When is the depth of the water four feet?

3. In modeling the behavior of tides using variations of the cosine and sine functions, you may have informally used the fact that the **period** of each of these functions is 2π and the **amplitude**, $\frac{1}{2}|maximum\ value - minimum\ value|$, of each is 1. Use similar reasoning to model the height of a Ferris wheel rider above the center line of a Ferris wheel that has a 6-meter radius and makes one revolution every 12 seconds. Using the diagram at the right, assume the wheel rotates in the counterclockwise direction.

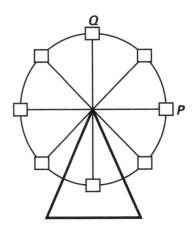

a. Write one rule assuming the rider begins at P.

b. Write another rule assuming the rider begins at Q.

c. How are your function rules in Parts a and b similar, and how are they different?

4. Work with partners to brainstorm a list of other variables in the world around you that change in periodic patterns. Then pick two of the variables and complete the following.

   a. Sketch graphs of each variable and estimate the period and amplitude.

   b. Describe how you would modify the basic cosine or sine function rules to fit the patterns in your graphs.

Checkpoint

In this investigation, you reviewed how to use variations of the trigonometric functions $s(x) = \sin x$ and $c(x) = \cos x$ to model periodic change.

a What clues in problem situations suggest using the cosine function as the basic building block? What clues suggest using the sine function?

b Suppose you are modeling a periodic phenomenon using the function $f(x) = a \cos (bx)$.

- How would you determine the value of a?

- How would you determine the value of b?

Be prepared to explain your modeling methods to the entire class.

On Your Own

Weather conditions and the interdependence of animal species sometimes produce periodic fluctuations in animal populations. Suppose the rabbit population in the Sleeping Bear Dunes National Forest is at a minimum of approximately 4,000 rabbits in January. By July the population reaches a maximum of about 12,500. It returns to a low of around 4,000 in the following January, completing the annual cycle.

a. Make a plot of the rabbit population for a two-year period, starting in January.

b. What is the amplitude and period of your graph?

c. How is your plot of the rabbit population as a function of time similar to and different from the graph of $c(x) = \cos x$? Of $s(x) = \sin x$?

INVESTIGATION 3 It's All in the Family

Studying the causes and effects of change in Earth's climate requires modeling and forecasting change in many variables. The functions that model relations among those variables and their patterns of change over time are often drawn from several important families that you've studied in earlier work: linear, exponential, power, and periodic. You've probably discovered that, to use those functions as descriptive and predictive models of change, it's important to know well the numeric, graphic, and symbolic patterns that are typical of each type.

The activities in this investigation ask you to construct and then extend an outline of the functions toolkit that you've been building throughout your study of algebra and trigonometry. As you complete this unit and other units in the *Contemporary Mathematics in Context* curriculum, you should add other function families to this toolkit outline.

1. On a copy of the functions toolkit outline on the next page, create your own toolkit by doing the following for each basic type of function.

    a. Give an example of a typical symbolic rule to calculate outputs from given inputs. Describe the domain and range of your sample function.

    b. Provide a table of sample (*input*, *output*) number pairs.

    ■ Explain how the table pattern can be predicted from the symbolic rule and how the rule can be predicted from the table pattern.

    ■ If possible, describe the pattern in the output values using a *NOW-NEXT* equation.

    c. Sketch a graph of the function. Explain how the graph pattern can be predicted from the symbolic rule and table pattern and how the rule and table pattern can be predicted from the graph.

2. Looking back at your toolkit of functions, you can see that the general symbolic rule for each function family involves one or more constants a and b, called **parameters**. For each function family, describe how different values of the parameters match different patterns in tables and graphs.

3. Examine this graph of the inverse power function $f(x) = \frac{1}{x}$.

    a. Note that for large values of x, either positive or negative, the graph gets closer and closer to the *x*-axis. Explain why the distance between the graph and the *x*-axis gets closer and closer to zero.

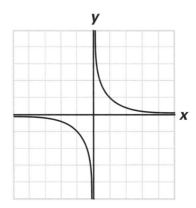

Functions Toolkit

Function Family/Example	Table	Graph
Linear Functions $\quad f(x) = a + bx$ $\quad f(x) = 0.5x + 3$ domain: all real numbers range:		

	x	f(x)
	0	3

Exponential Functions
$\quad f(x) = a(b^x),\ a \neq 0,$
$\quad b > 1 \text{ or } 0 < b < 1$
$\quad f(x) =$
domain:
range:

x	f(x)

Power Functions
Direct: $\ f(x) = ax^n,\ a \neq 0,$
$\qquad n$ a positive integer
$\qquad f(x) =$
domain:
range:

x	f(x)

Inverse: $\ g(x) = ax^n,\ a \neq 0,$
$\qquad n$ a negative integer
$\qquad g(x) =$
domain:
range:

x	g(x)

Periodic Functions
$\quad s(x) = a\sin x,\ a \neq 0$
$\quad s(x) =$
domain:
range:

x	s(x)

$\quad c(x) = a\cos x,\ a \neq 0$
$\quad c(x) =$
domain:
range:

x	c(x)

b. The graph of $f(x) = \frac{1}{x}$ is said to have the x-axis as a **horizontal asymptote**. This graph also has a **vertical asymptote**, which is the y-axis. Explain why this is the case.

c. Describe the asymptotes of the family of power functions.

d. What other function families have graphs with *asymptotic behavior*? What are the asymptotes?

e. What conditions in problem situations suggest function models with one or more asymptotes?

Checkpoint

In this investigation, you organized, in a systematic way, characteristics of several important families of functions.

a Compare your examples of linear, exponential, power, and periodic functions to those of other groups. Explain how the specific parameters in your function rules relate to the patterns in your sample tables and graphs. Then, as a class, develop general statements for each function family summarizing the effects of the parameters in symbolic rules on corresponding tables and graphs.

b Write a general statement summarizing how the integer exponent in direct power models relates to patterns in corresponding tables and graphs. Write a corresponding statement about inverse power models.

c Where do quadratic functions fit in your functions toolkit?

Be prepared to share your analyses and provide arguments supporting your generalizations.

On Your Own

In Course 2 of *Contemporary Mathematics in Context,* you explored the **square root function** $f(x) = \sqrt{x}$, where $x \geq 0$.

a. Include this function model in your toolkit. Supply a sample table of (*input, output*) pairs, a graph, and information on the domain and range.

b. Describe at least two specific problem contexts that you think are good illustrative examples of this function model.

Modeling

1. Many variables are involved in operating a business delivery van. Write function models for the relationships described below. Then use those models to sketch the graphs you would expect in each case. For each function model, write several specific questions that could be answered by use of an equation or inequality and show at least two methods of answering each question.

a. One company calculated that the annual operating cost of its business delivery van was $4,000 for insurance and a part-time driver, plus $0.40 per mile for gas, oil, and maintenance. How does total operating cost depend on number of miles driven *x*?

b. The company decides to buy a new delivery van for $25,000. The van's resale value decreases at a rate of 20% per year. What is the resale value of the van *x* years after its purchase?

c. Accounting rules allow the company to recognize the expense from wear and tear by reducing the value of its new van on its records by $2,500 per year. This expense, called *depreciation*, reduces income and thus saves the company money on income taxes. What is the accounting value of the van *x* years after its purchase?

d. Inflation adds to the operating cost of the van at a rate of about 5% per year. If the total operating cost in 1998 was $8,800, what operating cost would be predicted for a time *x* years later?

2. Storage containers often are rectangular or cylindrical in shape. The volume V of a cylinder is a function of its radius r and height h. The relationship among these variables is given by the equation $V = \pi r^2 h$. One of the most common uses of cylindrical containers is in tanks for fuel storage at refineries, factories, filling stations, and apartments or houses. Tanks can be designed and built to a variety of specifications.

a. If the design for a home oil tank calls for a radius of 2 feet and a height of 5 feet, what is the volume of that tank in cubic feet? What is the volume in gallons? (There are about 7.5 gallons to a cubic foot.)

b. The functions $V = (\pi r^2)(5)$ and $V = \pi(2^2)h$ show how volume depends on radius when height is fixed at 5 and on height when radius is fixed at 2. Which change in the design will produce the greatest change in volume: increasing or decreasing the radius or the height by some given amount? How is your answer shown in the graphs of the functions?

c. Suppose that you need to design a tank with fixed volume of 10,000 cubic feet (about 75,000 gallons).

■ Write an equation showing the relationship among radius r, height h, and this fixed volume.

■ Solve your equation for r to show how the required radius depends on the choice of height. Use this equation to find the required radius if the height is 20 feet.

■ Solve your original equation for h to show how the required height depends on the choice of radius. Use this equation to find the required height if the radius is 15 feet.

d. Study the relationships in Part c to see how changes in the two design options, height and radius, affect each other. How will increasing the design height of the tank change the required radius? How will increasing the design radius change the required height? What will the graphs of those relations look like?

3. There are many important situations in which variables are related by a function. Here are graphs and descriptions of several such situations. Match the descriptions to the graphs that seem to fit best. Then for each situation, describe the following:

- The sorts of numerical values you would expect for each variable
- A reasonable domain and range for each function
- The function family (if any) that would probably provide a good modeling rule

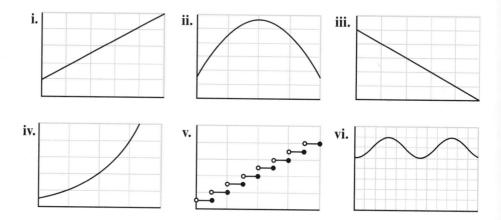

a. When a football team's punter kicks the ball, the ball's height changes as time passes from kick to catch. What pattern seems likely to relate time and height?

b. The senior class officers at Lincoln High School decided to order and sell souvenir baseball caps with the school insignia and name on them. One supplier said it would charge $100 to create the design and then an additional $4 for each cap made. How would the total cost of the order be related to the number of caps in the order?

c. The number of hours between sunrise and sunset changes throughout the year. What pattern seems likely to relate time and hours of sunlight?

d. In planning a bus trip to Florida for spring break, a travel agent worked on the assumption that each bus would hold at most 40 students. How would the number of buses be related to the number of student customers?

e. When the Lincoln High School sophomore class officers decided to order and sell T-shirts with the names of everyone in their class on the shirts, they checked with a sample of students to see how many would buy a T-shirt at various proposed prices. How would sales be related to price charged?

f. The population of the world has been increasing for as long as records have been available. What pattern of population growth has occurred over that time?

4. The following graph shows oscillation of the water depth in a shipping channel of an ocean harbor over two days.

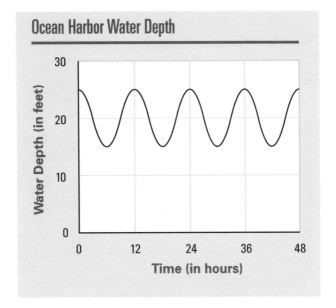

Ocean Harbor Water Depth

a. Based on information in the graph, estimate the maximum and minimum, the period, and the amplitude of periodic change in the water depth of the channel.

b. Write a function rule giving the depth of the channel as a function of time.

5. The surface area of Earth's oceans is about 145 million square miles, and they contain about 350 million cubic miles of water. Use these facts to answer the following questions about the effects of glaciers on ocean sea levels.

a. In the greatest ice age, sea levels were nearly 600 feet lower than they are today. How much more water could have been contained in the glaciers of that ice age than exists now? How does your answer compare to the current figure of about 7 million cubic miles?

b. Sea levels also rise when ocean temperatures rise and cause the saline water in the oceans to expand. What is the average depth of the oceans? What percent expansion of the ocean waters would be required to produce a one-foot rise in sea levels?

Organizing

1. Without using a graphing calculator or computer software, sketch graph patterns that you would expect for each of the following functions. Then use your calculator or computer software to produce each graph and check your symbol sense. Explain how you knew what to expect in those cases for which your sketches were correct, and explain what your errors were in those cases for which your sketches were incorrect.

   a. $f(x) = 5 - 4x$ **b.** $g(t) = 3(2^t)$ **c.** $h(s) = -3s^2$

   d. $j(t) = 0.5 \sin t$ **e.** $k(r) = 2.5(0.4^r)$ **f.** $m(x) = \dfrac{5}{x}$

2. Describe the domain and range for each of the functions in Organizing Task 1, and be prepared to explain how you could determine each answer by examining the symbolic rule.

3. Write *NOW-NEXT* equations that correspond to each of the following function rules:

   a. $f(x) = 3 + 2x$ **b.** $g(x) = 4(1.5^x)$ **c.** $h(x) = -2x + 4.5$

4. Graphs of periodic functions, by definition, have translation symmetry. Reproduced below is the graph (from Investigation 2, Activity 1, page 428) of the cyclic pattern of depth of water in a tidal bay. Also shown is the **midline** of the graph.

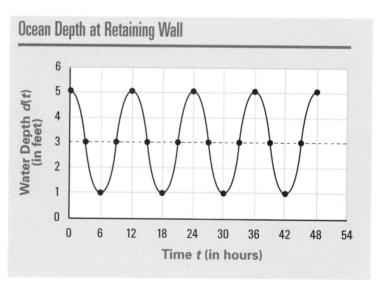

Ocean Depth at Retaining Wall

a. Assuming the pattern of the graph continues to the left and to the right, what is the magnitude of the translation that maps the curve onto itself?

b. What other types of symmetry are present in this graph?

c. How is the amplitude of this function related to the midline?

d. What is the midline of the graphs of $s(x) = \sin x$ and $c(x) = \cos x$? How is the midline related to the amplitude of each of these functions?

Reflecting

1. When you think about the various function families, do you think about them *first* in terms of their symbolic rules, their graphs, or their table patterns? Why?

2. News stories that involve consideration of change in some variable over time or the relation between two or more variables often use phrases like "growing exponentially," "periodic," or "directly or inversely related." What do you think people generally mean when they use each of those descriptive terms? How do the common usages relate to the technical mathematical usage?

3. Examine each of the following graphs.

   a. Which show relationships between variables in which *y* is a function of *x*?

   b. For each function, identify, if possible, the function family to which it

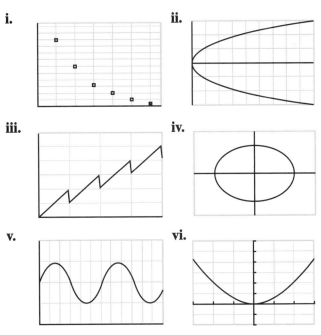

   belongs.

4. Some function families have the property that for the entire domain, function values are always increasing or always decreasing. For other function families, function values increase on some intervals and decrease on others. Sort the function families by these criteria.

Extending

1. In Activity 3 of Investigation 3, page 431, you saw that the graph of the inverse function $f(x) = \frac{1}{x}$ has the x-axis as a horizontal asymptote and the y-axis as a vertical asymptote.

   a. Describe the asymptotic behavior of this variation of the basic inverse function: $g(x) = \frac{5}{x+2}$.

   b. Make and test a conjecture about the asymptotic behavior of $h(x) = \frac{a}{x+b}$, where $a > 0$ and $b > 0$.

Each of the following displays in Tasks 2 through 5 shows graphs for two functions $f(x)$ and $g(x)$. In each case, the rules for the two functions are closely related to each other. For the pair of given graphs in each task, do the following:

   a. Explain the relation between rules for $f(x)$ and $g(x)$.

   b. Write function rules for $f(x)$ and $g(x)$ that you expect to give graphs with the same basic patterns as shown.

   c. Test your function rules to see how their graphs compare to those that are given. Then explain why the graphs turned out to be the same as or different from what you had expected.

2.

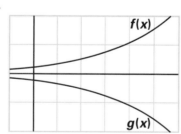

3.

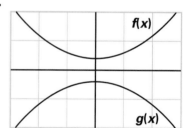

4.

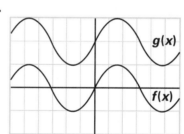

5.

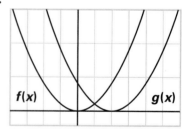

Customizing Models 1: Reflections and Vertical Transformations

If you take a warm soft drink can and place it in a freezer that is at 20° Fahrenheit, the drink will chill in a pattern like the one shown by this graph:

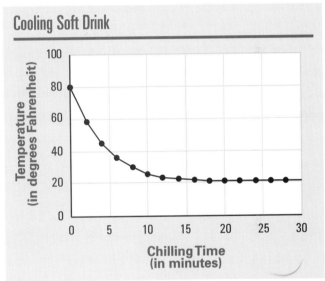

Cooling Soft Drink

Temperature (in degrees Fahrenheit) vs. Chilling Time (in minutes)

Think About This Situation

What family of functions is suggested by the numeric and graphic patterns of the cooling data above?

a What sort of function rule is associated with this function family?

b How is the cooling graph different from those in the function family it most resembles?

c How could you customize a function rule to account for the differences?

Trial-and-error testing of options or using calculator-based regression methods are effective ways to find models for data patterns. It is also helpful to know some general principles for modifying and combining the rules of basic function families to build new model rules for more complex situations. As you complete the following investigations, look for general methods to build symbolic rules so you can apply those methods in many different situations.

INVESTIGATION 1 ▶ Vertical Translation

The cooling function on the previous page looks a lot like an exponential decay function whose graph had been translated up about 20 units. In this investigation, you will explore connections between the forms of symbolic rules for functions whose graphs are related by *vertical translations*. For each graph, the scale on both coordinate axes is 1.

1. This diagram shows the graph of an important special function called the **absolute value function**. For each input value of x, the output is the distance from x to 0. The rule for the absolute value function can be written $f(x) = |x|$ or, in calculator and computer notation, $f(x) = \text{abs}(x)$. For example, $|-3| = 3$ and $|5.4| = 5.4$.

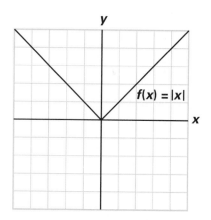

   a. Use the graph to complete a table of sample $(x, f(x))$ pairs.

x	−4	−3	−2	−1	0	1	2	3	4	5
f(x)										

   b. Describe in words the rule for finding outputs from the absolute value function.

   c. What value would you expect for $f(23.5)$? For $f(-14.7)$?

   d. Include the absolute value function in your functions toolkit. Supply information on the domain and range.

2. Consider what variation of the absolute value function rule might produce a rule for the function $g(x)$ with the graph shown here. (Assume that the graph continues in the pattern shown.)

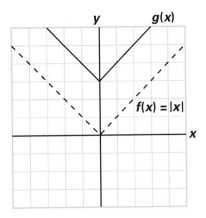

a. Use the graph to complete a table of sample $(x, g(x))$ pairs.

x	−4	−3	−2	−1	0	1	2	3	4	5
g(x)										

b. What value would you expect for $g(23.5)$? For $g(-14.7)$?

c. What rule would produce a graph and table for the function $g(x)$? Test and, if necessary, modify your conjecture.

3. Find a variation of the absolute value function that will produce a rule for the function $h(x)$ with the graph shown below. (Again, assume that the graph continues in the pattern shown.) Compare your rule to the rules found by other groups. Resolve any differences.

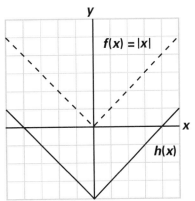

4. In general, if c is a positive number, how are the graphs of $f(x) = |x|$ and $g(x) = |x| + c$ related? How are the graphs of $f(x) = |x|$ and $h(x) = |x| - c$ related? Provide evidence or an argument that supports your conjectures.

5. The diagram below shows a graph of the function $s(x) = 0.5x^2$.

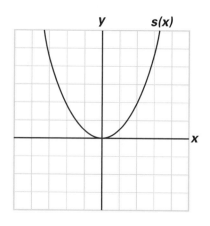

a. Complete a table of sample $(x, s(x))$ pairs.

x	−4	−3	−2	−1	0	1	2	3	4
s(x)									

b. Consider the function $t(x) = 0.5x^2 + 2$. Without using your calculator, do the following:

- Sketch graphs of $t(x)$ and the function $s(x) = 0.5x^2$ on the same set of coordinate axes. If possible, use different color pens or pencils.

- Complete a table like the one below.

x	−4	−3	−2	−1	0	1	2	3	4
t(x)									

c. Sketch a graph of $u(x) = 0.5x^2 - 3$ on the same coordinate axes you used in Part b. Then, without your calculator, complete a table like the one below.

x	−4	−3	−2	−1	0	1	2	3	4
u(x)									

6. In general, if c is a positive number, how are the graphs of $f(x) = x^2$ and $g(x) = x^2 + c$ related? How are the graphs of $f(x) = x^2$ and $g(x) = x^2 - c$ related? Explain your reasoning.

7. Draw a careful sketch of the function $c(x) = \cos x$ for $-2\pi \le x \le 2\pi$. Use *critical points* such as intercepts, maximums, and minimums. Then on the same coordinate axes, draw sketches of $f(x) = \cos(x) + 2$ and $g(x) = \cos(x) - 1$. Compare your sketches to those of other group members.

As you've studied variations of the functions $f(x) = |x|$, $s(x) = 0.5x^2$, and $c(x) = \cos x$, you've probably discovered patterns that can help you find rules for other functions that are variations of familiar models.

a Suppose $f(x)$ and $g(x)$ are any two functions. What connection between the rules for these functions would you expect when the graph of $f(x)$ is a vertical translation (up or down) of the graph of $g(x)$?

b What similarities in table patterns correspond to functions with graphs that can be translated vertically onto each other?

Be prepared to explain your ideas to the entire class.

On Your Own

Check your understanding of connections among graphs, tables, and symbolic rules of related functions.

a. The diagram at the right shows graphs of three functions, one of which is the basic linear model with rule $f(x) = x$. The scale on both axes is 1. What are the rules for the other two functions, $g(x)$ and $h(x)$? (Remember to assume that the graphs continue in the same pattern shown.)

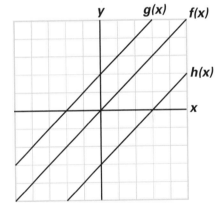

b. The next diagram shows graphs of the function $i(x) = 8(0.8)^x$ and another function $j(x)$. Which graph is $i(x)$, and what rule would match the graph pattern of $j(x)$?

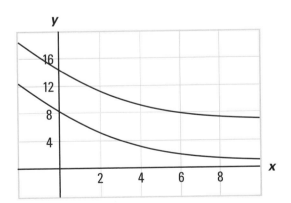

c. The table that follows shows a sample of (*input*, *output*) pairs for the function $c(x) = x^3$ and another function $d(x)$.

x	−3	−2	−1	0	1	2	3	4
c(x)	−27	−8	−1	0	1	8	27	64
d(x)	−32	−13	−6	−5	−4	3	22	59

- How are the graphs of $c(x)$ and $d(x)$ related to each other?
- What rule matches the given $(x, d(x))$ values?

INVESTIGATION 2 Reflection across the x-axis

In many situations, you'll find data patterns that look like graphs of familiar functions that have been reflected across the *x*-axis. That observation often makes it easy to find symbolic rules for the new relation.

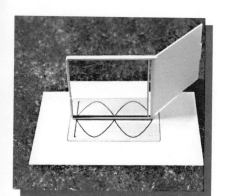

1. Study the pairs of function graphs and tables shown below and find the missing symbolic rule in each case.

a. $f(x) = 0.8x$

$g(x) = ?$

X	Y₁	Y₂
−3	−2.4	2.4
−2	−1.6	1.6
−1	−.8	.8
0	0	0
1	.5	−.5
2	2	−2
3	4.5	4.5

X= −3

b. $h(x) = 0.5x^2$

$i(x) = ?$

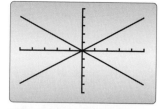

X	Y₁	Y₂
−3	4.5	−4.5
−2	2	−2
−1	.5	−.5
0	0	0
1	.5	−.5
2	2	−2
3	4.5	−4.5

X= −3

c. $j(x) = \dfrac{1}{x}$

$k(x) = ?$

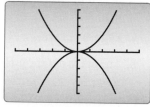

X	Y₁	Y₂
0	ERROR	ERROR
1	1	−1
2	.5	−.5
3	.3333	−.3333
4	.25	−.25
5	.2	−.2
6	.1667	−.1667

X= 0

d. $s(x) = \sin x$

$t(x) = ?$

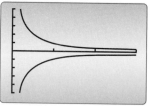

X	Y₁	Y₂
0	0	0
.7854	.70711	−.7071
1.5708	1	−1
2.3562	.70711	−.7071
3.1416	0	0
3.927	−.7071	−.70711
4.7124	−1	1

X= 0

2. The next graph shows the way an ice cream bar warms up when set out in a hot summer sun. The basic shape probably looks a bit familiar but not exactly like one of the basic function types you've encountered before.

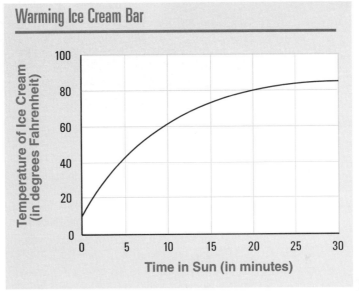

To construct a function rule matching this graph pattern, it might help to solve some related problems first, combining strategies you have studied thus far.

a. In the following diagram, the rule for one function is $f(x) = |x|$. The scale on both coordinate axes is 1. What rule gives the indicated graph of $g(x)$?

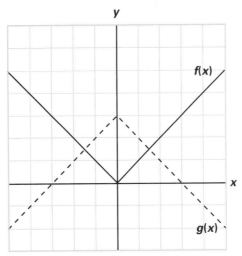

b. In the next diagram, the rule for one function is $h(x) = 0.2x^2$. The scale on both coordinate axes is 1. What rule would give the indicated graph of the function $i(x)$?

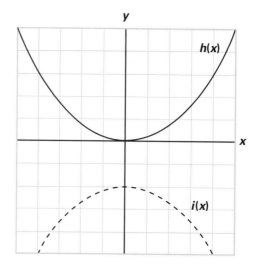

c. Now construct a function rule to match the "ice cream warming" function graphed at the beginning of this activity. As a hint to get you started, try building your function rule as a variation of $f(x) = 80(0.9^x)$.

3. Write a rule for a function whose graph is the graph of $c(x) = \cos x$ reflected across the x-axis and translated up 1 unit. How does the amplitude and period of this new function compare to those of $c(x) = \cos x$? Why does this make sense?

Checkpoint

As you've studied rules and graphs of the functions in this investigation, you've probably discovered some ways to build more variations on the basic linear, power, exponential, absolute value, and periodic models. What connection between the rules for two functions $f(x)$ and $g(x)$ would you expect:

a when the graph of $f(x)$ is a vertical translation of the graph of $g(x)$?

b when the graph of $g(x)$ is a reflection across the x-axis of the graph of $f(x)$?

c when the graphs of the two functions are related by a combination of reflection across the x-axis and then vertical translation (up or down)?

Be prepared to explain your ideas to the entire class.

▶ **On Your Own**

The calculator display below shows a graph of $f(x) = \frac{1}{x}$ for $-4 \le x \le 4$.

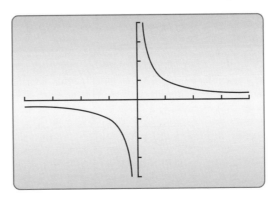

a. Describe the pattern of change in $f(x)$ values as x increases from -4 to 4, and explain how that overall pattern could be predicted from studying the function rule alone, without specific calculations.

b. Without using a graphing calculator, sketch the general pattern of the graphs you'd expect for the following functions.

- $g(x) = -\dfrac{1}{x}$
- $h(x) = \dfrac{1}{x} + 2$
- $i(x) = 3 - \dfrac{1}{x}$

INVESTIGATION 3 ▶ Vertical Stretching and Shrinking

In many important problems, the key variables change in periodic patterns as time passes. For example, the pendulum on a grandfather clock swings from right to left and back again. The depth of water in an ocean harbor rises and falls as tides move in and out. As you have previously seen, the trigonometric functions $s(x) = \sin x$ and $c(x) = \cos x$ are the basic tools for modeling periodic variables, since they give graphs that oscillate up and down in repeating patterns.

To model different patterns of periodic change, you need variations of the basic sine and cosine rules. For example, recall that the basic sine and cosine functions oscillate between $y = -1$ and $y = 1$, but a pendulum might swing through a range that is 5 inches left and right of vertical. The depth of water in an ocean harbor might vary from 15 to 20 feet as time passes. The electricity in a standard AC circuit oscillates between -150 and $+150$ volts. In order to model these situations, you will have to *stretch* the basic trigonometric graphs.

1. The two diagrams below show graphs for two variations of $s(x) = \sin x$. In each case, the scale on both axes is 1. The graphs were produced using radian measure for the input variable x.

How could you adapt the basic sine function rule to model the patterns in these graphs? Compare your customized function rules to those of other groups.

a.

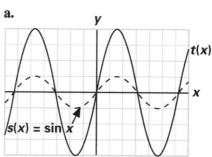

b.

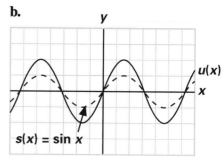

2. The next diagram shows a slightly different variation of the graph of the basic sine function.

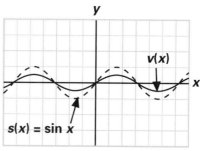

a. How would you describe the relationship between the two graphs?

b. Find a variation of the basic sine function that will give a rule for the function $v(x)$.

3. Now, use your calculator to compare graphs and tables of values for these functions:

- $c(x) = \cos x$ ■ $d(x) = 5 \cos x$ ■ $e(x) = 0.5 \cos x$ ■ $f(x) = 5 \cos(x) - 2$

a. How is the graph of $d(x)$ similar to and different from the graph of $c(x)$ for $-2\pi \le x \le 2\pi$? How is $e(x)$ similar and different? How is $f(x)$ similar and different?

b. Produce tables of the four functions for $0 \le x \le 2\pi$, and describe ways that the table for $d(x)$ is similar to and different from the table for $c(x)$. Then compare the tables for $e(x)$ and $f(x)$ to the table for $c(x)$.

4. Look back at your work in Activities 1 through 3 and think about general patterns you found in Investigation 2.

a. How does a vertical stretch or a vertical translation affect the amplitude of a periodic graph? How does each affect the period?

b. What can you say about the amplitude and period of $f(x) = a \sin(x) + b$ and $g(x) = a \cos(x) + b$? Why does this make sense?

c. The graph of $g(x) = a \cos(x) + b$ involves a vertical stretch and translation of the graph of the basic function $c(x) = \cos x$.

  ■ Which transformation is applied first, the stretch or the translation? How do you know?

  ■ Would you get the same graph if you reversed the order of the transformations of the given graph? Explain.

5. Find variations of the basic sine or cosine function rules that model these four graph patterns. The scale on both axes is 1.

a.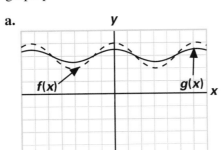

b.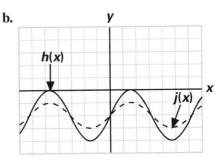

6. Now, combine what you have noticed about variations of $s(x) = \sin x$ and $c(x) = \cos x$ to build a model for depth of water in an ocean harbor, rising and falling between a maximum of 20 feet and a minimum of 16 feet.

  a. What additional information about the behavior of tides would you need to know to refine your model?

  b. Make an assumption about this information and then produce a graph of a possible function model. Write a symbolic rule that matches your graph.

  c. Compare your function model to those of other groups. Resolve any differences.

7. In Investigations 1 and 2, you explored the connection between the symbolic rules and the position and shape of graphs for variations of $f(x) = |x|$ and $g(x) = x^2$. Study tables and graphs of several functions with rules in the form $y = a|x|$ and $y = ax^2$ with various values of a.

  a. How are the graphs of $f(x) = |x|$ and $h(x) = a|x|$ related by shape and position, if $a > 1$? If $0 < a < 1$? If $a < 0$? How do those relations show up in tables of the basic function and the variations?

  b. Do the relationships that you discovered in Part a also apply to the functions $g(x) = x^2$ and $k(x) = ax^2$? Explain your reasoning.

  c. Determine if the relationships that you discovered in Part a also apply to the functions $u(x) = x$ and $v(x) = ax$.

  d. Do the relationships that you discovered in Part a also apply to the functions $e(x) = b^x$ and $h(x) = a(b^x)$ for $b > 1$? For $0 < b < 1$?

As in the case of vertical translations and reflections across the *x*-axis, you may have discovered that vertically stretching or shrinking graphs is related to the form of symbolic rules and patterns in tables of values.

ⓐ What connection between rules for functions $h(x)$ and $k(x)$ would you expect when the graph of one is found by vertically stretching or shrinking the other?

ⓑ What table patterns correspond to vertically stretching and shrinking graphs?

ⓒ What connection between rules for functions $f(x)$ and $g(x)$ would you expect when the graph of one is vertically stretched (shrunk) and then translated?

Be prepared to explain your findings to the entire class.

▶**On Your Own**

The following graph again shows the function $y = \sin x$. The scale on each coordinate axis is 1.

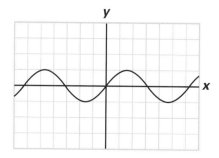

What variations of the basic sine function rule model the patterns in the graphs below?

a.

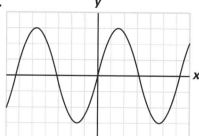

b.

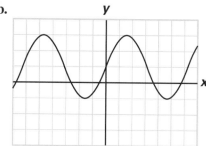

c. In Unit 3, "Symbol Sense and Algebraic Reasoning," you studied the function $h(t) = 30\sin(t) + 35$ giving the height of a Ferris wheel rider at any time t during a ride.

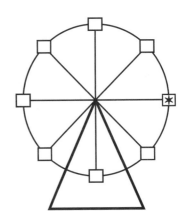

- How does the graph of this function relate to the graph of the basic sine function? How does that relation appear in a table of values for the two functions?

- What do the numbers 30 and 35 tell about the Ferris wheel and a rider's height at various times during the ride?

MORE
Modeling • Organizing • Reflecting • Extending

Modeling

1. Home security systems are a big business in many urban areas. One such service offers a package that costs $99 for installation and $24.50 per month for monitoring.

   a. What rule gives the total cost of using that service for x months?

   b. How would that rule change if the installation charge was reduced to $49.95? How would the graph of this new cost function be related to the graph of the rule for the original offer?

   c. How would the cost function rule change if the monthly fee was reduced to $19.95 (but the installation charge remained $99)? How would the graph of that new cost function be related to the graphs of the rules for the original offer and the modification in Part b?

2. Consider again the cooling graph from the lesson introduction, page 441, reproduced here:

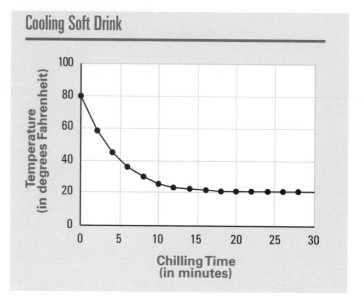

Cooling Soft Drink

Temperature (in degrees Fahrenheit) vs. *Chilling Time (in minutes)*

a. Complete the following data table with estimates for a function $g(t)$ that has the same shape as this cooling curve but asymptotically approaches the t-axis rather than the line $y = 20$.

t	0	2	4	6	8	10	12	14	16	18	20	22
$g(t)$												

b. Use a statistical curve-fitting tool or other analysis to find an exponential function rule that fits $g(t)$.

c. Use your rule for $g(t)$ to write a rule for $f(t)$ that models the actual soft drink temperature data in the graph.

3. The M. L. King High School marching band is so good that it gets invited to perform all over the country. The band members often have to find ways to raise money for their trips. On one occasion, the director proposed selling tickets for a raffle, with the prize being an all-expense-paid trip for two to Walt Disney World®.

a. Some students surveyed their classes to estimate how many raffle tickets would be sold at various prices. Based on their sampling, they estimated the following relations between ticket price and ticket sales:

Raffle Prospects			
Ticket Price	$1	$5	$10
Number of Tickets Sold	1,425	1,125	750

Find a rule for a linear function $S(p)$ that models the pattern in these data relating predicted ticket sales to ticket price p.

b. Use the result of Part a to write a rule for the function $I(p)$ that gives predicted income from raffle ticket sales. Find the maximum income predicted.

c. The raffle-prize trip will cost $1,500. Write a rule for the function $N(p)$ that gives net income or profit from the raffle. Explain how the graph of this function is related to the graph of the income function and how you can find the ticket price leading to maximum profit without further calculation.

4. In many problems, you've worked with the quadratic relationship between time and distance traveled for objects dropped from high places. For action near Earth's surface, the function rule $d(t) = 4.9t^2$ gives the distance in meters that an object has fallen t seconds after being dropped.

a. Graph $d(t)$ and explain what the shape of that graph says about the change in speed of the falling object as time passes.

b. Use the rule for distance to write a rule for the function $h(t)$ giving the height of the object t seconds after it has been dropped from a tower that is 200 meters high. Explain how the graphs of $h(t)$ and $d(t)$ are related to each other and how the rule could be modified to fit different drop heights.

c. Use symbolic reasoning to find the time when the object in Part b will reach the ground. Explain how that point could also be located on graphs and in tables of values of $d(t)$ and $h(t)$.

d. The coefficient 4.9 is determined by the gravity of our planet, Earth. Gravitational force near the surface of the Moon is only about one-sixth of the force on Earth. So in any time period, objects falling toward the Moon's surface move only one-sixth the distance that they would move if falling toward Earth's surface.

Assuming an object is dropped from a height of 200 meters above the Moon's surface, write rules for the distance fallen by the object and for the height of the object above the Moon's surface. Explain how the graphs of these Moon-based distance and height functions are related to those for Earth-based activity.

5. If the temperature in a restaurant's pizza oven is set at 500°F, it will actually vary above and below that setting as time passes. Suppose the actual temperature, after the oven is heated, is a function of time in minutes with rule $t(x) = 10\sin(x) + 500$.

   a. What are the high and low temperatures that will occur in this oven after it has been preheated?

   b. What is the pattern of the temperature function's graph?

   c. What patterns of variation in temperature of different pizza ovens are predicted by each of the following functions?

   - $u(x) = 15\sin(x) + 500$
   - $v(x) = 10\sin(x) + 550$

Organizing

1. Given below are graphs of a function $f(x)$ and four functions whose graphs are closely related to the graph of $f(x)$.

   Graph of $f(x)$:

   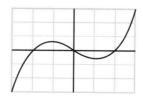

   Related Function Graphs:

   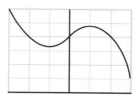
   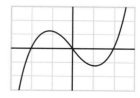

   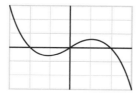
   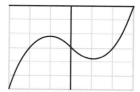

   Match each graph to the function rule below that best fits it, and explain the reasoning that supports each match. Make your matches without using a calculator.

   a. $g(x) = -f(x)$

   b. $h(x) = f(x) - 3$

   c. $j(x) = 2f(x)$

   d. $k(x) = 4 - f(x)$

2. For each of the functions in Parts a through d below, use what you know about the relationships between function rules and geometric transformations of graphs to sketch graphs of the following:

- $f(x)$
- $f(x) + 2$
- $-f(x)$
- $0.5f(x)$
- $-2f(x) - 3$

Sketch the graphs without using your calculator. Check your ideas and then, with another color pen or pencil, note any corrections needed.

a. $f(x) = |x|$

b. $f(x) = x^2$

c. $f(x) = \cos x$

d. $f(x) = 1.5^x$

3. The rule for the original function in Organizing Task 1, page 456, was $f(x) = x^3 - 4x$.

    a. Write rules for the related functions $g(x)$, $h(x)$, $j(x)$, and $k(x)$ whose graphs were given in Task 1. Use what you know about equivalence of algebraic expressions to write each rule in two different symbolic forms, one of which is the standard polynomial form.

    b. Check your ideas with a graphing calculator or computer software. Make notes of errors and make any needed corrections.

4. Shown below is the graph of the square root function, $f(x) = \sqrt{x}$, for $0 \le x \le 20$.

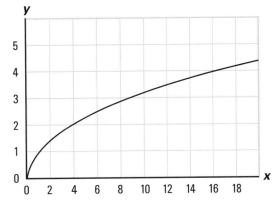

Sketch graphs of the following variations of the square root function, and then check your ideas. With another color pen or pencil, note any needed corrections.

    a. $g(x) = 3\sqrt{x}$ **b.** $h(x) = 0.5\sqrt{x}$ **c.** $j(x) = -\sqrt{x}$

    d. $k(x) = \sqrt{x} + 5$ **e.** $m(x) = -\sqrt{x} + 5$ **f.** $n(x) = 2\sqrt{x} + 2$

5. The graph at the right is a parabola with *x*-intercepts at –2 and 3.

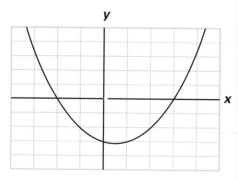

a. Write two different but equivalent symbolic rules, one in factored form and the other in standard polynomial form, for a quadratic function *f(x)* that has the given graph. Use symbolic reasoning to prove the two forms are equivalent.

b. Without using your calculator, sketch graphs of the following related functions. Explain why the zeroes and maximum or minimum points on their graphs will be the same as or different from those for *f(x)*.

- $g(x) = -f(x)$
- $h(x) = 15f(x)$
- $j(x) = f(x) + 5$
- $k(x) = -4f(x)$

Reflecting

1. Which of the following functions will have graphs that are *congruent* to the graph of *f(x)*? Explain your reasoning.

a. $g(x) = -f(x)$ b. $h(x) = f(x) + c$

c. $j(x) = cf(x)$, with $|c| \neq 1$ d. $k(x) = -f(x) + c$

2. Below are graphs of functions with rules formed by modifying basic exponential, power (both direct and inverse), and periodic function rules. In each case, identify as specifically as possible the basic function family that you would use in constructing a rule to match the given graph. Then, also explain the type of transformations that would probably be needed: translation, reflection, stretch or shrink, or some combination of these.

a.
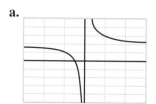

b.
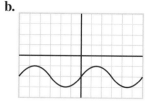

c.
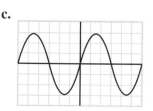

d.
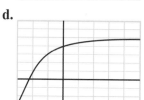

e.
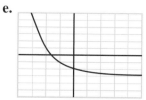

f.
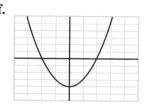

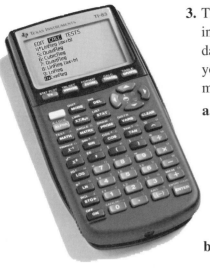

3. The statistical curve-fitting routines of calculators and computer software help in many situations in which you need to find a function rule that matches a data pattern. In fact, those routines will almost always give "an answer" when you enter some data. However, there are times when the technology-produced models are not very useful.

a. Make a scatterplot of the following data and use an exponential curve-fitting routine to produce a model for the pattern in the data. Then, compare a graph of the indicated function model to the data plot.

x	–2	–1	0	1	2	3	4
y	19.7	13	9	6.6	5.2	4.3	3.8

b. The (x, y) data used in Part a were actually generated using $y = 6(0.6^x) + 3$. How does that fact help explain the poor fit of the calculator's exponential model to the actual data?

c. What sort of adjustment could you have made in finding a good function model for the data if you knew that the pattern was tending to a lower limit of $y = 3$? Test your idea and see how well it works.

4. In one class that was working on problems involving transformations of graphs and their associated function rules, a student conjectured that zeroes of any function are not changed when the graph is reflected, translated, or stretched vertically. Do you agree with this conjecture? Explain your reasoning.

5. When a major news event occurs, such as a coming hurricane, a plane crash, or a spectacular crime, word about the event spreads rapidly through the media and by word of mouth. Models for predicting the rate of news spread often use the general form $K(t) = 100 - a(b^t)$, where t represents time since the event occurred, a and b are numbers that can be estimated from previous experience with spread of news, and $K(t)$

is the percent of the population who know the news after t hours.

a. If $a = 99$ and $b = 0.85$, what is the shape of the graph of $K(t)$?

b. What familiar function type is the basis of this news-spread model?

c. What geometric transformations would convert the basic graph type into the graph of the new function $K(t)$?

d. Why does the pattern of this function graph seem reasonable for the situation being modeled?

Extending

1. Rules of familiar functions can be modified to produce new functions that model graphs or data patterns that are vertical translations, reflections, or stretches of both the basic functions (linear, exponential, power, and periodic) and special functions such as the absolute value or square root functions. Below are rules for functions based on a general function, $f(x)$. Try to predict what geometric transformations of the graph of $f(x)$ will give the graphs for the new functions. Then explore each pattern with several specific basic functions for $f(x)$ to test your predictions. Record any general patterns that you believe will hold for any $f(x)$.

   a. $g(x) = f(x + 5)$

   b. $h(x) = f(-x)$

   c. $j(x) = f(5x)$

   d. $k(x) = f(0.5x)$

   e. $m(x) = f(x - 5)$

2. Rules for basic linear and exponential models can be expressed in "$y = ...$" form or in *NOW-NEXT* form. However, customizing linear and exponential patterns to fit more complex situations changes things a bit.

   a. What *NOW-NEXT* equation matches the linear function $f(x) = a + bx$? How, if at all, will that equation change if the function needs to be modified to fit a graph that is

   ■ translated up or down by some number c?

   ■ reflected across the x-axis?

   ■ stretched vertically by a factor k?

   b. What *NOW-NEXT* equation matches the exponential function with rule $f(x) = a(b^x)$? How, if at all, will that equation change if the function needs to be modified to fit a graph that is

   ■ translated up or down by some number c?

   ■ reflected across the x-axis?

   ■ stretched vertically by a factor k?

3. When a shoe company launches a new model, it has certain startup costs for design and advertising. Then, it has production costs for each pair of shoes that is made. When the planning department of Start Line Shoes estimated costs of a proposed new model bearing a popular athlete's name, it reported that the average cost per pair of shoes would depend on the number made, with the equation $C(x) = 29 + \frac{25,000,000}{x}$.

   a. Describe the asymptotic behavior of the graph of $C(x)$.

   b. What connection is there between the graph of $C(x)$ and one of the basic function types you reviewed in this unit?

4. One limitation on the growth of atmospheric CO_2 is the finite supply of fossil fuels like coal, oil, and gas that produce greenhouse gases when burned. However, modeling of both supply and consumption of those resources is not a simple matter.

a. Around 1970, estimates placed the world's proven oil reserves at 100 billion tons, with annual extraction of about 3 billion tons. If that rate of extraction held constant over many years, what function would predict world oil reserves x years after 1970? When would that model predict supplies to run out?

b. The growing world population and industrial development will actually increase usage each year. Suppose that those factors produce a 5% increase in annual usage each year. Use this assumption to write a *NOW-NEXT* equation showing how annual consumption will increase as years pass. Then use your equation to produce a table of annual consumption estimates for the 30 years from 1970 to 2000.

c. Use the assumptions of Part b to write a *NOW-NEXT* equation showing how the remaining world oil supplies $v(x)$ will decline as time passes. Then use your equation to produce a table giving world oil supply estimates for the 30 years from 1970 to 2000.

d. As you know, the world has not depleted its reserves of oil, as the 1970 prediction suggested. What factors do you believe contributed to the fact that world oil reserves have not been completely drained?

Customizing Models 2: Horizontal Transformations

Many important physical variables, such as ocean tides, positions of the planets in orbit around the sun, and household electrical currents, oscillate in periodic patterns that suggest modeling by the trigonometric functions sine and cosine.

$s(x) = \sin x$

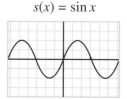

The periods of these basic trigonometric functions are both 2π (approximately 6.28). But ocean tides typically vary, with a period of about 12 hours, and the voltage of standard alternating current electricity has a period of $\frac{1}{60}$ of a second. As you previously have seen, the graphs of the required function models will be similar to sine and cosine, but stretched or squeezed horizontally (and vertically). In this lesson, you will investigate how to write symbolic function rules that correspond to these variations in graph patterns.

$c(x) = \cos x$

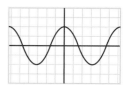

Think About This Situation

What modification of the rules for $s(x) = \sin x$ and $c(x) = \cos x$ might produce functions with graphs that are stretched, squeezed, or shifted like those below? (The scale on each x-axis is 1, and the scale on each y-axis is 0.5.)

a Longer period:

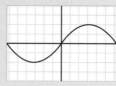

b Shorter period:

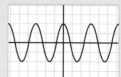

c Shifted; not symmetric about the y-axis or the origin:

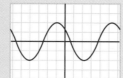

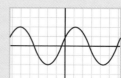

INVESTIGATION 1 ▸ Horizontal Shifts

In previous work, you studied several function families with graphs that are symmetric about a vertical line. In the simplest cases, the line of symmetry is the *y*-axis, but there are also some natural ways to modify the rules for those basic functions to produce graphs with other vertical lines of symmetry.

1. The diagram at the right shows the graph of $f(x) = |x|$. The scale on both axes is 1. Consider two variations of the absolute value function:

   $g(x) = |x + 3|$

   $h(x) = |x - 3|$

   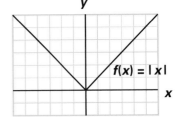

   a. Make and complete copies of the following table of values for these functions. Then match the table and rules for $g(x)$ and $h(x)$ to the given graphs.

x	–5	–4	–3	–2	–1	0	1	2	3	4	5
$g(x) = \|x + 3\|$											
$h(x) = \|x - 3\|$											

   i.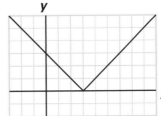

   ii.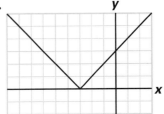

   b. Examine your work in Part a for ideas that could be used to adjust other function rules so they match **horizontal translations** of graphs of other basic functions. Test your ideas with specific functions in your functions toolkit.

2. In this activity, you will explore more complex variations of the familiar function with rule $f(x) = x^2$. In each part, the scale on both axes is 1. Complete Parts a and b without using a graphing calculator or computer software.

   a. Which rule matches the graph below: $g(x) = (x - 2)^2$ or $h(x) = (x + 2)^2$?

   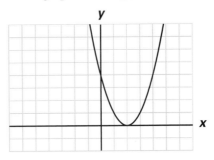

b. Match these rules with the graphs below:

- $f(x) = -x^2 + 4$
- $g(x) = -(x - 4)^2 + 4$
- $h(x) = -(x + 4)^2 + 4$

i. 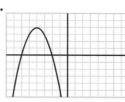 **ii.** 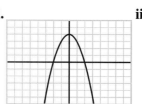 **iii.**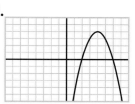

c. Write symbolic rules matching these graphs and check your ideas with a graphing calculator or computer software.

i. 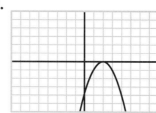 **ii.**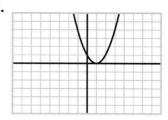

iii. 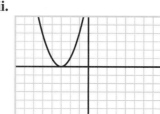 **iv.**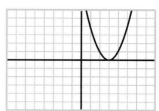

d. Explain why it is reasonable for the graph of $g(x) = (x - 3)^2$ to be positioned 3 units to the right of the graph of $f(x) = x^2$.

3. Use ideas you have from studying the graphs in Activities 1 and 2 to answer these questions about other functions and their graphs.

a. How will the graphs of $g(x) = \cos(x - 2)$ and $h(x) = \cos(x + 2)$ be related to the graph of the basic cosine function $c(x) = \cos x$?

b. How will the graphs of $r(x) = \sin(x + 1)$ and $t(x) = \sin(x - 1)$ be related to the graph of the basic sine function $s(x) = \sin x$?

c. Use the idea of horizontal translation to find a variation of the basic cosine function $c(x) = \cos x$ whose graph coincides with the graph of $s(x) = \sin x$.

d. How do horizontal translations of the graph of a periodic function affect the period? How do they affect the amplitude? Explain your reasoning.

4. Now combine your strategies for matching function families to data patterns and customizing rules so you can model the following probability situation: Suppose two six-sided dice are rolled and the sum of the dots on the upper faces is computed. The plot at the right shows the probabilities associated with the possible sums.

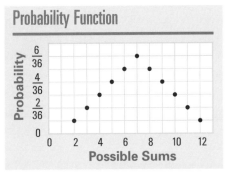

Probability Function

a. Verify that the plot is accurate and accounts for all possibilities. Share the workload among your groupmates.

b. What basic function type is suggested by the pattern in the plot?

c. Use your understanding of graph transformations to build a function rule that models the pattern in the data.

d. Compare your function rule to the rules built by other groups. Resolve any differences.

e. What are the practical domain and range of this function?

Checkpoint

You have now explored how to build models for graphs and data patterns that are related to basic function models by horizontal translation.

a What variations of the rule for $f(x) = |x|$ will produce graphs like these (where k and r are fixed, positive numbers):

■ $g(x) = ?$ ■ $h(x) = ?$

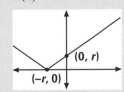

b How will the graphs of the following functions be related to $f(x) = x^2$? (Both r and s are fixed, positive numbers.)

■ $g(x) = (x - r)^2$ ■ $h(x) = (x + r)^2$

■ $i(x) = (x - r)^2 + s$ ■ $j(x) = (x + r)^2 - s$

■ $k(x) = -(x - r)^2 + s$

c How will the graph of $g(x) = a \cos (x - b) + c$, where a, b, and c are fixed, positive numbers, be related to the graph of $c(x) = \cos x$?

d What reasoning would you use to convince someone that your answers to Parts a through c are correct?

Be prepared to share your group's ideas and reasoning with the rest of the class.

The following graph shows the function $f(x) = -|x| + 3$.

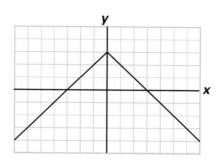

Without using a calculator or computer software, sketch graphs for the following related functions. Then check your ideas with a calculator or computer software, make any needed corrections, and explain your reasoning in the first attempt and in any revisions.

a. $a(x) = -|x - 3| + 3$

b. $b(x) = -|x + 4| + 3$

c. $c(x) = -|x + 4| + 1$

INVESTIGATION 2 Horizontal Stretching and Compression

The connection between vertical and horizontal translation of function graphs and the modification of rules to match those geometric transformations might suggest a strategy for constructing rules for functions with graphs obtained by *horizontal stretching* or *compression* of a familiar graph.

1. The following graphs show two useful variations of the basic sine function. The scale on both axes is 1.

$r(x) = \sin(2x)$ $\qquad\qquad\qquad q(x) = \sin\left(\frac{1}{2}x\right)$

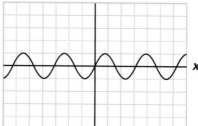 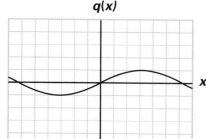

a. Estimate, as accurately as possible, the period of each function.

b. How do the periods of the graphs relate to the period of $s(x) = \sin x$?

2. Now consider other variations on the basic sine function rule.

    a. Which of the following variations of $s(x) = \sin x$ have a period that is longer than the period of $s(x)$, and which have a shorter period than $s(x)$?

- $p(x) = \sin(3x)$
- $h(x) = \sin\left(\frac{1}{5}x\right)$
- $k(x) = \sin(4.5x)$

    b. For the function $p(x) = \sin(kx)$, what positive values of k will produce periodic functions that have

- shorter periods than $s(x) = \sin x$?
- longer periods than $s(x) = \sin x$?

3. The function $s(x) = \sin x$ has a period of 2π (approximately 6.28).

    a. Estimate as accurately as possible the period for the following functions.

- $f(x) = \sin(3x)$
- $d(x) = \sin\left(\frac{1}{3}x\right)$
- $e(x) = \sin(10x)$

    b. In general, how is the period of $f(x) = \sin(kx)$ related to the period of $s(x) = \sin x$? How can this fact be used to explain your answers in Part a?

4. Investigate the periods for variations of the basic cosine function with symbolic rules of the form $g(x) = \cos(kx)$. Write a summary of your findings on the relation between the number k and the period of $g(x) = \cos(kx)$.

5. The following table shows the average monthly Fahrenheit temperatures for Des Moines, Iowa.

Average Temperatures, Des Moines

Month	Jan	Feb	Mar	Apr	May	June	July	Aug	Sept	Oct	Nov	Dec
Temperature	19	25	37	51	62	72	77	74	65	54	39	24

Source: *The World Almanac and Book of Facts 1997.* Mahwah, NJ: World Almanac, 1996.

ical Center in Des Moines, Iowa

    a. Plot the (*month, temperature*) data using 0 for January, 1 for February, and so on. On the same plot, sketch a graph which fits the data.

    b. What function family best fits the data?

    c. What is the amplitude of the modeling function?

    d. What is the period of the modeling function?

    e. Do the data indicate a horizontal shift from the basic toolkit function for this function's family? Do the data indicate a vertical shift?

f. Write a symbolic rule that gives average monthly temperature as a function of the month.

g. Compare your function rule to the rules of other groups. Resolve any differences.

h. Use your function model to estimate the average monthly temperature for the month of April. Compare the temperature as reported in the table to your estimate.

Checkpoint

In this investigation, you explored modifications of the basic sine and cosine functions to describe variables changing with a variety of periods.

a How is the graph of a function with rule $f(x) = \sin(kx)$ related to the graph of $s(x) = \sin x$ when $k > 1$? When $0 < k < 1$? How is the situation similar for $g(x) = \cos(kx)$ and $c(x) = \cos x$?

b How can you construct variations of the basic sine and cosine function rules with period p different from 2π?

c What reasoning would you use to convince someone that your answers to Parts a and b are correct?

Be prepared to share your group's ideas and reasoning with the entire class.

▶ On Your Own

The voltage in standard household alternating current circuits oscillates between −150 and 150 volts with period $\frac{1}{60}$ of a second.

a. What modification of the function $s(x) = \sin x$ will model the periodic variation of voltage in an AC circuit, with x measured in seconds?

b. What geometric transformations of the graph of $s(x) = \sin x$ will give the graph of your answer to Part a?

Modeling • Organizing • Reflecting • Extending

Modeling

1. The number of hours between sunrise and sunset at any location on Earth varies in a predictable pattern with a period of 365 days, not 2π like the basic sine and cosine functions. In the Northern Hemisphere, the shortest days occur very near to the first day of each calendar year.

   a. What modification of the basic sine function will have a period of 365?

   b. What modification of your answer in Part a will have an amplitude of 3, representing the maximum deviation from yearly average sunlight hours in many cities, such as Chicago, Illinois?

   c. What modification of your answer in Part b will shift the graph to the right so the minimum point occurs when $x = 0$, with x measured in days?

   d. What modification of your answer in Part c will represent the fact that the average number of hours of sunlight per day is 12?

2. Suppose that the tides in an ocean harbor cause a change in water depth from 18 to 22 feet from low to high tide, with a period of 12 hours.

   a. Experiment with variations of the rule $y = \sin x$ or $y = \cos x$ to find a function that models this situation.

   b. Explain how the numbers in your symbolic rule are related to the behavior of the tide.

3. Suppose that a Ferris wheel with radius 50 feet makes one complete rotation every 10 seconds and that the ride starts (the last passengers are loaded into their seats) when you are at the top of the ride.

   a. The bottom of the Ferris wheel is 2.5 feet above the ground. Sketch a graph of the relation between elapsed time and your height above the ground during the ride described in this situation.

b. What are the period and amplitude of a function modeling the (*time*, *height*) relation?

c. What geometric transformations of the graph of $c(x) = \cos x$ produce your graph in Part a?

d. What modification of the function $c(x) = \cos x$ models your height above the ground as a function of time?

e. Use your modeling function to predict your height above the ground 12 seconds into the ride.

4. In Activity 5 of Investigation 2, page 467, you saw that the average monthly temperature for a location on Earth varies *sinusoidally* with a period of 12 months. For Phoenix, Arizona, the highest average monthly Fahrenheit temperature is 94° and occurs in July. The lowest average monthly temperature occurs in January and is 54°. (Source: *The World Almanac and Book of Facts 1997.* Mahwah, NJ: World Almanac, 1996.)

Phoenix, Arizona

a. Find a variation of $s(x) = \sin x$ that models the pattern of change in average monthly temperature for Phoenix.

b. Use your modeling rule to predict the average temperature for Phoenix in October.

c. Find a variation of $c(x) = \cos x$ that models the pattern of change in average monthly temperature for Phoenix. What would this model predict for the average monthly temperature for October?

5. In Unit 3, you studied the equation for the height above the road surface of a cable suspended between two 30-foot towers of a 100-foot-long bridge. The minimum height above the road surface was 5 feet in the center.

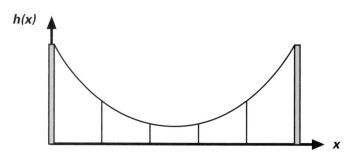

a. Which family of functions is most appropriate to model the height of the suspension cable?

b. Use the given information about tower height, bridge length, and the low point of the suspension cable to find an equation to model the height of the suspension cable.

c. Modify your function rule so that the vertex is at $(0, 0)$ instead of $(50, 5)$. Calculate output from this new function rule for $x = -50, 0$, and 50. Explain what those results tell about the bridge and its suspension cable.

d. Use algebraic reasoning to write the quadratic expression obtained in Part c in equivalent standard polynomial form.

6. All over the world, the number of hours between sunrise and sunset changes in a periodic pattern with the seasons, longer in summer and shorter in winter, with an average of 12 hours that is reached in late March and late September. For regions north of the tropic of Cancer, the deviation from average is a function of the day of the year and the latitude. For a city near the tropic of Cancer, such as Havana, Cuba, the deviation from average is modeled reasonably well by the function $C(x) = \sin(0.017x - 1.5)$, where x is the day of the year using the first of January as day 1. (Source: *The World Almanac and Book of Facts 1992.* Mahwah, NJ: World Almanac, 1991.)

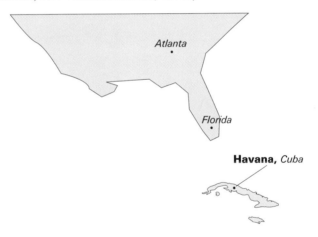

a. Study the function $C(x)$ to find the amplitude of the variation in hours of sunlight in Havana. Find the times of the year when sunlight hours are maximum, minimum, and near the average of 12 hours.

b. Modify the rule for $C(x)$ to give another function $S(x)$ that tells the actual number of hours between sunrise and sunset in Havana on any given day.

c. For cities that are farther north than Havana, the change in hours of sunlight from summer to winter is greater. For example, in Washington, D.C., the longest day is about 15 hours, and the shortest is about 9 hours. What modification of the rule for $C(x)$ will give the variation in hours of sunlight in Washington as a function of the day of the year? What rule will give the actual number of hours of sunlight there on any given day?

d. For cities that are even farther north, such as Oslo, Norway, or Stockholm, Sweden (both near 60° north latitude), the longest day has about 18 hours of sunlight, and the shortest has only about 6 hours of sunlight. What rule gives the variation in hours of sunlight in those cities as a function of the day of the year? What rule gives the actual number of hours of sunlight on any given day?

e. For cities in the Southern Hemisphere, such as Rio de Janeiro, Brazil, or Melbourne, Australia, the seasons are the opposite of those in the Northern Hemisphere. For example, Melbourne and Washington, D.C., are about equidistant from the equator, and Melbourne's longest day is the same day as Washington's shortest day. Similarly, Rio de Janeiro and Havana are about equidistant from the equator. Use that information to write rules giving the variation in hours of sunlight for Rio de Janeiro and Melbourne as a function of the day of the year. Then modify those functions to produce rules giving the actual number of hours of sunlight on any given day in the two cities.

Rio de Janeiro

Organizing

1. Consider the absolute value function $A(x) = |x|$. Modify the rule for $A(x)$ to give functions with graphs that have the following properties. Check each answer with a graphing calculator or computer and make any needed corrections. For any errors you make in your first attempt, make notes on how they can be avoided in the future.

a. Minimum point at (3, 0)

b. Minimum point at (–2, 0)

c. Maximum point at (0, 0)

d. Maximum point at (5, 0)

e. Minimum point at (3, –2)

2. The graph of $f(x) = x^3 - x$ with unit scales on the axes is shown at the right. What modifications of the rule for $f(x)$ gives each of the following graphs, in the same window with the same scales?

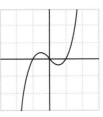

a.

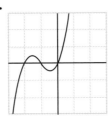

b.

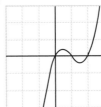

c.

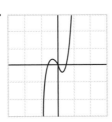

d.

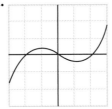

3. Consider the basic parabola defined by the function $f(x) = x^2$. What function rules will produce graphs related to the graph of $f(x)$ in the following ways?

   a. Translated 5 units to the left

   b. Translated 4 units to the right

   c. Compressed by a factor of 3 toward the y-axis

   d. Stretched by a factor of 4 away from the y-axis

   e. Vertex at $(5, 0)$ and opening downward

   f. Vertex at $(5, 3)$ and opening upward

   g. Vertex at $(-2, 4)$ and opening upward

   h. Vertex at (h, k) and opening downward

4. Describe how the graph of each function in Column 2 is related to the graph of the corresponding function in Column 1.

	Column 1	Column 2
a.	$f(x) = x^2$	$g(x) = -(x - 6)^2 + 8$
b.	$h(x) = \lvert x \rvert$	$i(x) = 0.5\lvert x \rvert - 2$
c.	$c(x) = \cos x$	$d(x) = 2\cos x$
d.	$s(x) = \sin x$	$t(x) = 3\sin(x) + 1$
e.	$u(x) = (0.3)^x$	$v(x) = 5 - (0.3)^x$
f.	$r(x) = \sqrt{x}$	$p(x) = \sqrt{x + 5}$
g.	$s(x) = \sin x$	$m(x) = -\sin\left(x - \frac{\pi}{2}\right)$
h.	$c(x) = \cos x$	$n(x) = \cos\left(\frac{\pi}{4}x - 2\right)$

5. Think back to coordinate representations of geometric transformations.

   a. Complete each coordinate rule below.

   - Reflection across the x-axis: $(x, y) \rightarrow$ (__ , __)
   - Translation with components (h, k): $(x, y) \rightarrow$ (__ , __)
   - Size transformation with center at the origin and scale factor k:
     $(x, y) \rightarrow$ (__ , __)

   b. What connections do you see between the coordinate representation of these transformations and the form of algebraic rules for transformed functions?

Reflecting

1. Which transformations of basic function graphs are easiest to predict simply by looking at the symbolic function rules? Which are most difficult to predict?

2. For most students it seems natural to expect that the graph of $g(x) = (x - k)^2$, where $k > 0$, should be congruent to the graph of $f(x) = x^2$ but translated k units to the *left*. As you now know, that isn't what happens; the graph of $g(x)$ is identical to that of $f(x)$ but translated k units to the *right*.

   a. How can you think about this pair of rules and graphs so that the correct relationship makes sense?

   b. How can you adapt your reasoning in Part a to include the case of $h(x) = (x + k)^2$?

3. For many students it seems natural to expect that when $k > 1$, the graph of $g(x) = (kx)^2$ should be similar to the graph of $f(x) = x^2$ but stretched out from the y-axis. As you now know, that isn't what happens; the graph of $g(x)$ is a compression of the graph of $f(x)$ toward the y-axis with a scale factor of $\frac{1}{k}$.

   a. How can you think about this pair of rules and graphs so that the correct relationship makes sense?

   b. How can you adapt your reasoning in Part a to include the case of $h(x) = (kx)^2$ when $0 < k < 1$?

4. In the Southern Hemisphere, the times at which summer and winter occur are reversed relative to the Northern Hemisphere. How would you modify your function rule in Activity 5 of Investigation 2, page 467, so that it models the pattern of change in average monthly temperature for a city in the Southern Hemisphere that geographically corresponds to Des Moines? Will the average monthly temperature in these two cities ever be about the same?

Des Moines, *Iowa*

Puertos Lobos,
Buenos Aires

5. In earlier work, you learned that the points of a circle with radius r and center at the origin have coordinates (x, y) satisfying the equation $x^2 + y^2 = r^2$. In the "Symbol Sense and Algebraic Reasoning" unit, you may have proven that a circle centered at some other point (h, k) has equation $(x - h)^2 + (y - k)^2 = r^2$. (See Extending Task 4 on page 252.)

  a. Write the equations of these circles:

   ■ Center $(2, 3)$ and radius 5

   ■ Center $(2, -3)$ and radius 4

   ■ Center $(-4, 5)$ and radius 3

   ■ Center $(-1.5, -2.9)$ and radius 7.2

  b. Explain how the connection between equations for circles centered at the origin and equations for circles centered away from the origin is in some ways similar to, and in some ways different from, the connection between rules for functions and rules for related functions with translated graphs.

Extending

1. Find rules for quadratic functions with graphs satisfying the following conditions. In each case, show how one or more correct rules can be obtained by the use of a statistical curve-fitting tool and also by algebraic reasoning alone. If there is more than one correct rule, include all such rules (using parameters such as k or c as needed).

  a. Zeroes at $x = 9$ and $x = 2$

  b. One zero at $x = 7$ and line of symmetry at $x = 5$

  c. Zeroes at $x = -3$ and $x = 5$ and minimum point with $y = -8$

  d. Zeroes at $x = -9$ and $x = -1$ and maximum point with $y = 168$

2. Modeling Task 5, page 470, involved finding the equation for the height above the road surface of a suspension cable of a long bridge suspended between two towers. Suppose that the towers are 50 feet high, the bridge road surface is 200 feet long, and the suspension cable has a minimum height at the center, 10 feet above the road.

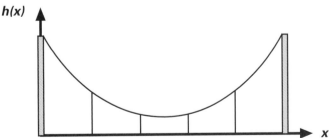

  a. How could you use the given information and statistical curve-fitting tools to find the equation of the height of the suspension cable above the bridge?

b. Use the following reasoning to reach the same equation.

   i. Consider first the basic parabola with the y-axis as the axis of symmetry. What would its equation be?

   ii. Modify your equation from Part i to get an equation $y = f(x)$ such that $f(100) = f(-100) = 40$.

   iii. Modify the result from Part ii to get an equation $y = g(x)$ with minimum point 10 feet above the x-axis and $g(100) = g(-100) = 50$.

   iv. Modify the result from Part iii to get $y = h(x)$ with $h(0) = h(200) = 50$ and $h(100) = 10$.

c. Use algebraic reasoning to prove that the quadratic expression obtained from curve-fitting in Part a is equivalent to the expression obtained from the reasoning outlined in Part b.

3. Shown below is a portion of a graph and a table of sample values for a periodic function $y = f(x)$.

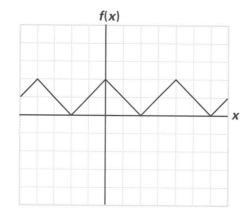

x	f(x)
−4	2
−2	0
0	2
2	0
4	2
6	0

a. What are the domain and range of this function?

b. Explain how a rule for $g(x)$, whose graph is shown below, is related to the rule for $f(x)$ and how tables of sample values for the two functions are related.

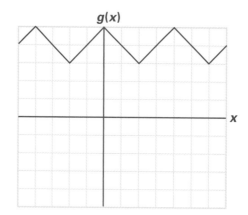

x	g(x)
−4	
−2	
0	
2	
4	
6	

c. Explain how a rule for $i(x)$, whose graph is shown below, is related to the rule for $f(x)$. Complete a table of sample values for $i(x)$.

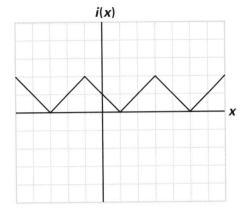

i(x)

x	i(x)
−4	
−2	
0	
2	
4	
6	

d. Explain how a rule for $j(x)$, whose graph is shown below, is related to the rule for the original function $f(x)$. Complete a table of sample values.

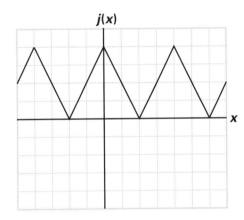

j(x)

x	j(x)
−4	
−2	
0	
2	
4	
6	

4. In this unit, you have seen how simple geometric transformations of a function graph are connected to corresponding transformations of the function rule. In this task, you will investigate how horizontal shifts are related to the zeroes of quadratic functions and, more generally, to the quadratic formula.

a. First examine each of the following pairs of quadratic functions and their graphs. For each pair of functions, do the following:

- Write rules for the lines of symmetry.
- Describe geometrically how the graphs are related.
- Explain how the zeroes of the two functions are related.
- Solve $f(x) = 0$ using algebraic reasoning.

i. $g(x) = x^2 - 10x + 16$ $f(x) = x^2 - 9$

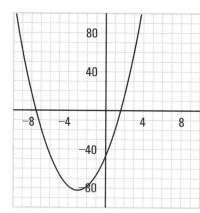
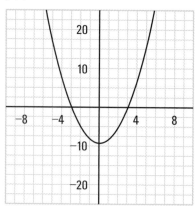

ii. $g(x) = 4x^2 + 24x - 45$ $f(x) = 4x^2 - 81$

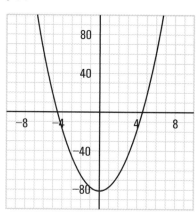
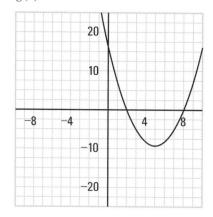

b. Just as you are able to transform the graph of $g(x)$ to the graph of $f(x)$ for each pair of functions above, you can similarly transform the function rule. Consider the function $g(x)$ in Part i above and the related equation:

$$x^2 - 10x + 16 = 0$$

■ Define a new variable z by $z = x - 5$. This is a transformation of the variable x to the variable z. Explain how the transformation $z = x - 5$ is related to the axis of symmetry of $g(x)$.

■ Solve $z = x - 5$ for x and substitute the resulting expression for each occurrence of x in $x^2 - 10x + 16 = 0$.

■ Now use algebraic reasoning to solve your new quadratic for the variable z.

■ Finally, use the fact that $z = x - 5$ to find the roots of $x^2 - 10x + 16 = 0$.

c. Use algebraic reasoning similar to what you used in Part b to find the zeroes of $g(x) = 4x^2 + 24x - 45$.

d. You can use the reasoning in Part c to provide another proof of the quadratic formula. To begin, use the fact that $x = -\dfrac{b}{2a}$ is the line of symmetry for the parabola $y = ax^2 + bx + c$ to define a new variable $z = x - (-\dfrac{b}{2a})$ or $z = x + \dfrac{b}{2a}$. So $x = z - \dfrac{b}{2a}$. Now use what you know about algebraic properties to show that if $ax^2 + bx + c = 0$ and $a \neq 0$, then

$$x = -\frac{b}{2a} \pm \frac{\sqrt{b^2 - 4ac}}{2a}.$$

5. Shown below is a graph of a function $y = h(x)$. On copies of this diagram, sketch and label graphs of each related function listed.

a. $y = -h(x)$

b. $y = h(x) - 3$

c. $y = 0.5h(x) + 1$

d. $y = h(x + 3)$

e. $y = h(2x)$

f. $y = h(0.5x)$

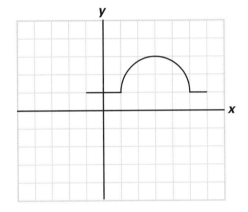

Looking Back

In the investigations of this unit, you have reviewed and extended the range of data table and graph patterns that you can model with function rules. By now, you should be able to recognize patterns of change that are matched well by linear, exponential, power, and periodic functions; by combinations of those function types; and by functions with graphs that are translations, reflections, and stretches or compressions of the basic forms. The activities and tasks in this final lesson will help you consolidate your understanding of function families and their applications.

1. The change from one year, decade, century, or millennium to another seems to prompt people to look back over time to see how things have changed in the past and to make some predictions about the near future. About 1,000 years ago, Earth's human population was about 250 million. One fourth of all those people lived in China. The world's largest city was Cordova, Spain, with a population of  450,000. Half of all children died before the age of five, so the population grew at a rate of only 0.1% per year until modern medicine and improved water and sewage systems emerged in the 1700s. (Source: *Making sense of the millennium*. 1998. *National Geographic*, January.)

   a. What type of function and what specific rule would model the pattern of world population growth described for the period from 1000 to 1700?

   b. How does the world population near the turn of the second millennium of about 6 billion compare to what would have happened if growth had continued at the rate of 0.1% from the year 1000 to the year 2000?

   c. Assume a world population in the year 2000 of about 6 billion and a growth rate of about 1.7%. What function would predict world population t years later? In particular, what population is predicted for the year 2100 and the end of the next millennium, 3000?

   d. How will the graphs of the two functions in Parts a and c be similar, and how will they be different?

   e. How do doubling times of world population compare in the cases of 0.1% and 1.7% growth rates?

f. Earth has a land area of about 57 million square miles (although not all is inhabitable). What functions give population density (people per square mile) as a function of time in the two cases in Parts a and c? How will graphs and tables of the two population density functions be similar to and different from those of the world population functions? (*Caution:* Be careful about units of measure.)

g. If the functions in Parts a and c are denoted by $P_a(t)$ and $P_c(t)$, what information would be given by the functions $f(t) = P_a(10t)$ and $g(t) = P_c(10t)$?

- Write algebraic rules for these new functions.

- How would the graphs of the new functions relate to the graphs of the originals?

h. If you assume that a world population of about 6 billion increases at a constant rate of 100 million people per year, what function would estimate the world population at any time t years in the future?

i. How will tables and graphs of the population function described in Part h compare to those of the percent growth rate model in Part c?

j. What is the population density function (people per square mile) associated with the population function described by the information in Part h?

- How will the tables and graphs of that density function compare to those of the population function in Part h?

- How will patterns of this new density function compare to those of the population density function derived from the percent growth rate assumptions of Part c?

k. Which patterns of change in the various questions of this activity can be represented by *NOW-NEXT* equations that describe the change from one time to the next?

2. When the Hale-Bopp comet flew within sight of Earth during 1996 and 1997, there was considerable discussion about the chances that other comets and asteroids might actually enter Earth's atmosphere. Some scientists even made estimates of the damage that would result if such an event did occur. One theory predicts that if an asteroid of only 3 miles in diameter were to

© Copyright 1997 Jerry Lodriguss

land in the middle of the North Atlantic Ocean, it would send a 300-foot tsunami crashing on the shores of the United States and Europe. Fortunately, such events are likely to occur only once in every 10,000,000 years! (Source: Newcott, William R. 1997. The age of comets. *National Geographic*, December, 94–109.)

Assume that the bodies of comets are roughly spherical in shape as you answer the following questions.

a. The sizes of comets and asteroids are usually described by estimates of their radii or diameters, but their visual appearance and the force of a collision would be more directly related to measures of area and volume. For an asteroid with radius measured in miles, what function rules would give the area of the circular disk that we see, the total surface area, and the volume of that asteroid? How would each of those function rules change if the given information was a diameter instead of a radius?

b. Although the tails of comets might be millions of miles long, the core is usually a much smaller body. For example, the core of comet Halley has diameter of less than 10 miles; Earth's diameter is about 8,000 miles. How will the surface area and volume of Earth compare to those of comet Halley? How can you make those comparisons by studying the area and volume formulas and not actually calculating each area and volume?

c. Earth's average density is about 5.5 billion metric tons per cubic kilometer. If other planets or asteroids had the same density, what function rule would give the masses (density × volume) of those bodies as a function of their radii (in kilometers)? How would the graph of this function be related to the volume function in Part a?

d. Comet Hale-Bopp last came near Earth over 4,200 years ago. Because of the gravitational pull of the planet Jupiter, its next return is predicted to occur in 2,400 years. Planets also affect the paths of asteroids. Look back in this unit to find the relationship between the gravitational attraction of two cosmic bodies and the distance between their centers. What does the graph of that relationship look like?

3. For residents of planet Earth, the most important planetary body (other than Earth itself) is the Moon. The visible Moon varies from a small slice to a full disk and then back to a small slice in phases that have names like first quarter, full moon, last quarter, and (when not visible at all) new moon. The full cycle takes roughly 30 days.

a. What function family seems likely to be the best starting point in building a model of the Moon's repeated pattern of phases, if you assume the cycle starts on a full moon?

b. What adjustments to the basic function rule chosen in Part a will give a model with the correct period?

c. What adjustments would give the correct model if you assumed the start of each cycle was the time of a new moon?

Scientists who study the planets and stars of the universe, the climate and geography of Earth, the animals and plants that live on Earth, or the political and economic activity of human beings and their societies often turn to mathematics for models of the patterns and relationships that they find. By now you should know well some of the most useful of those modeling tools (linear, exponential, power, polynomial, and periodic functions) and ways to adjust the basic rules for those functions to match unique conditions.

4. Match the following algebraic rule forms to the corresponding function family.

   a. $f(x) = a + bx$ Periodic

   b. $g(x) = x^b$ Exponential

   c. $h(x) = \sin x$ Power

   d. $i(x) = b^x$ Linear

   e. $j(x) = \dfrac{1}{x}$ Polynomial

   f. $k(x) = \cos x$

   g. $m(x) = ax^2 + bx + c$

5. For each of the following graphs and tables, identify the family of functions from which it makes most sense to build a model for the data pattern. Then construct a function model that best fits the pattern. Be prepared to explain the reasoning that led to your choice of a basic function model type and the adjustments needed to make the rule fit the specific pattern of the given table or graph.

a.

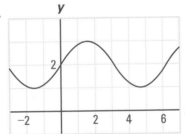

b.

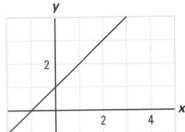

c.

x	−2	−1	0	1	2	3	4
y	6	4	3	2.5	2.25	2.125	2.0625

x	5	6	7	8	9	10	11
y	2.0313	2.0156	2.0078	2.0039	2.0020	2.0010	2.0005

d.

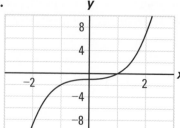

e.

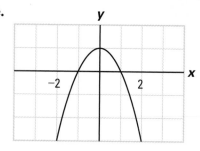

f.

x	−1.571	−0.7854	0	0.7854	1.5708	2.3562	3.1416
y	0	0.7071	1	0.7071	0	−0.7071	−1

x	3.9270	4.7124	5.4978	6.2832	7.0686	7.8540	8.6394
y	−0.7071	0	0.7071	1	0.7071	0	−0.7071

g.

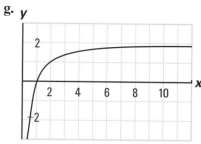

h.

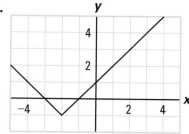

i.

x	−4	−3	−2	−1	0	1	2
y	36	25	16	9	4	1	0

x	3	4	5	6	7	8	9
y	1	4	9	16	25	36	49

6. Draw sketches and find algebraic rules for the functions that meet the following conditions.

   a. $f(x)$ has a graph that is a translation 3.5 units upward of the graph of $y = \frac{1}{x}$.

   b. $g(x)$ has a graph that is a translation 3.5 units to the right of the graph of $y = \frac{1}{x}$.

   c. $h(x)$ has a graph that is a reflection of the graph of $y = \sqrt{x}$ across the x-axis.

   d. $i(x)$ has a graph that is a compression with factor of 4 toward the x-axis of the graph of $y = \sin x$.

   e. $j(x)$ is periodic with amplitude 5, period $\frac{\pi}{2}$, and $j(0) = 0$.

f. $k(x)$ has a graph that is a reflection of the graph of $y = 1.5^x$ across the x-axis and then translated so that the line $y = 15$ is an asymptote.

g. $m(x)$ has a graph that is a translation 4 units to the left of the graph of $y = \sin x$.

h. $n(x)$ has a graph that is a translation 3 units to the right of the graph of $y = -2.5x + 4$.

i. $p(x)$ has a graph that is a translation 6 units to the left and 4 units upward of the graph of $y = 2x^2$.

Checkpoint

In this unit, you have organized your thinking about functions in terms of families whose members share symbolic rules that are alike in form, graphs that have a characteristic shape, and tables that display similar patterns. You have also reviewed how functions belonging to the same family share properties that serve to make them useful as models of real-world phenomena.

a What table and graph patterns and problem conditions are clues to use the following types of functions as models?

- Linear
- Exponential
- Quadratic polynomial
- Trigonometric
- Direct power
- Absolute value
- Inverse power
- Square root

b What is the general form of an algebraic rule for each of the above types of functions, and how can the patterns in tables and graphs of specific cases be predicted by inspection of the parameters in those rules?

c How can you adjust the algebraic rules of the basic function types to match graphs that are related to one of the basic function graphs by these transformations?

- Vertical translation
- Vertical stretching or compression
- Horizontal translation
- Horizontal stretching or compression
- Reflection across the x-axis

d How can the sine and cosine function rules be adjusted to give functions with period P and amplitude A?

Be prepared to compare your responses to those of other groups.

Discrete Models of Change

Modeling Sequential Change Using Recursion

We live in a changing world. In previous units, you have used equations, tables, and graphs to investigate linear, exponential, polynomial, and periodic patterns of change. You have used coordinates and matrices to model geometric change in position, size, and shape. In many situations, it is important to also understand **sequential change**, for example, change from year to year. You have already used equations involving the words *NOW* and *NEXT* to describe this type of change. In this unit, you will examine sequential change more fully.

Think About This Situation

Wildlife management has become an increasingly important issue as modern civilization puts greater demands on wildlife habitat. As an example, consider a fishing pond that is stocked with trout from a Department of National Resources hatchery. Suppose you are in charge of managing the trout population in the pond.

a What are some factors to consider in managing the trout population in the pond? List as many factors as you can.

b How could you estimate the current trout population?

c Why would it be useful to be able to predict the year-to-year changes in the trout population? Why would knowledge of the long-term population changes be useful?

INVESTIGATION 1 ▶ Modeling Population Change

In this lesson, you will build and use a mathematical model to help you predict the changing trout population. As you have seen before, a typical first step in mathematical modeling is simplifying the problem and deciding on some reasonable assumptions. Three factors that you may have listed in the "Think About This Situation" discussion are initial trout population in the pond, annual growth rate of the population, and annual restocking amount, that is, the number of trout added to the pond each year. For the rest of this investigation, use just the following assumptions:

■ There are about 3,000 trout currently in the pond.

■ Regardless of restocking, the population decreases by about 20% each year due to the combined effect of all causes, including natural deaths and trout being caught.

■ 1,000 trout are added at the end of each year.

1. Using these assumptions, build a mathematical model to analyze the population growth in the pond.

   a. Find the population after each of the first two years.

   b. Write an equation using the words *NOW* and *NEXT* to model this situation.

   c. Use the equation from Part b and the last-answer feature of your calculator or computer software to find the population after seven years. Explain how the keystrokes or software features you used correspond to the words *NOW* and *NEXT* in the equation.

2. Now think about the patterns of change in the long-term population of trout in the pond.

   a. Do you think the population will grow without bound? Level off? Die out? Make a conjecture about the long-term population. Compare your conjecture to those made by other students in your group.

   b. Determine the long-term population. Was your conjecture correct? Explain, in terms of the fishing pond ecology, why the long-term population you have determined is reasonable.

   c. Does the trout population change faster around year 5 or around year 25? How can you tell?

3. What do you think will happen to the long-term population of trout if the initial population is different but all other conditions remain the same? Make an educated guess. Then check your guess by finding the long-term population for a variety of initial populations. Describe the pattern of change in long-term population as the initial population varies.

4. Investigate what happens to the long-term population if the annual restocking amount changes but all other conditions are the same as in the original assumptions. Describe your findings about the relationship between long-term population and restocking amount.

5. Describe what happens to the long-term population if the annual decrease rate changes but all other conditions are the same as in the original assumptions.

6. Now consider a situation in which the trout population shows an annual rate of *increase*.

   a. What do you think will happen to the long-term population if the population *increases* at an annual rate? Make a conjecture and then test it by trying at least two different annual increase rates.

   b. Write equations using *NOW* and *NEXT* that represent your two test cases.

   c. Do you think it is reasonable to model the population of trout in a pond with an annual rate of increase? Why or why not?

Checkpoint

Consider this population modeling equation: $NEXT = 0.6NOW + 1{,}500$.

a Describe a situation involving a population of fish that could be modeled by this equation.

b What additional information is needed to be able to use this equation to predict the population in 3 years?

c What additional information is needed to be able to use this equation to predict the long-term population?

d Consider the following variations in a fish-population situation modeled by an equation like the one above.

- If the initial population doubles, what will happen to the long-term population?

- If the annual restocking amount doubles, what will happen to the long-term population?

- If the annual population decrease rate doubles, what will happen to the long-term population?

e How would you modify the equation above so that it represents a situation in which the fish population increases annually at a rate of 15%? What effect does such an increase rate have on the long-term population?

Be prepared to share your group's thinking with the entire class.

Situations involving sequential change, as in the case of the trout population, are sometimes called **discrete dynamical systems**. A discrete dynamical system is a situation (system) involving change (dynamical) in which the nature of the change is step-by-step (discrete). The method of describing the next step in terms of previous steps is called **recursion**. An important part of analyzing discrete dynamical systems is determining long-term behavior, as you did when you found the long-term population of trout.

On Your Own

A hospital patient is given an antibiotic to treat an infection. He is initially given a 30-mg dose and then receives another 10 mg at the end of every six-hour period thereafter. Through natural body metabolism, about 20% of the antibiotic is eliminated from his system every six hours.

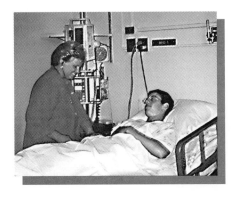

a. Estimate the amount of antibiotic in his system after the first six hours and after the second six hours.

b. Write an equation using the words *NOW* and *NEXT* that models this situation.

c. Find the amount of antibiotic in the patient's system after two weeks.

d. Suppose his doctor decides to modify the prescription so that the long-term amount of antibiotic in his system will be about 25 mg. How should the prescription be modified?

INVESTIGATION 2 The Power of Notation

A compact notation can be used for equations involving *NOW* and *NEXT* that allows for a detailed analysis of the equations and the situations they model. Using the context of a changing trout population from the last investigation, the **subscript notation** P_n can be used to represent the population after n years. (The notation P_n is read "P sub n.") Thus, P_0 (P sub 0) is the population after 0 years, that is, the initial population. P_1 is the population after 1 year, P_2 is the population after 2 years, and so on.

Recall that the trout-population problem from Investigation 1 was based on these three assumptions:

- There are about 3,000 trout currently in the pond.
- Regardless of restocking, the population decreases by 20% each year due to natural causes and trout being caught.
- 1,000 trout are added at the end of each year.

1. Calculate P_0, P_1, P_2, and P_3 and then sketch a graph of n versus P_n. Describe the pattern of change.

2. The subscript notation relates closely to the way you have used the words NOW and NEXT to describe sequential change in many contexts.

   a. In the context of a changing fish population, if P_1 is the population NOW, what subscript notation represents the population NEXT year?

   b. If P_{24} is the population NEXT year, what subscript notation represents the population NOW?

   c. If P_n is the population NEXT year, what subscript notation represents the population NOW?

   d. An equation that models the annual change in trout population as described in Investigation 1 is

   $$NEXT = 0.8NOW + 1,000.$$

   Rewrite this equation using P_n and P_{n-1} notation.

3. The equations in Part d of Activity 2 don't tell you what the population is for any given year; they show only how the population changes from year to year. You can analyze situations that involve sequential change, like this one, by using the "recursion mode" on a calculator or computer software. (This activity assumes a calculator is being used.)

   a. Set the mode on your calculator so that you get equations that look like "$P_n = ...$" or "$U_n = ...$" or "$u(n) = ...$" Different calculators may have different names for this mode, and the letters and notation may differ slightly.

   $$U_n =$$
   $$V_n =$$

   b. Rewrite the population equation $NEXT = 0.8NOW + 1,000$ using the notation system of your calculator. (For example, if your calculator uses U_n, then write the equation in the form "$U_n = ...$") Then enter the rule into your calculator.

   c. Use your calculator to produce a table and graph of the rule, with n as the input variable.

   d. Describe any patterns of change you see in the table and graph. Compare the information you get from the table and graph to your analysis of the trout-population situation in Investigation 1. Be sure to describe how the long-term population trend shows up in the table and graph.

4. Reasoning with recursion, as you have been doing with the trout-population problem, is useful in many other contexts. For example, it is often necessary to borrow money for major purchases. Suppose you borrow $5,000 to buy a pre-owned sports utility vehicle, at 12% annual interest, with repayment due in 48 monthly payments. You are told that your monthly payment will be $135. As a wise consumer, you should check to see if this payment amount is correct.

a. Working as a group, decide how you can determine the amount you still owe, called the *balance*, after a given month's payment. Then find the balance of the auto loan after each of the first three payments. Compare your balances to those of other groups.

b. Write an equation using the words *NOW* and *NEXT* that models the month-by-month change in the balance of the loan. Write an equivalent equation using subscript notation. Be sure to specify the initial balance.

c. If the monthly payment of $135 is correct, what should the balance be after the 48th payment? Use the equations from Part b and your calculator to see if $135 is the correct payment for this loan. If the payment is incorrect, is it too high or too low? How can you tell? Experiment to find the correct monthly payment.

5. Investigate further the loan situation from Activity 4.

a. How much total interest was paid on the $5,000 loan, using the correct monthly payment?

b. Is the balance of the loan reduced faster at the beginning of the repayment period or at the end? Explain and give evidence to support your answer.

c. Suppose someone offers you a "great deal" whereby you have to pay only $45 per month until the loan is paid off. Describe what happens to the repayment process in this situation. Is this such a great deal after all?

Checkpoint

Consider a wildlife population that is modeled by these equations:

$$U_n = 0.4U_{n-1} + 2,500, \ U_0 = 11,000$$

ⓐ Describe what these equations tell you about the population.

ⓑ The size of the population after 3 years is 4,604. Find the population after 4 years:

- without using a calculator or computer software.
- using the last-answer feature of a calculator or computer software.
- using the recursion mode on a calculator.

ⓒ Describe the pattern of population change, including the long-term population trend.

ⓓ Rewrite the "$U_n = ...$" equation using the words *NOW* and *NEXT*.

ⓔ Explain why this situation involves sequential change and why it is an example of recursion.

Be prepared to share your group's responses and thinking with the entire class.

Equations involving recursion, like those you have been using in this investigation, are called **recursion equations**. They are also called *recurrence relations* or *difference equations*. The recursion equations you have studied in this lesson have all been of the general form $A_n = rA_{n-1} + b$, with A_0 as the initial value. Different values for r and b allow you to model many different situations.

▶ **On Your Own**

Recall the situation involving a hospital patient taking an antibiotic to treat an infection. He was initially given a 30-mg dose, and then he took another 10 mg at the end of every six hours. Through natural body metabolism, about 20% of the antibiotic was eliminated from his system every six hours.

a. Write a recursion equation in the form "$U_n = ...$" that models this situation.

b. Using your calculator, produce a table and graph of n versus U_n, with n as the input variable.

c. Describe how the amount of antibiotic in the patient's system changes over time, including the long-term change.

MORE
Modeling • Organizing • Reflecting • Extending

Modeling

1. Every ten years, the United States Census Bureau conducts a complete census of the nation's population. In 1990, the census report said that there were about 248 million residents in the United States and its territories. The population changes quite a lot between census reports, but it is too expensive to conduct the census more often. So the Census Bureau estimates annual changes, such as the following:

- Births will equal about 1.6% of the total population.
- Deaths will equal about 0.9% of the total population.
- Immigrants from other countries will add about 0.9 million people each year.

a. Using the statistics on the previous page, what population is estimated for the United States in 1991? In the year 2000?

b. Write an equation using the words *NOW* and *NEXT* that represents this situation.

c. Write a recursion equation that represents this situation, and specify the initial value.

d. Produce a table and a graph that show the population estimates through the year 2010. Describe the expected long-term trend in population change over time.

e. Describe some hypothetical birth and death rates that would result in a population that levels off over time. Represent this situation with a recursion equation, a table, and a graph.

2. Commercial hunting of whales is controlled to prevent the extinction of some species. Because of the danger of extinction, scientists conduct counts of whales to monitor their population changes. A 1991 research study on the bowhead whales of Alaska reported that the population of these whales was between 5,700 and  10,600 and that the difference between births and deaths yielded an annual growth rate of about 3%. No hunting of bowhead whales is allowed, except that Alaskan Inuit are allowed to take, or harvest, about 50 bowhead whales each year for their livelihood. (Source: Zeh, Judith, et al., 1991. Rate of increase, 1978–88, of bowhead whales, *Balaena Mysticetus*, estimated from ice-based census data. *Marine Mammal Science*, no. 2. (April): 105–122.)

a. Compute the mean of the high and low population estimates from the report. Use that figure as your estimate of the 1991 population for the rest of this task.

b. Write an equation using the words *NOW* and *NEXT* to model this situation.

c. Write a recursion equation that models this situation; include the initial value.

d. Produce a table and graph showing the change in the bowhead whale population over time. Describe any trends in that change.

e. Suppose that, because of some natural disaster, the current bowhead whale population is reduced to 1,500, but growth rate and number harvested by the Inuit stay the same. Under these conditions, what happens to the long-term population?

3. Retirement is probably not something you are currently concerned about! However, working adults, even very young working adults, should have a financial plan for retirement. If you start saving early and take advantage of compound interest, then you should be in great financial shape by the time you retire. Consider twin sisters with two different retirement savings plans.

Plan I: Cora begins a retirement account at age 20. She starts with $2,000 and then saves $2,000 per year at 8% interest, compounded annually, for 10 years. (*Compounded annually* means that her money will grow at a rate of 8% each year.) Then she stops contributing to the account but keeps her savings invested at the same rate.

Plan II: Mawiyah doesn't save any money in her twenties, but when she turns 30, she starts with $2,000 and then saves $2,000 per year at 8% interest, compounded annually, for 35 years.

Both sisters retire at age 65. Who do you think will have more retirement savings at age 65? Test your conjecture.

4. Chlorine is used to keep swimming pools safe by controlling certain harmful microorganisms. However, chlorine is a powerful chemical, so just the right amount must be used. Too much chlorine irritates swimmers' eyes and can be hazardous to their health; too

little chlorine allows the growth of microorganisms to be uncontrolled, which can be harmful. A pool manager must measure and add chlorine regularly to keep the level just right. The chlorine is measured in parts per million (ppm) by weight. That is, one ppm of chlorine means that there is one ounce of chlorine for every million ounces of water.

Chlorine dissipates in reaction to bacteria and to the sun at a rate of about 15% of the amount present per day. The optimal concentration of chlorine in a pool is from 1 to 2 ppm, although it is safe to swim when the concentration is as high as 3 ppm.

a. Suppose you have a summer job working at a swimming pool, and one of your responsibilities is to maintain a safe concentration of chlorine in the pool. You are required to add the same amount of chlorine to the pool every day. When you take the job, you find that the concentration is 3 ppm. How much chlorine (in parts per million) do you need to add each day in order to maintain a long-term optimal concentration? Write a recursion equation that models your optimal chlorine maintenance plan.

b. There are three key factors in this problem: the initial concentration, the daily increase in concentration due to the amount you add, and the dissipation rate. Systematically explore changes in each of these three factors and record the corresponding effects on the long-term chlorine concentration in the swimming pool.

c. Suppose the chlorinating pellets you use are 65% active chlorine, by weight. If the pool contains 50,000 gallons of water, and water weighs 8.337 pounds per gallon, how many pounds of chlorine pellets must you add to the pool each day?

5. If you have money in an interest-bearing savings account, the interest is probably compounded at a rate between 4% and 5.5%. Recursion equations can be used to analyze how money grows due to compounding of interest. For this task, assume you make no withdrawals from the savings account.

a. Suppose you deposit $100 in a savings account that pays 4% interest, compounded annually. (*Compounded annually* means that your money will grow at a rate of 4% per year.) Write a *NOW-NEXT* equation and a recursion equation that show how the amount of money in your account changes from year to year. Find the amount of money in the account after 10 years.

b. Most savings accounts pay interest that compounds more often than annually. Suppose that you make an initial deposit of $100 into an account that pays 4% annual interest, compounded monthly.

■ Write a recursion equation that models the month-by-month change in the amount of money in your account.

■ How much money is in the account after 1 month? After 2 months? After 2 years?

■ How much money is in the account after 10 years? Compare your answer to the answer you got in Part a. Which kind of interest is a better deal, compounding annually or compounding monthly? How much better?

c. Suppose that, in addition to the initial $100, you deposit another $50 at the end of every year, and the interest rate is 4% compounded annually.

■ Write a recursion equation that models this situation.

■ How much money is in the account after 10 years?

■ Describe the pattern of growth of the money in the savings account.

Organizing

1. In this lesson, you have investigated recursion equations of the form $A_n = rA_{n-1} + b$. Different values for r and b yield models for different situations. Consider some of the possibilities by completing a table like the one below. For each entry in the table, do the following.

   ■ Describe a situation that could be modeled by a recursion equation. (You may use examples from the lesson if you wish.)

   ■ Write the recursion equation.

   ■ Describe the long-term trend.

	$0 < r < 1$	$r > 1$
$b < 0$	A whale population is decreasing by 5% per year due to a death rate higher than the birthrate, and 50 whales are harvested each year. $A_n = 0.95A_{n-1} - 50$ Long-term trend: Extinction	
$b > 0$		

2. In this lesson, you used a specific and very common subscript notation to represent sequential change. However, there are other ways to represent sequential change with subscript and related notation. You may see some of these other ways when using different textbooks and calculators. Consider again the trout population modeling equation $NEXT = 0.8NOW + 1{,}000$, which you represented as $P_n = 0.8P_{n-1} + 1{,}000$.

   a. If U_n is the population *NOW*, what subscript notation represents the population *NEXT* year? Rewrite the *NOW-NEXT* equation above using U_n and U_{n+1}.

   b. If $A(n)$ is the population *NOW*, what notation represents the population *NEXT* year? Rewrite the *NOW-NEXT* equation above using $A(n)$ and $A(n+1)$.

   c. You now have four different equations representing the same trout population: an equation using the words *NOW* and *NEXT*, an equation using P_n and P_{n-1}, an equation using U_n and U_{n+1}, and an equation using $A(n)$ and $A(n+1)$. Suppose that one of your classmates has not completed this task. Write a paragraph or two to the classmate explaining how all four equations accurately represent the changing trout population.

3. In Activity 2 of Investigation 2 (page 492), you found the following recursion equation to model a trout population:

$$P_n = 0.8P_{n-1} + 1,000, \text{ with } P_0 = 3,000$$

Another equation that represents this situation is the following:

$$P_n = -2,000(0.8)^n + 5,000$$

   a. Using ideas from the "Families of Functions" unit, explain why this new equation is reasonable.

   b. Verify that the new equation gives the same values for P_1 and P_5 as those found using the recursion equation.

   c. Verify that the new equation yields an initial population of 3,000.

   d. Use the new equation to verify the long-term population you found in Activity 3 of Investigation 1 (page 489). Explain your thinking. How is the long-term population revealed in the symbolic form of the new equation?

4. You can represent recursion equations with subscript notation or function notation. For example, in the trout-population problem, you can represent the population P as a function of the number of years n and write P_n or $P(n)$. In the case of the trout-population problem, what are the practical domain and practical range of the function P?

5. Think about how matrix multiplication can be used to calculate successive values generated by recursion equations of the form $A_n = rA_{n-1} + b$. For example, consider the recursion equation for the original trout-population situation at the beginning of this lesson: $P_n = 0.8P_{n-1} + 1,000$, with $P_0 = 3,000$.

   a. A first attempt at a matrix multiplication that would be equivalent to evaluating the recursion equation might use the following matrices.

$$A = [3,000 \ 1] \quad \text{and} \quad B = \begin{bmatrix} 0.8 \\ 1,000 \end{bmatrix}$$

   Compute AB and compare it to P_1.

   b. AB is just a 1×1 matrix and so is not much good for repeated multiplication. Thus, you can't use repeated multiplication of these matrices to successively evaluate the recursion equation. A better try might be to use the following matrices.

$$A = [3,000 \ 1] \quad \text{and} \quad C = \begin{bmatrix} 0.8 & 0 \\ 1,000 & 1 \end{bmatrix}$$

   Compute AC and compare it to P_1. What matrix multiplication would you use next to find P_2? To find P_3?

c. There is just one finishing touch needed: Modify the matrices so that the multiplication computes not only the successive values but also the number of the year. Consider the following matrices.

$$A = [0 \quad 3{,}000 \quad 1] \quad \text{and} \quad D = \begin{bmatrix} 1 & 0 & 0 \\ 0 & 0.8 & 0 \\ 1 & 1{,}000 & 1 \end{bmatrix}$$

Compute AD, AD^2, AD^3, AD^4, and AD^5, and compare the results to P_1 through P_5.

d. Use matrix multiplication to generate three successive values of the recursion equation $P_n = 1.04P_{n-1} - 350$, with $P_0 = 6{,}700$.

e. Explain why this matrix multiplication method works to find successive values of a recursion equation.

Reflecting

1. When using some graphing calculators, you have the option of graphing in "connected" mode or "dot" mode. Find out what the difference is between these two modes of graphing. Which do you think is more appropriate for the graphing you have been doing in this lesson? Why?

2. You can use a calculator to produce the successive values of a recursion equation in several different ways. For example, you can use the last-answer key, you can use recursion mode to generate a table, or you can use recursion mode to generate a graph and then trace the graph.

   a. Use each of the above methods to find the successive values of the recursion equation $A_n = 0.65A_{n-1} + 90$, with $A_0 = 200$.

   b. Use any other method you can think of to find some successive values.

   c. Do you prefer one method over the others? If you have your choice of methods, how will you decide which one to use?

3. In this lesson, you used recursion equations to model sequential change in several situations, such as population growth, drug concentration, chlorine concentration, and money saved or owed. Describe one result of your investigations that was particularly interesting or surprising.

4. Recursion equations are also sometimes called *difference equations*. What difference would be of interest in studying a recursion equation?

Extending

1. Spreadsheets are designed to take advantage of the power of recursion. In particular, recursion equations can be evaluated and analyzed using spreadsheets. Use some spreadsheet software to complete one of the Modeling tasks from this lesson.

	A	B	C	
1	2			
2	14			
3	50			
4				
5				
6				
7				
8				
9				
10				

2. In this lesson, you modeled a trout population with the recursion equation $P_n = 0.8P_{n-1} + 1,000$, with $P_0 = 3,000$. You can get another modeling formula for this situation by fitting a curve to the population data and finding the equation for that curve. Use the following steps to carry out this plan.

   a. Use the formula $P_n = 0.8P_{n-1} + 1,000$, with $P_0 = 3,000$, to generate the sequence of population figures for 20 years and put these figures into a data list, say L_2, on your calculator or computer. Generate another list, say L_1, that contains the sequence of years 0 through 20. Produce a scatterplot of L_1 versus L_2.

   b. Modify your scatterplot by transforming the data in the lists so that the plot matches one of the standard regression models of your calculator or computer software. Use the regression model feature to find an equation that fits the transformed data.

   c. Now, transform your regression equation so that it fits the original data.

   d. Test your equation. Does the graph fit the original scatterplot? Compare the function value for $n = 20$ to what you get when you find P_{20} using the recursion equation $P_n = 0.8P_{n-1} + 1,000$, with $P_0 = 3,000$.

3. These days, almost every state has a lottery, and the jackpots are often quite large. But are they really as large as they seem? Suppose you win $500,000 in a lottery (which you will, of course, donate to the mathematics department at your school). Typically, these large jackpots are paid over time. For example, suppose you receive your $500,000 over 20 years at $25,000 per year. To accurately analyze how much you have *really* won in this situation, you need to include the effect of compound interest.

a. Suppose you deposit $500,000 in a bank account paying 6% annual interest, and you withdraw $25,000 at the end of every year. Write a recursion equation that models this situation, and calculate how much money will be in the account after 20 years.

b. Experiment to find an initial deposit that will yield a balance of $0 after 20 years.

c. The result from Part b is called the **present value** of your lottery winning. The present value is the lump sum amount that, if deposited now at 6% annual interest, would generate payments of $25,000 per year for 20 years. The present value is what your lottery winning is really worth, taking into account the reality of compound interest. So in this situation, how much is a $500,000 jackpot paid over 20 years really worth?

d. Find the actual value, that is, the present value, of a lottery winning of $1,000,000 that is paid at $50,000 per year for 20 years, given that you can invest money at 8% annual interest.

e. Actual present values are even lower than what you have calculated here. What do you think causes even lower present values?

4. The Towers of Hanoi is a mathematical game featured in an old story about the end of the world. As the story goes, monks in a secluded temple are working on this game, and when they are finished, the world will end! The people of the world would like to know how long it will take the monks to finish the game.

The game is played with 3 pegs mounted on a board and 64 golden disks of successively larger sizes with holes in the center. (Commercial games such as the example above have much fewer disks.) The game begins with all 64 disks stacked on one peg, from largest to smallest. The goal of the game is to move all 64 disks onto another peg, subject to these rules: (1) Only one disk may be moved at a time. (2) You are not allowed to put a larger disk on top of a smaller disk. (3) Disks may be placed temporarily on any peg, including the one on which the disks were originally stacked. (4) Eventually, the disks must be stacked from largest to smallest on a new peg.

a. You may not have 64 golden disks to play this game, but to get an idea of how it works, you can play with some homemade disks and pegs. Cut out 4 successively larger squares of paper to use as disks (or use different size coins for the disks). Put 3 large dots on a piece of paper to use as pegs mounted on a board. Play the game several times, first with just one disk stacked on the starting peg, then with two disks, then three, and so on. As you play each game, keep track of the *fewest* number of moves it takes to finish the game. Make a table listing the number of disks in the game and the fewest number of moves it takes to finish the game.

b. By thinking about strategies for how to play the game with more and more disks and by looking for patterns in the table from Part a, find a recursion equation and any other formula you can for the fewest number of moves needed to finish the game with *n* disks.

c. What is the fewest number of moves needed to finish a game with 64 disks? If the monks in the story move one disk every second and work nonstop, should we worry about the world ending soon? Explain.

5. You undoubtedly have noticed how a hot drink will cool down as it sits in a room. In the 1700s, Sir Isaac Newton discovered a mathematical model for this situation, called **Newton's Law of Cooling**: The change in an object's temperature from one time period to the next is proportional to the difference between the temperature of the object at the earlier time period and the temperature of the surrounding environment.

a. To say that one thing, X, is proportional to another, Y, means that there is some constant, k, such that $X = kY$. If t_n is the temperature of a cup of hot coffee after n minutes, s is the temperature of the surrounding environment, and k is the constant of proportionality, find a formula for Newton's Law of Cooling.

b. Suppose that the temperature of a cup of hot coffee is initially 180°F and that, after sitting in a room at temperature 72°F for one minute, the coffee cools down to 171°F. Use this information to find t_0, s, and k. Rewrite the formula from Part a so that it models this particular situation.

c. Rewrite the formula from Part b in the "standard" form $A_n = rA_{n-1} + b$.

d. Find the temperature of the cup of hot coffee if it remains sitting in the room for 5 minutes. How long will you have to wait before it cools down to 110°F?

e. Use the formula to compute the long-term behavior of the temperature of the cup of coffee. Did you expect this behavior? Explain why this behavior makes sense in terms of the cooling coffee.

f. *Optional:* Compare your analysis of the cooling coffee to actual data. Obtain a temperature probe that will connect to your calculator or to an available computer.

Use the probe to gather data on the minute-by-minute temperature of a cooling cup of hot coffee. Use Newton's Law of Cooling to predict the cooling behavior. Compare the observed temperature changes to the predicted changes. Discuss any discrepancies. Use the statistical regression capability of your calculator or computer to fit a curve to the observed data and get another formula describing the cooling. Check that your new formula produces results reasonably close to the results using your original formula. Which of these formulas is recursive?

Lesson 2

A Discrete View of Function Models

In the previous lesson, you investigated a variety of situations that were modeled by recursion equations, including population growth, consumer loans, and medicine dosage. In each of these situations, you examined a sequence of numbers and looked for patterns. In this lesson, you will take a closer look at sequences of numbers. As you do so, you will extend your understanding of recursion, and you will revisit three important function families: linear, exponential, and polynomial. To begin, consider the exciting but dangerous sport of skydiving.

Think About This Situation

Imagine a sky diver jumping from a plane at a height of about 5,000 feet. Because of Earth's gravity and ignoring wind resistance, the sky diver will fall 16 feet in the first second. Thereafter, until the parachute opens, the distance fallen during each second will be 32 feet more than the distance fallen during the previous second.

a Think about the pattern of change in the distance the sky diver falls each second. How would you describe the number of feet fallen during each second:

- using a recursion equation?
- as a function of the number of seconds n?

b Now consider the pattern of change in the *total* distance fallen. How far has the sky diver fallen after each of the first five seconds? Describe any patterns you see in this sequence of numbers. Compare this sequence to the sequence of distances fallen during each second.

c How would you describe the total distance fallen after each second using an algebraic equation? How might the sky diver use this equation in planning the jump?

INVESTIGATION 1 ▸ Arithmetic and Geometric Sequences

As you can imagine, skydiving requires considerable training and careful advance preparation. Although the sport of bungee jumping may require little or no training, it too requires careful preparation to ensure the safety of the jumper. In Course 1, you may have explored the relationship between jumper weight and bungee cord length by conducting an experiment with rubber bands and weights.

1. In one such experiment, for each ounce of weight added to a 3-inch rubber band, the rubber band stretched about $\frac{1}{2}$ inch.

   a. Describe the relationship between weight added and rubber band length, using words, graphs, tables, and equations. What type of function models this relationship?

   b. Complete a data table like the one below.

Bungee Experiment												
Weight (in ounces)	0	1	2	3	4	5	...	50	...	99	...	n
Length (in inches)								...		...		...

   c. The sequence of numbers that you get for the lengths is called an *arithmetic sequence*. An **arithmetic sequence** of numbers is one in which you add the same constant to each number in the sequence to get the next number. An arithmetic sequence models **arithmetic growth**. Explain why the sequence of rubber band lengths is an arithmetic sequence.

   d. Which, if any, of the sequences in the "Think About This Situation" section is an arithmetic sequence? Why?

2. There are several different equations that can be used to represent the weight-length relationship.

   a. Write an equation using the words *NOW* and *NEXT* that shows how the length changes as weight is added.

   b. Write a recursion equation that models this situation; that is, write an equation for this situation that looks like

$$L_n = (\text{expression involving } L_{n-1}).$$

   An equation in this form is called a **recursive formula** for the sequence.

c. Use the recursive formula to predict the rubber band length when 15 ounces of weight are attached.

d. Write an equation for this situation that looks like

$$L_n = \text{(expression involving } n \text{ with no subscripts).}$$

An equation in this form can be called a **function formula** for the sequence of lengths. Explain why it makes sense to call such a formula a function formula.

e. Use the function formula to predict the rubber band length when 15 ounces of weight are attached.

f. Describe the difference between the processes of using the recursive formula and using the function formula to compute the rubber band length when 15 ounces of weight are attached.

3. Cellular phones, pagers, and telephone calling cards afford convenient ways to stay in contact with friends and family. A typical calling card at a convenience store may cost $1.25 plus 40 cents per minute.

a. Determine recursive and function formulas for the sequence of calling card prices.

b. Compare these formulas to those you found for the rubber band experiment in Activity 2. How are they similar? How are they different?

4. Now think about possible connections between arithmetic sequences and other mathematical models you have studied.

a. What type of function is represented by each of the function formulas in Activities 2 and 3?

b. In each case, describe the shape of the graph of the function formula.

c. What is the slope of each graph? How does the slope appear in each of the recursive and function formulas you have been examining?

5. Suppose t_0 is the initial term of a *general* arithmetic sequence for which you add d to each term of the sequence to get the next term of the sequence.

a. Write the first five terms of this sequence and then find recursive and function formulas for the sequence. Compare your formulas to those of other groups. Resolve any differences.

b. How would you interpret t_0, d, and n in the context of the rubber band experiment?

c. The constant d is sometimes called the **common difference** between terms. Explain why it makes sense to call d the common difference.

d. Suppose an arithmetic sequence t_0, t_1, t_2, ... begins with $t_0 = 84$ and has a common difference of -6. Find function and recursive formulas for this sequence and then find the term t_{87}.

6. Now consider the growth sequence of bacteria cells if a cut by a rusty nail puts 25 bacteria cells into a wound and then the number of bacteria doubles every quarter-hour.

a. Use words, graphs, tables, and equations to describe the relationship between the number of quarter-hours and the number of bacteria. What type of function models this relationship?

b. Complete a data table like the one below for this situation.

Bacterial Growth

Number of Quarter-Hours	0	1	2	3	4	5	...	50	...	99	...	n
Bacteria Count							...		...		...	

c. The sequence of numbers that you get for the bacteria count is called a *geometric sequence*. A **geometric sequence** of numbers is one in which each number in the sequence is multiplied by a constant to get the next number. A geometric sequence models **geometric growth**. Explain why the sequence of bacteria counts is a geometric sequence.

d. Which, if any, of the sequences in the "Think About This Situation" section is a geometric sequence? Why?

7. If B_n represents the bacteria count after n quarter-hours, then there are several different equations that can be used to model this situation.

a. Write an equation using the words *NOW* and *NEXT* that shows how the bacteria count increases as time passes.

b. Write a recursive formula beginning "$B_n = ...$" for the sequence of bacteria counts. Use the recursive formula to predict the bacteria count after 18 quarter-hours.

c. Write a function formula beginning "$B_n = \dots$" for the sequence of bacteria counts. Use the function formula to predict the bacteria count after 18 quarter-hours.

d. Describe the difference between the processes of using the recursive formula and using the function formula to compute the bacteria count after 18 quarter-hours.

8. One of the simplest fractal patterns is the *Sierpinski carpet*. Starting with a solid square "carpet" one meter on a side, smaller and smaller squares are cut out of the carpet. The first two stages in forming the carpet are shown below.

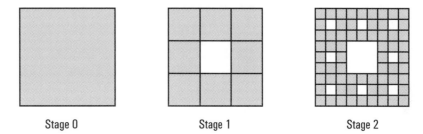

Stage 0   Stage 1   Stage 2

a. Find recursive and function formulas for the sequence of carpet area that remains at each stage.

b. Compare your formulas to those you found for the bacteria present after a cut by a rusty nail, in Activity 7. How are they similar? How are they different?

9. Now, suppose t_0 is the initial term of a *general* geometric sequence for which each term of the sequence is multiplied by r ($r \neq 1$) to get the next term of the sequence.

a. Write the first five terms of this sequence and then find recursive and function formulas for the sequence. Compare your formulas to those of other groups. Resolve any differences.

b. What are t_0, r, and n in the situation involving bacterial growth?

c. The constant r is sometimes called the **common ratio** of terms. Explain why it makes sense to call r the common ratio.

d. Suppose a geometric sequence t_0, t_1, t_2, $\dots$ begins with $t_0 = -4$ and has a common ratio of 3. Find function and recursive formulas for this sequence and then find the term t_{17}.

10. Working individually, write the first five terms for three different sequences. One sequence should be arithmetic, one should be geometric, and the third should be neither. Challenge your groupmates to correctly identify your sequences. Similarly, identify the sequences prepared by the other members of your group. Write a summary of how you can tell by inspection whether a given sequence is arithmetic, geometric, or neither.

In this investigation, you studied two important patterns of growth: arithmetic growth, modeled by arithmetic sequences, and geometric growth, modeled by geometric sequences.

ⓐ How are arithmetic and geometric sequences different? How are they similar? Describe one real-world situation different from those you studied in this investigation that could be modeled by an arithmetic sequence. Do the same for a geometric sequence.

ⓑ What is the connection between arithmetic and geometric sequences and linear and exponential functions?

ⓒ Describe the difference between a recursive formula and a function formula for a sequence. What information do you need to know to find each type of formula?

ⓓ What is one advantage of a recursive formula for a sequence? What is one disadvantage? What is one advantage of a function formula? What is one disadvantage?

ⓔ In the first lesson of this unit, you investigated situations that could be modeled by recursion equations of the form $A_n = rA_{n-1} + b$. Such equations are sometimes called **combined recursion equations**. What is the connection between combined recursion equations and recursive formulas for arithmetic and geometric sequences? Why does it make sense to call these equations "combined recursion equations"?

Be prepared to share your group's thinking with the entire class.

On Your Own

For each of the sequences below and on the next page, do the following.

- Complete a copy of the table.
- State whether the sequence is arithmetic, geometric, or neither.
- For those sequences that are arithmetic or geometric, find a recursive formula and a function formula.
- If a sequence is neither arithmetic nor geometric, find whatever formula you can that describes the sequence.

a.

n	0	1	2	3	4	5	6	...	10	...	100	...
A_n	2	6	18	54	162			...		...		...

b.

n	0	1	2	3	4	5	6	...	10	...	100	...
B_n	1	2	5	10	17			...		...		...

c.

n	0	1	2	3	4	5	6	...	10	...	100	...
C_n	3	7	11	15	19			...		...		...

INVESTIGATION 2 Some Sums

In the "Think About This Situation" section at the beginning of this lesson, you considered the distance fallen by a sky diver during each second of a free fall and the total or *accumulated* distance fallen. Predicting the accumulated distance for various times in the jump is critical to determining when to open the parachute.

1. The table below shows the distance in feet fallen by a sky diver, assuming no wind resistance, during each of the first 10 seconds of a jump.

Skydiving

Time n (in seconds)	1	2	3	4	5	6	7	8	9	10
Distance Fallen D_n (in feet)	16	48	80	112	144	176	208	240	272	304

  a. What is the total distance fallen after three seconds? After five seconds? After 10 seconds?

  b. What kind of sequence is D_n?

  c. Notice that the sequence of distances fallen, $D_1, D_2, D_3, ...,$ begins with subscript 1 rather than subscript 0 like the other sequences you have studied in this lesson. From Investigation 1, you know that the function formula for an arithmetic sequence beginning with subscript 0 and having common difference d is $t_n = t_0 + nd$. As you know from the "Families of Functions" unit, a horizontal shift will affect the function formula in a predictable way. Since the D_n sequence has subscripts shifted by 1, the corresponding function formula is $D_n = 16 + (n - 1)(32)$. (To explore the situation of shifted subscripts more fully, see Extending Task 2 on page 526.)

  ■ Use the function formula to verify the entries for D_1 and D_5.

  ■ Use the function formula to find $D_{18}, D_{19},$ and D_{20}.

  d. How would you determine the total distance fallen by the sky diver after 20 seconds?

e. One approach to finding the sum of the first 20 terms of the sequence D_n is based on a method reportedly discovered by Carl Friedrich Gauss (1777–1855) when he was only 10 years old. Gauss, considered to be one of the greatest mathematicians of all time, noticed that the sum of the terms of an arithmetic sequence, such as $16 + 48 + 80 + ... + 560 + 592 + 624$, could be quickly calculated by first writing the sum in reverse order and then adding pairs of corresponding terms.

$$\begin{array}{r} 16 + 48 + 80 + ... + 560 + 592 + 624 \\ 624 + 592 + 560 + ... + 80 + 48 + 16 \\ \hline 640 \end{array}$$

- What is the sum of each pair of terms? How many pairs are there?
- What is the total distance fallen after 20 seconds?

f. Use your function formula from Part c and Gauss's method to determine the total distance the sky diver would fall in 30 seconds and in 35 seconds.

g. An expert sky diver typically free-falls to about 2,000 feet above Earth's surface before pulling the rip cord on the parachute. If the altitude of the airplane was about 5,000 feet when the sky diver began the jump, how much time can the sky diver safely allow for the free-fall portion of the flight?

2. You can use Gauss's idea in Activity 1 and algebraic reasoning to derive a general formula for the *sum of the terms of an arithmetic sequence* with common difference d.

a. If a_0, a_1, a_2, ..., a_n is an arithmetic sequence with common difference d, explain why the sum S_n of the terms a_0 through a_n can be expressed by the equation

$$S_n = a_0 + (a_0 + d) + (a_0 + 2d) + ... + (a_n - 2d) + (a_n - d) + a_n.$$

b. If you rewrite S_n in reverse order and then add pairs of corresponding terms as in Activity 1, what is the sum of each pair of terms? How many pairs are there?

c. Write a formula for S_n in terms of a_0, a_n, and n. Compare your formula to those of other groups and resolve any differences.

d. Toni developed the following formula for the sum of the terms of an arithmetic sequence:

$$S = \frac{(\textit{initial term} + \textit{final term})(\textit{number of terms})}{2}$$

Explain why this formula makes sense.

e. Now combine your ideas to find the sum of the terms of the sequence

$$7, 12, 17, 22, ..., 52.$$

In modeling a situation involving sequential change, it is important to decide whether the situation involves a pattern of change in *additional* amount or a pattern of change in *accumulated* amount.

3. It may happen that in two different situations, you get the same sequence of numbers, but it makes sense to add the terms of the sequence in only one of the situations. Consider an epidemic that begins with one infected person and spreads rapidly through a population. A health official states, "The number of sick people triples every day."

   a. Suppose the statement is interpreted to mean, "The *accumulated* number of sick people triples every day." Write the first six terms of the sequence of accumulated numbers of sick people. What is the total number of sick people at the end of five days (assuming no sick person gets well in that time)?

   b. Suppose the statement is interpreted to mean, "The *additional* number of sick people triples every day." Write the first six terms of the sequence of additional numbers of sick people. Under this interpretation, what is the total number of sick people at the end of five days (assuming no sick person gets well in that time)?

   c. Look back at Parts a and b. Explain why it makes sense to sum the terms of the sequence in one situation but not in the other.

4. In the epidemic example from Activity 3, assume that the epidemic begins with one sick person and the *additional* number of sick people triples every day. Then the total number of sick people at the end of n days is given by
$$S_n = 1 + 3 + 3^2 + 3^3 + 3^4 + \ldots + 3^n.$$

   a. Using algebraic reasoning, you can derive a formula for quickly calculating this sum, as shown below. Provide reasons for each step in the following derivation.
   $$S_n = 1 + 3 + 3^2 + 3^3 + 3^4 + \ldots + 3^n$$
   $$3(S_n) = 3(1 + 3 + 3^2 + 3^3 + 3^4 + \ldots + 3^n)$$
   $$= 3 + 3^2 + 3^3 + 3^4 + \ldots + 3^n + 3^{n+1}$$
   $$3(S_n) - S_n = 3^{n+1} - 1$$
   $$(3 - 1)S_n = 3^{n+1} - 1$$
   $$S_n = \frac{3^{n+1} - 1}{3 - 1}$$

   b. Use this formula to calculate the total number of sick people at the end of five days. Compare your answer to your response to Part b of Activity 3.

   c. Using similar reasoning, prove that the *sum of the terms of the geometric sequence* $1, r, r^2, r^3, r^4, \ldots, r^n$, where $r \neq 1$, is
   $$1 + r + r^2 + r^3 + r^4 + \ldots + r^n = \frac{r^{n+1} - 1}{r - 1}.$$

5. Consider sums of geometric sequences when the initial term is not 1.

   a. Suppose an epidemic begins with two infected people and the additional number of infected people triples every day. What is the total number of sick people at the end of four days?

b. Suppose an ice cream store sold 22,000 ice cream cones in 1998. Based on sales data from other stores in similar locations, the manager predicts that the number of ice cream cones sold will increase by 5% each year. Find the total predicted number of ice cream cones sold during the period from 1998 to 2004. Show how this problem can be solved using the formula for the sum of a geometric sequence, which you developed in Part c of Activity 4. (You may find it helpful to write the sum term-by-term and then factor out 22,000.)

6. Now suppose $a_0, a_1, a_2, ..., a_n$ is a geometric sequence with common ratio r, where $r \neq 1$. Write a formula for calculating the sum S_n in terms of a_0, r, and n. Provide an argument for why your formula is correct.

7. It is also possible to use the geometric sum formula when the common ratio is less than 1. Consider a geometric sequence with initial term $t_0 = 48$ and common ratio of $\frac{1}{4}$.

a. Find a recursive formula and a function formula for this sequence.

b. Find the sum of the terms of this sequence through t_8.

Checkpoint

In this investigation, you examined total change in situations involving arithmetic growth and geometric growth or decay.

ⓐ In such situations, it may be that the *accumulated* amount increases by a constant d or a factor r every time period, or it may be that the *additional* amount increases by a constant d or a factor r every time period. Give an example of each case for each growth model. In which case would you sum an arithmetic sequence to find the total amount after 12 time periods? In which case would you sum a geometric sequence to find the total amount?

ⓑ Suppose an arithmetic sequence has initial term a_0 and common difference d.

- Write recursive and function formulas for the sequence.
- Write a formula for the sum of the terms up through a_n.

ⓒ Suppose a geometric sequence has initial term a_0 and common ratio r.
- Write recursive and function formulas for the sequence.
- Write a formula for the sum of the terms up through a_n.

Be prepared to explain your group's thinking and formulas to the entire class.

An expression denoting the sum of the terms of a sequence is called a **series**. The series $a_0 + a_1 + a_2 + \ldots + a_n$ is called an **arithmetic series** or a **geometric series**, depending on the sequence that generates the terms.

▶ **On Your Own**

Find the indicated sum for each of the sequences below.

a. If $t_0 = 8$ and $d = 3$ in an arithmetic sequence, find S_{10}.

b. If $t_0 = 1$ and $r = 2.5$ in a geometric sequence, find the sum of the terms up through t_{12}.

c. Find the sum of the first 15 terms of each sequence below.

n	0	1	2	3	4	5	6	...	14	...
A_n	2	6	18	54	162				...	...

n	0	1	2	3	4	5	6	...	14	...
B_n	95	90	85	80	75				...	...

d. A popular shoe store sold 5,700 pairs of athletic shoes in 1998. Projections were for a 3% increase in sales each year for several years after 1998. What was the projected total number of athletic shoes sold during the period from 1998 to 2004?

INVESTIGATION ▶ 3 Finite Differences

So far, you have been able to find a function formula for a sequence by detecting and generalizing a pattern. Sometimes that is not so easily done. In this investigation, you will explore a method called *finite differences* to find the function formula for certain sequences.

1. To see how the method works, it's best to start with a sample function formula. Suppose you *toss* a rock straight down from a high bridge. If the rock is thrown from a bridge 300 feet above the river with an initial velocity of 10 feet per second, then the distance D_n of the rock from the river after n seconds is given by the function formula

$$D_n = -16n^2 - 10n + 300.$$

An analysis of the pattern of change in the distance between the rock and the river is shown in the following table.

Number of Seconds n	D_n	1st Difference	2nd Difference
0	300		
		−26	
1	274		−32
		−58	
2	216		—
		—	
3	—		—
		—	
4	—		

a. Make a copy of the table and complete the second column.

b. The third column contains differences between consecutive terms of the sequence D_n. How was the "−58" calculated? Find the remaining entries in the "1st Difference" column.

c. The fourth column contains differences between consecutive terms of the "1st Difference" column. Verify the entry "−32" and find the remaining entries in the "2nd Difference" column.

d. A table like this is called a **finite differences table**. Describe any patterns you see in the completed table.

It is a fact that for any function formula that is a quadratic equation, such as the equation in Activity 1, the 2nd differences in a finite differences table will be a constant. (See Extending Task 4 on page 528.) Conversely, if the 2nd differences are a constant, then the function formula is a quadratic. For example, consider the following counting problem involving vertex-edge graphs.

2. A **complete graph** is a graph in which there is exactly one edge between every pair of vertices. The diagram below shows a complete graph with 4 vertices. In this activity, you will investigate the number of edges E_n in a complete graph with n vertices.

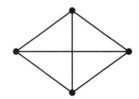

a. Complete a table like the one below. Draw complete graphs to help you, as needed.

Complete Graphs						
Number of Vertices n	0	1	2	3	4	5
Edge Count E_n						

b. Make a finite differences table for the sequence of edge counts E_n. Describe any patterns you see in the table.

c. What pattern in the finite differences table tells you that the function formula for the sequence of edge counts must look like $E_n = an^2 + bn + c$?

d. How could you find the coefficients a, b, and c? With some classmates, brainstorm some ideas and try them out.

e. One way to find a, b, and c is to set up and solve a system of three linear equations. You can get this system of equations by letting n equal any three values, for example, 1, 2, and 3.

   i. To get the first equation, suppose $n = 1$.

- Explain what the value of E_1 in your table means in terms of complete graphs and numbers of edges.

- If you substitute $n = 1$ in the equation $E_n = an^2 + bn + c$, you get
$$E_1 = a(1)^2 + b(1) + c = a + b + c.$$

   So you know that $E_1 = a + b + c$ and, from your table, that $E_1 = 0$. Thus, one equation is $a + b + c = 0$.

   ii. Use similar reasoning with $n = 2$ to get the second equation.

   iii. To get the third equation, let $n = 3$. What is the equation that results from this choice of n?

f. Compare the system of three linear equations you found in Part e to the systems found by other groups. Resolve any differences.

g. You can solve systems of three equations like these using matrices, as you did for the case of systems of two linear equations in "Matrix Models," Unit 1 of Course 2. Written in matrix form, the system looks like this (fill in the missing entries):

$$\underbrace{\begin{bmatrix} 1 & 1 & \rule{0.5em}{0.1pt} \\ \rule{0.5em}{0.1pt} & 2 & 1 \\ 9 & \rule{0.5em}{0.1pt} & 1 \end{bmatrix}}_{A} \cdot \underbrace{\begin{bmatrix} a \\ b \\ c \end{bmatrix}}_{X} = \underbrace{\begin{bmatrix} 0 \\ 1 \\ \rule{0.5em}{0.1pt} \end{bmatrix}}_{C}$$

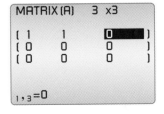

Solve this matrix equation.

h. Use the results of Part g to write the function formula for the number of edges in a complete graph with n vertices. Use this formula to check the entries in the table from Part a.

i. Now find a recursive formula for the sequence of edge counts by examining the table in Part a.

3. So far in this investigation, you have examined situations in which the function formula is a quadratic equation. Now consider the case of a higher-degree function formula. Suppose $A_n = 4n^3 + 2n^2 - 5n - 8$. Make a prediction about which column in the finite differences table for this sequence will be constant. Construct the finite differences table to check your conjecture.

In general, it is possible to compute more than just 2nd or 3rd differences. If the function formula is an rth degree polynomial, then the rth differences will be constant. The converse is also true. These facts can be used to find function formulas for certain sequences.

Checkpoint

Think about the method of finite differences and how it can be used.

ⓐ Describe how to construct the finite differences table for a sequence of numbers.

ⓑ If the 4th differences in the finite differences table for a sequence are constant, what do you think the function formula for the sequence will look like? How would you go about finding the specific formula?

ⓒ In general, what kind of function formulas can be found using finite differences tables?

Be prepared to share your group's descriptions and thinking with the entire class.

▶On Your Own

Use a finite differences table and matrices to find a function formula for the sequence below.

n	0	1	2	3	4	5	6	7	8	9	10	11
A_n	3	12	25	42	63	88	117	150	187	228	273	322

Modeling • Organizing • Reflecting • Extending

Modeling

1. For many people, a college education is a desirable and worthwhile goal. But the cost of a college education is growing every year. Suppose that the average cost for a year of college education is now $9,500 and that the cost is rising at a rate of 8% per year.

   a. Make a table showing the average cost of a year of college education for the next 5 years.

   b. Is the sequence of increasing costs arithmetic, geometric, or neither?

   c. Determine a recursive and function formula for the sequence of costs.

   d. Use your formulas to predict the average cost of a year of your college education.

   e. Predict the cost of four years of college for a child born this year.

2. Animal behavior often changes as the outside temperature changes. One curious example of this is the fact that the frequency of cricket chirps varies with the outside temperature in a very predictable way. Consider the data below for one species of cricket.

Cricket Chirps

Temperature (in degrees F)	45	47	50	52	54	55	60
Frequency (in chirps/min)	20	28	41	50	57	61	80

   a. If you were to choose an arithmetic sequence or a geometric sequence as a model for the frequency sequence, which type of sequence would you choose? Why?

   b. As is often the case in mathematical modeling, the model you chose in Part a does not fit the data exactly. Nevertheless, it may be quite useful for analysis of the situation. Find a recursive formula for the frequency sequence, based on the sequence you chose in Part a. Use the formula to predict the frequency of cricket chirps for a temperature of 75°F.

   c. At what temperature would you expect crickets to stop chirping?

   d. You can use the relationship between the frequency of cricket chirps and the temperature as a kind of thermometer. What would you estimate the temperature to be if a cricket is chirping at 100 chirps per minute?

3. Sandy has a sales job which pays him a monthly commission. He made $250 in his first month. His supervisor tells him that he should be able to increase his commission income by 10% each month for the next year. For this problem, assume that the supervisor's prediction is correct.

   a. Find recursive and function formulas for the sequence of monthly commission income.

   b. How much total commission income will Sandy earn in his first ten months on the job?

4. In this task, you will use the idea of sequential change to investigate the number of diagonals that can be drawn in a regular n-sided polygon.

   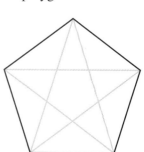

   a. Draw the first few regular n-gons and make a table showing the number of diagonals that can be drawn in each of them.

   b. Determine a recursive formula for the number of diagonals that can be drawn in a regular n-gon.

   c. Use the method of finite differences to find a function formula for the number of diagonals that can be drawn in a regular n-gon.

   d. Use your formulas to predict the number of diagonals in a regular 20-gon.

   e. What other methods might you use to find a function formula for the sequence in Part a?

5. The square Sierpinski carpet you constructed in Investigation 1, page 509, is an example of a *fractal* in that small pieces of the design are similar to the design as a whole. Other fractal shapes can also be constructed using recursive procedures.

   a. A *Sierpinski triangle* is constructed through a sequence of steps illustrated by the figures below.

      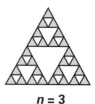

   | $n = 0$ | $n = 1$ | $n = 2$ | $n = 3$ |

   At stage $n = 0$, you construct an equilateral triangle whose sides are all of length 1 unit. In succeeding stages, you remove the "middle triangles," as shown in stages $n = 1$, 2, and 3. This process continues indefinitely. Consider the sequence of areas of the figures at each stage. Find recursive and function formulas for the sequence of areas.

b. Another interesting fractal is the *Koch snowflake*. The procedure for constructing the Koch snowflake also begins with an equilateral triangle whose sides are of length 1 unit. At each stage you remove the segment that is the middle third of each side and replace it with two outward-extending segments of the same length, creating new equilateral triangles on each side as shown. This process is illustrated in the diagrams below. The process continues indefinitely.

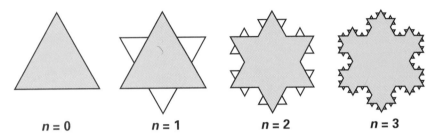

$n = 0$ $n = 1$ $n = 2$ $n = 3$

Find recursive and function formulas for the sequence of perimeters of the snowflake.

6. *Glottochronology* is the study of changes in languages. Over time, certain words in a language are no longer used. In effect, they disappear from the language. Suppose a linguist examines a list of 500 words used in a language 1,000 years ago. Let $W(n)$ be the percentage of the words in this list that are still in use n years later, given as a decimal. It is commonly assumed that $W(n)$ is proportional to $W(n-1)$. Glottochronologists have determined that the constant of proportionality can be estimated to be about 0.9999. Find recursive and function formulas for this sequence. What type of sequence is this?

Organizing

1. In Modeling Task 2, page 519, you may have established that the sequence of chirping frequencies for one species of cricket is approximately an arithmetic sequence with recursive formula

$$C_n = C_{n-1} + 4.$$

a. Plot the (*temperature, frequency*) data from the table on page 519 and find an equation that fits the data.

b. Using the equation from Part a, write a function formula for the sequence. Check that your formula does generate the values given in the table for the chirping frequencies at temperatures of 47°F and 60°F.

2. In the "Think About This Situation" section for Lesson 2, page 505, you considered two sequences related to the free fall of a sky diver: the sequence D_n of distance fallen each second and the sequence T_n of total distance fallen after each second.

a. Verify that the two sequences below, D_n and I_n, are accurate models if you assume Earth's gravity and no air resistance.

Distances Fallen

n	D_n	T_n	n	D_n	T_n
1	16	16	6	176	576
2	48	64	7	208	784
3	80	144	8	240	1,024
4	112	256	9	272	1,296
5	144	400	10	304	1,600

b. Use the method of finite differences to find a function formula that describes the sequence of total distance fallen.

c. Use calculator- or computer-based regression methods to find a function formula relating total distance fallen to the number of seconds in the fall.

d. For the "Think About This Situation" questions, you wrote a recursive formula for the sequence D_n. Note that each term (after the first) of T_n is the result of adding the corresponding term of D_n to the previous term of T_n. Use this fact to help you find a recursive formula for T_n.

3. Below is the sequence from the "On Your Own" activity on page 518.

n	0	1	2	3	4	5	6	7	8	9	10	11
A_n	3	12	25	42	63	88	117	150	187	228	273	322

a. Produce a scatterplot of n versus A_n using a graphing calculator or computer software. Describe the shape of the graph. Which function family would best model this data pattern?

b. Use calculator- or computer-based regression methods to find the equation of the model that seems to best fit the scatterplot. Compare this equation to the function formula you derived in the "On Your Own" activity using the finite differences method. Describe and resolve any differences in the two solutions.

c. Do you think statistical regression methods will work to find a function formula for any sequence? Explain.

4. Use a finite differences table and matrices to find the function formula for the sequence given by $B_n = B_{n-1} + 3n$, with $B_0 = 2$.

5. In this lesson, you found function formulas for arithmetic and geometric sequences. In Lesson 1, you studied combined recursion equations of the form $A_n = rA_{n-1} + b$. You can now use what you know about geometric sequences and their sums to find a **function formula for combined recursion equations**.

a. Complete the following list of terms for the combined recursion equation $A_n = rA_{n-1} + b$. Examine the list for patterns so that you can write a function formula for A_n.

$$A_0 = A_0$$

$$A_1 = rA_0 + b$$

$$A_2 = rA_1 + b = r(rA_0 + b) + b = r^2A_0 + rb + b$$

$$A_3 = r(r^2A_0 + rb + b) + b = r^3A_0 + r^2b + rb + b$$

$$A_4 = ?$$

$$A_5 = ?$$

$$\vdots$$

$$A_n = ?$$

b. The expression you have for A_n at the end of Part a is a function formula, but it can be simplified. To simplify, use what you know about the sum of the terms of a geometric sequence.

c. Now reconsider the combined recursion equation that modeled the trout-population problem in Lesson 1: $A_n = 0.8A_{n-1} + 1,000$, with $A_0 = 3,000$. Use the general function formula from Part b to write a function formula that models the trout population. Then use that formula to find A_2 and A_{10}. Choose a year far in the future and find the long-term population. Compare your results to those you found in Lesson 1, using other methods.

d. Suppose the combined recursion equation $A_n = rA_{n-1} + b$ represents year-to-year population change. Assume that r is a positive number less than 1. Use the function formula from Part b to explain why the long-term population in this situation is $\frac{b}{1-r}$. Use this fact to find the long-term population in the trout-population problem, and compare it to what you found before.

e. Compare the function formula you obtained in Part c to the one given in Organizing Task 3 of Lesson 1, page 499. Explain and resolve any differences.

6. As you complete this task, think about the defining characteristics of arithmetic and geometric sequences and how those characteristics are related to the sum of their terms. For each sequence below, determine if the sequence is arithmetic, geometric, or neither. Then find the sum of the indicated terms.

a. 13, 26, 52, 104, ..., 6,656

b. 13, 12.25, 11.5, 10.75, ..., 1

c. 1, 4, 9, 16, ..., 225

d. 5, 4, 3.2, 2.56, ..., 0.8388608

7. In Course 2 of *Contemporary Mathematics in Context*, you may have investigated the waiting-time distribution in the context of a modified Monopoly® game in which 36 students are in jail and a student must roll doubles to get out of jail.

a. The probability of rolling doubles is $\frac{1}{6}$. Thus, the probability of getting out of jail on any given roll of the dice is similarly $\frac{1}{6}$. What is the probability of remaining in jail on any given roll of the dice?

b. Complete the following table. The waiting-time distribution refers to the first two columns, since you want to know how long a student has to wait to get out of jail. The last column provides important related information.

Rolling Dice to Get Doubles

Number of Rolls to Get Doubles	Expected Number of Students Released on the Given Number of Rolls	Expected Number of Students Still in Jail
1	6	30
2	5	
3		
4		
5		

c. Consider the sequence of numbers in the last column.

- Is the sequence an arithmetic or geometric sequence? Why?
- Determine the recursive and function formulas for the sequence. (Use 36 as the initial term of the sequence since that is the initial number of students in jail.)
- Use the formulas to find the expected number of students left in jail after 20 rolls.

d. Sketch a histogram for the waiting-time distribution shown in the first two columns.

- Write a recursion equation that shows how the height of any given bar compares to the height of the previous bar.
- What kind of sequence is the sequence of bar heights?

Reflecting

1. Suppose you want to find the 100th term of a sequence of numbers. You have both a recursive formula and a function formula. Which formula would you use? Why?

2. Describe one situation in your daily life or in the daily newspaper that could be modeled by a geometric sequence. Describe another situation that could be modeled by an arithmetic sequence.

3. A series $a_0 + a_1 + a_2 + ... + a_n$ can be written in a more compact form using sigma notation: $\sum_{i=0}^{n} a_i$. You used sigma notation (without subscripts) when writing a formula for standard deviation in Unit 5.

   a. Suppose $x_1, x_2, x_3, ..., x_n$ are sample data values. Use sigma notation with subscripts to write an expression for

   ■ the mean of this distribution.

   ■ the standard deviation of this distribution.

   b. Write $\sum_{k=0}^{12} 3k$ in *expanded form* and then find the sum.

   c. Write $\sum_{i=3}^{10} 2^i$ in expanded form and then find the sum.

   d. Complete this equation: $3 + 5 + 7 + 9 + 11 + 13 + 15 = \sum_{n=?}^{?} (2n + 1)$.

4. The English economist Thomas Malthus (1766–1834) is best remembered for his assertion that *food supply grows arithmetically while population grows geometrically*. Do some research and write a brief essay about this idea. Your essay should address the following questions: What is the meaning of Malthus's statement in terms of sequences you have studied? Do you think it is a reasonable statement? What are its consequences? Why has this statement been called "apocalyptic"? Have the events of the last 200 years borne out the statement? What can we learn from the statement even if it is not completely accurate?

5. You have represented sequences using recursive and function formulas.

   a. A function formula for a sequence is sometimes called an *explicit formula*. Why do you think the term "explicit" is used? What is explicit about a function formula?

   b. A function formula is also sometimes called a *closed-form formula*. Why do you think this term is used?

6. On page 517, you solved the matrix equation $AX = C$ to find the coefficients of a quadratic equation. Examine matrix A on page 517. Do you think this matrix will change if you work a similar problem that involves different data? Explain.

Extending

1. You may have seen a stack of oranges in a grocery store that was in the shape of a pyramid with a square base. The number of oranges in such a stack depends on the number of layers in the stack.

   a. Complete a table like the one below.

   ### Pyramid of Oranges

Number of Layers in a Stack	0	1	2	3	4	5	6
Number of Oranges in a Stack	0	1	5				

   b. Find a recursive formula for the sequence of number of oranges in a stack.

   c. Use the method of finite differences to find a function formula for the sequence of number of oranges in a stack. How many oranges are in a stack with 15 layers?

2. In this lesson, you mainly considered sequences that started with subscript 0; that is, A_0 was the initial term. It is certainly possible to use other notation. For example, you might represent the initial term as A_1. Changing the notation like this does not, of course, change the pattern of the sequence, but it will change the form of the function formula. Consider the arithmetic sequence 4, 7, 10, 13, ...

   a. Determine a recursive formula and a function formula for this sequence, using $A_0 = 4$.

   b. Now determine the function formula for the sequence labeling the initial term, 4, as A_1 instead of A_0. (That is, $A_1 = 4$.)

   c. The recursive formula doesn't change, no matter how you label the initial term, because it just describes how you get from one term to the next. However, the function formula will change if you change the subscript of the initial term, as you saw in Parts a and b. What will be the function formula for this same sequence if you label the initial term A_2?

   d. Sometimes a sequence may start with a much higher value of n. Consider the sequence of chirping frequencies for the species of crickets in Modeling Task 2, page 519. That sequence is reproduced below.

   ### Cricket Chirps

Temperature (in degrees F)	45	47	50	52	54	55	60
Frequency (in chirps/min)	20	28	41	50	57	61	80

   It is probably easiest to consider the part of the sequence shown in the table as beginning with $n = 45$ (*temperature* = 45°); that is, the initial term is A_{45}. Find a function formula for this sequence.

e. What is the function formula for an arithmetic sequence with initial term t_1 and common difference d?

f. What is the function formula for a geometric sequence with initial term t_1 and common ratio r?

g. Investigate and prepare a brief report on how the formulas for the sum of the terms of arithmetic and geometric sequences change if the initial term is a_1 instead of a_0.

3. In this unit, you have investigated recursion equations and sequences that can be modeled by equations using the words *NOW* and *NEXT*. This means that to find *NEXT,* you need to use only *NOW*, one step before *NEXT*. However, there are sequences for which finding *NEXT* requires using more than one step before *NEXT*. One of the most famous sequences of this type is called the *Fibonacci sequence*, named after the mathematician Leonardo Fibonacci (c.1175–c.1250), who first studied the sequence.

a. Here is the Fibonacci sequence: 1, 1, 2, 3, 5, 8, 13, 21, 34, 55, 89, 144, ... Using the words *NEXT*, *NOW*, and *PREVIOUS*, describe the pattern of the sequence.

b. Let F_{n+1} represent *NEXT*, and use F_{n+1}, F_n, and F_{n-1} to write a recursive formula for the Fibonacci sequence.

c. Here is a recursive formula for a sequence similar to the Fibonacci sequence: $A_n = 2A_{n-1} - A_{n-2}$.

  ■ Why can't you list the terms of this sequence?

  ■ Choose some initial values and list the first six terms of the sequence. Then choose different initial values and list the first six terms of the sequence. Compare the two sequences. Describe any patterns you see.

  ■ Write a recursive formula for this sequence that uses only A_n, A_{n-1}, A_1, and A_0.

d. Consider the sequence given by $A_n = A_{n-1} + A_{n-2} + 7A_{n-3}$. Choose some initial values and list the first six terms of this sequence.

e. *Optional:* The Fibonacci sequence has many interesting patterns and shows up in the most amazing places. In the photo at the left, the flower has 34 spirals in the counterclockwise direction and 55 in the clockwise direction; these two numbers are successive terms in the Fibonacci sequence. Sunflowers and pine cones also have spirals with numbers from the Fibonacci sequence, as do many other things in nature.

In fact, entire books and journals have been written about this sequence. Find an article or book about the Fibonacci sequence and write a brief report on one of its patterns or applications.

4. In Investigation 3, pages 515–518, you used the method of finite differences to find a function formula for certain sequences. You used the fact that the function formula for a sequence is a quadratic equation if and only if the 2nd differences in a finite differences table are constant. In this task you will prove that fact.

a. Suppose a sequence has a quadratic function formula ($A_n = an^2 + bn + c$). Construct a finite differences table and verify that the 2nd differences are constant. Describe any relationship you see between the constant 2nd differences and the function formula.

b. Now, conversely, suppose the 2nd differences are constant. Show that the function formula is a quadratic equation.

5. In Activity 6 of Investigation 2, page 514, you found a formula for the sum of a *finite* number of terms of a geometric sequence. A sequence can also have an *infinite* number of terms. It is possible to analyze mathematically the sum of an infinite number of terms. Consider the sequence $\frac{1}{2}, \frac{1}{4}, \frac{1}{8}, \frac{1}{16} \cdots, \frac{1}{2^n}, \cdots$.

a. Explain why this is a geometric sequence. Find recursive and function formulas for this sequence.

b. Find the sum of the terms up through $\frac{1}{2^n}$.

c. This sequence has infinitely many terms. Does the geometric model of this sequence shown below suggest what the infinite sum of all the terms of the sequence might be?

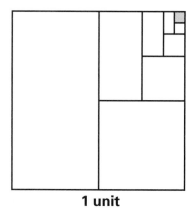

1 unit

d. A mathematical analysis of infinite sums involves thinking about what happens to the sum of n terms as n gets very large. Examine the formula for the sum of terms up through $\frac{1}{2^n}$ from Part b. What happens to this formula as n gets very large? Your answer should give you the infinite sum.

e. Consider a general geometric sequence with terms t_n and common multiplier r. Suppose that $0 < r < 1$. Determine a general formula for the infinite sum by considering what happens to the finite sum formula if n is very large.

f. Use the general infinite sum formula for $0 < r < 1$ to find the infinite sum of the sequence $\frac{1}{2}, \frac{1}{4}, \frac{1}{8}, \frac{1}{16} \dots, \frac{1}{2^n}, \dots$. Compare the sum to your answer for Part d.

g. Construct a geometric sequence of your choice with $0 < r < 1$. Use the general infinite sum formula from Part e to find the infinite sum.

6. Extending Task 5 involved infinite geometric sums. Infinite sums lead to some surprising results. Consider a figure that consists of the rectangles of width 1 and height $\frac{1}{2^n}$ arranged as shown below.

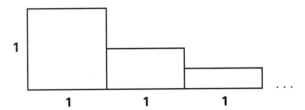

There are infinitely many rectangles that comprise this figure. Find the area of this figure. Find the perimeter. Do you think it is possible for a figure to have finite area but infinite perimeter? Explain.

Iterating Functions

Functions and recursive (*NOW-NEXT*) thinking are both important and unifying ideas in the *Contemporary Mathematics in Context* curriculum. In this lesson, you will explore a connection between recursion equations and functions, and you will use this connection to further analyze processes of sequential change.

A function can be considered a process that accepts inputs and produces outputs. For example, for the function $f(x) = x^2$, an input of 2 produces an output of 4. Imagine starting with a specific input, such as 2, and then sequentially feeding the outputs back into the function as new inputs.

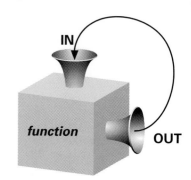

Think About This Situation

Think about the function $f(x) = x^2$ as an input-output process.

a Start with an input of 2. The resulting output is 4.

- Put 4 in as a new input. What is the new output?

- Put the new output in as the next input. What is the next output?

- Continue this process of feeding outputs back in as new inputs for several more steps.

- What do you think will be the long-term behavior of the sequence of numbers generated by this process?

b Suppose you carry out the same process for the same function, except this time start with an input of $\frac{1}{2}$. What do you think will be the long-term behavior of the resulting sequence of numbers in this case?

c What happens when you carry out the same process with a starting input of $x = 1$?

d In what way is this process of feeding outputs back in as inputs a recursive process?

INVESTIGATION 1 ▶ Play It Again ... and Again

The process of feeding the outputs of a function back into itself as inputs is called **iterating a function**. Imagine making a reduced copy on a copying machine, then making a reduced copy of your copy, then making a reduced copy of that copy, and so on.

As you might expect, there is a close connection between iterating a function and evaluating a recursion equation.

1. Consider the equation $NEXT = 2(NOW)^2 - 5$.

   a. Use an initial value of 1 and find the next three values.

   b. Rewrite the equation as a recursion equation using U_n and U_{n-1}. Let $U_0 = 1$ and then find U_1, U_2, and U_3.

   c. Now think about iterating a function, as illustrated in the diagram before the "Think About This Situation" on page 530. Iterate $f(x) = 2x^2 - 5$ three times, starting with $x = 1$.

   d. Compare the sequences of numbers you got in Parts a, b, and c.

2. Think about iterating the function $f(x) = 3x + 1$, starting with $x = 2$. A table that shows the iteration process is similar to function tables you have used before, but with a new twist.

   a. Complete a table like the one below.

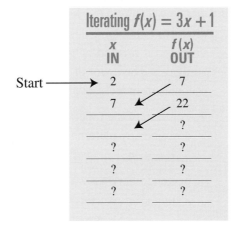

Iterating $f(x) = 3x + 1$	
x IN	$f(x)$ OUT
2	7
7	22
?	?
?	?
?	?
?	?

   Start ⟶

   b. How would the table be different if you started with $x = 0$?

3. Consider the recursion equation $U_n = (U_{n-1})^2 + 3U_{n-1} + 4$, with $U_0 = 1$.

   a. Rewrite the recursion equation as an equation using the words *NOW* and *NEXT*.

   b. What function can be iterated to yield the same sequence of numbers generated by the recursion equation? Check your answer by iterating your function, starting with an input of 1, and comparing the result to the corresponding sequence generated by the recursion equation.

4. Now consider the function $g(x) = -0.7x + 6$.

   a. What recursion equation yields the same sequence of numbers generated by iterating $g(x)$?

   b. Use the last-answer feature of your calculator or computer software to iterate $g(x)$ at least 30 times, starting with 14. Describe any patterns that you see in the iteration sequence.

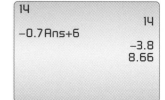

   c. Use the recursion mode on your calculator or computer software to produce a graph illustrating the iteration of $g(x)$, starting with $x = 14$.

As with any process of sequential change, it is important to study the long-term behavior of function iteration.

5. Suppose $f(x) = \sqrt{x}$. Iterate this function, starting with $x = 256$. Describe the long-term behavior of the resulting sequence of numbers.

6. Now suppose $h(x) = 1 - x$. Iterate this function and describe the long-term behavior of the iteration sequence for each of the following starting values.

   a. $x = 5$

   b. $x = -28$

   c. $x = \frac{1}{2}$

In the next activity, you will iterate functions of the form $f(x) = rx(1 - x)$. This is a broadly useful equation in mathematics, called the **logistic equation**. For different values of r, you get different functions, each of which may have a different behavior when iterated. Iterating these functions has proven to be a very useful method of modeling certain population growth situations. Also, the study of the behavior of these functions has contributed to many important developments in modern mathematics over the last several decades.

7. For each of the function iterations below, use $x = 0.02$ as the starting value and describe any patterns you see, including the long-term behavior.

   a. Iterate $f(x) = 2.7x(1 - x)$.

   b. Iterate $g(x) = 3.2x(1 - x)$.

   c. Iterate $h(x) = 3.5x(1 - x)$.

   d. Iterate $j(x) = 3.83x(1 - x)$.

   e. Iterate $k(x) = 4x(1 - x)$.

Function iteration is an interesting and useful way to think about the input-output process of a function.

a Describe some of the possible long-term behaviors that can occur when a function is iterated.

b Explain the connection between function iteration and recursion equations.

c Consider evaluating the equation $NEXT = (NOW)^3 + 5$, starting with 2.

- What recursion equation, when evaluated, will produce the same sequence?
- What function, when iterated, will generate the same sequence?

Be prepared to share your group's descriptions and thinking with the entire class.

Function iteration is a relatively new field of mathematical study. There are many unanswered questions in this area, including questions about the behavior of logistic equations like the ones you investigated in Activity 7. Function iteration is related to such contemporary mathematical topics as *fractals* and *chaos*. Applications of function iteration are being discovered every day, in areas like electronic transmission of large

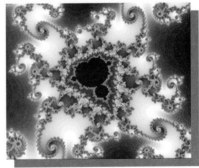

The Mandelbrot Set (fractal)

blocks of data, computer graphics, and modeling population growth. You will explore some of these ideas and applications in the MORE set at the end of this lesson.

▶On Your Own

Function iteration can be applied to any function.

a. Iterate $g(x) = \cos x$, starting with $x = 10$. (Be sure you are using radian mode, not degrees.) Describe the long-term behavior of the iteration sequence.

- What recursion equation yields the same sequence as iterating $g(x)$?
- Rewrite your recursion equation using the words *NOW* and *NEXT*.

b. Choose any function not used in this investigation and several different starting points. Iterate your function, starting with each of your starting points, and describe the long-term behavior of the iteration sequences.

INVESTIGATION 2 Iterating Linear Functions

In Investigation 1, you iterated a variety of functions, both linear and nonlinear. The iterative behavior of nonlinear functions is not yet completely understood and is currently a lively area of mathematical research. On the other hand, iteration of linear functions is understood well.

1. Just as with many other ideas in mathematics, the process of function iteration can be represented visually. To see how *graphical iteration* works, consider the function $f(x) = 0.5x + 2$. The graphs of $y = x$ and $y = 0.5x + 2$ are shown below on the same set of axes. Think graphically about how an input becomes an output, which then becomes the next input, which produces the next output, and so on.

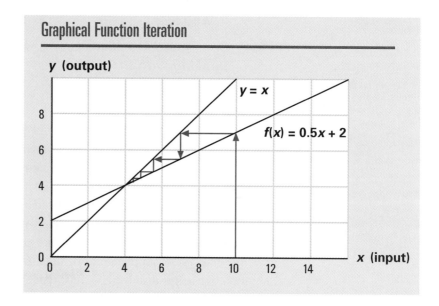

In the diagram above, 10 has been chosen as the original input. To find an input's (x value's) resulting output (y value), you go up to the graph of the function you are iterating. Next, according to the process of function iteration, the output gets put back into the function as an input. This is accomplished graphically by moving horizontally to the $y = x$ graph, since on this line the y value (the current output) is identical to the x value (the new input). Now go vertically again to find the output associated with the new input. The process continues in this way until, in this example, you are drawn into the intersection point of the two graphs. This is the process of **graphical iteration**.

  a. From this graphical perspective, what is the long-term behavior of the function $f(x) = 0.5x + 2$ when iterated? Use your calculator to iterate $f(x)$, starting with $x = 10$, and see if the numerical result matches the graphical result.

b. Now, think about the process of graphical iteration as illustrated in the diagram on the previous page.

- Explain, in your own words, why you can graphically find the output of a function for a given input by moving vertically to the graph of the function.

- Explain, in your own words, why you can graphically turn an output into the next input by moving horizontally from the graph of the function to the graph of $y = x$.

c. Carefully draw the graphs of $y = 0.5x + 2$ and $y = x$ on graph paper and illustrate the process of graphical iteration using $x = 1$ as the original input. What do you notice?

2. Sketch graphs and illustrate the process of graphical function iteration for the function $g(x) = -0.5x + 8$. Choose your own starting value. Compare the overall pattern of the graphical iteration to the patterns you saw in Activity 1. Make a conjecture about what kinds of linear function rules yield graphical iteration patterns like the one you found in this activity. You will test your conjecture later in this lesson.

3. As you have seen, sometimes when you iterate a function, you are drawn to a particular value, and if you reach that value, you never leave it. Such a value is called a *fixed point*.

a. Look back at Activity 1. What is the fixed point when iterating the function $f(x) = 0.5x + 2$?

b. What is the fixed point when iterating the function $f(x) = -0.7x + 6$?

c. The precise definition of a **fixed point** is a value x such that $f(x) = x$. Explain why this definition fits the above description of a fixed point: "If you reach that value, you never leave it."

4. One method that sometimes works to find a fixed point is iterating the function, either numerically or graphically, and seeing what happens. Another method for finding a fixed point is to use the definition of a fixed point. That is, set the rule for the function equal to x and solve. Use this symbolic method to find the fixed point when iterating the function $f(x) = 0.5x + 2$, and compare your answer to your response in Part a of Activity 3.

5. For each of the functions on the following page, try to find a fixed point using each of these three methods.

- Iterate by using the last-answer feature of your calculator or computer software or by producing a table (numeric method).

- Iterate graphically (graphic method).

- Solve the equation $f(x) = x$ (symbolic method).

Organize your work as follows.

- Try a variety of starting values for each function.

- Keep a record of what you try, the results, and any patterns that you notice.

Each student should use all three of the methods on the previous page for Parts a and b.

a. $s(x) = 0.6x + 3$

b. $u(x) = 4.3x + 1$

For Parts c through h, share the workload among members of your group.

c. $t(x) = 0.2x - 5$ **d.** $v(x) = 3x - 4$

e. $w(x) = x + 2$ **f.** $f(x) = -0.8x + 4$

g. $h(x) = -x + 2$ **h.** $k(x) = -2x + 5$

6. Three important characteristics to look for when iterating functions are *attracting fixed points*, *repelling fixed points*, and *cycles*. An **attracting fixed point** is a fixed point such that iteration sequences that start close to it get pulled into it. In contrast, iteration sequences move away from a **repelling fixed point**, except of course for the sequence that begins at the fixed point. A **cycle** is a set of numbers that an iteration sequence repeats over and over.

    a. For each of the linear functions you iterated in Activity 5, decide as a group whether it has an attracting fixed point, a repelling fixed point, a cycle, or none of these.

    b. Is there a connection between the slope of the graph of a linear function and the function's behavior when iterated? If so, explain how you could complete Part a of this activity simply by knowing the slope of each linear function's graph.

Checkpoint

In this investigation, you have seen that linear functions have rich and varied behavior when iterated.

ⓐ Describe what a fixed point is and how to find one. Give as many different descriptions of how to find a fixed point as you can.

ⓑ Attracting fixed points seem to pull you into them. But do you ever actually get to a fixed point? Explain.

ⓒ Describe the different long-term behaviors that can occur when a linear function is iterated. For each of the behaviors described, explain how that behavior is completely characterized by the slope of the graph of the iterated function.

ⓓ In the first lesson of this unit, you investigated situations that could be modeled by combined recursion equations $A_n = rA_{n-1} + b$. What is the connection between combined recursion equations and iterating linear functions?

Be prepared to share your group's descriptions and thinking with the entire class.

On Your Own

At the beginning of this unit, you modeled the trout population of a fishing pond. The pond had an initial population of 3,000 trout. There were 1,000 trout added at the end of each year, and regardless of restocking, the population decreased by 20% each year due to the combined effect of several causes. One of the equations that models this situation is

$$NEXT = 0.8NOW + 1,000.$$

a. Rewrite this equation as a recursion equation.

b. What function can be iterated to produce the same sequence of population numbers generated by the recursion equation? With what value should you start the function iteration?

c. Iterate the function in Part b and describe the long-term behavior of the iteration sequence. Compare this behavior to the long-term behavior of the trout population that you discovered in Investigation 1 of Lesson 1, page 489.

d. Graphically iterate this function, starting with $x = 3,000$.

e. Find the fixed point by solving an equation. Is the fixed point attracting or repelling? How can you tell by examining the slope of the function's graph?

f. Explain what the fixed point and its attracting or repelling property tell you about the changing trout population.

MORE
Modeling • Organizing • Reflecting • Extending

Modeling

1. Experiment with iterating the function $f(x) = x^3 - x^2 + 1$.

  a. Describe the behavior of the iteration sequence when you iterate $f(x)$ with the following beginning values.

    ■ Begin with $x = 1$.

    ■ Begin with $x = 0.8$.

    ■ Begin with $x = 1.2$.

  b. Find a fixed point for $f(x)$. Is this fixed point repelling, attracting, some combination of repelling and attracting, or none of these? Explain.

2. Experiment with iterating $g(x) = 3.7x - 3.7x^2$.

   a. Find the fixed points of $g(x)$ by writing and solving an appropriate equation.

   b. Iterate $g(x)$ starting with $x = 0.74$, which is close to a fixed point. Carefully examine the iteration sequence by listing these iterations:

      ■ List iterations 1 through 6.

      ■ List iterations 16 through 20.

      ■ List iterations 50 through 55.

      ■ List iterations 64 through 68.

   c. Describe any patterns you see in the iteration sequence. Does the iteration sequence get attracted to the fixed point? Does it get steadily repelled? A fixed point is called repelling if iteration sequences that begin near it get pushed away from the fixed point at some time, even if such sequences occasionally come back close to the fixed point. Is the fixed point at about 0.73 repelling?

3. Consider iterating $h(x) = 3.2x - 0.8x^2$.

   a. The fixed points of $h(x)$ are repelling. Do you think you will find them by numerical iteration? Explain your reasoning.

   b. Find the fixed points of $h(x)$ using symbolic reasoning.

   c. Experiment with iterating $h(x)$, starting with initial values just above and below each fixed point. Carefully describe the characteristics of each fixed point.

4. Function iteration can be used to model population change. Consider, for example, the bowhead whale population described in Modeling Task 2 of Lesson 1, page 495. A 1991 research study on the bowhead whales of Alaska reported that the population of this stock was between 5,700 and 10,600 and that the difference between births and deaths yielded an annual growth rate of about 3%. No hunting of bowhead whales is allowed, except that Alaskan Inuit are allowed to take, or harvest, about 50 bowhead whales each year for their livelihood.

   a. Write a recursion equation and an equivalent function that can be iterated to model this situation.

b. Using the low population estimate as the initial value, iterate and describe the long-term behavior of the population. Do you think this model is a good one to use for predicting the bowhead whale population hundreds of years from now? Why or why not?

c. Find the fixed point. By examining the slope of the graph of the iterated function, decide if the fixed point is attracting or repelling. Confirm your conclusions by graphically iterating the function.

d. Write a brief analysis of the changing bowhead whale population, as described by your model. As part of your analysis, describe the role played by the fixed point and make some long-term predictions based on different initial whale populations.

Organizing

1. It is possible to use function iteration to solve equations. Consider the equation $x - 3 = 0.5x$.

a. Before solving the equation by using function iteration, solve it using at least two other methods. In each case, explain your method.

b. To solve $x - 3 = 0.5x$ by function iteration, you will make use of fixed points. Consider the equation written in an equivalent form: $x = 0.5x + 3$.

■ Explain why this form is equivalent to the original form.

■ For what function does this equation define a fixed point?

c. Iterate the function you identified in Part b for some initial value. Describe the long-term behavior. Explain why the observed long-term behavior gives you a solution to the original equation. Compare the solution you obtained to what you found in Part a.

d. Use the method of function iteration to solve $2x + 5 = 6x - 7$. (If at first you do not succeed, try rewriting the equation in an equivalent form.)

e. Summarize the method of function iteration to solve linear equations.

2. In this task, you will find and use a general formula for the fixed point of a linear function.

a. Use the algebraic method for finding fixed points to derive a general formula for the fixed point of the linear function $f(x) = rx + b$.

b. Use the general formula to find the fixed point for $h(x) = 0.75x - 4$.

c. If the fixed point is attracting, then you can find it by iteration.

■ How can you tell from the formula for $h(x)$ that this function has an attracting fixed point?

■ Iterate $h(x)$ to find the fixed point and compare it to what you found using the general formula in Part b.

3. In Lesson 1, you investigated recursion equations of the form $A_n = rA_{n-1} + b$. Suppose such a recursion equation represents year-to-year change in some population. Assume that r is a positive number less than 1.

   a. Explain why the long-term population in this situation can be found by finding the fixed point of the function $f(x) = rx + b$.

   b. Use the general fixed point formula from Part a of Organizing Task 2 to explain the following patterns you previously discovered about the trout-population problem in Lesson 1.

     ■ Changing the initial population does not change the long-term population.

     ■ Doubling the restocking amount doubles the long-term population.

     ■ Doubling the population-decrease rate cuts the long-term population in half.

4. Consider iteration of an arbitrary function, $y = f(x)$.

   a. Represent the process of iterating $f(x)$ by an equation using the words *NOW* and *NEXT*.

   b. Represent the process of iterating $f(x)$ by a recursion equation.

5. In Activity 7 of Investigation 1, page 532, you investigated the logistic equation, $f(x) = rx(1 - x)$. You found that different values of r produce different long-term iteration behavior. You can program a computer to play "music" that corresponds to the long-term behavior. For example, consider the BASIC program below.

```
10 volume = 50
20 duration = 0.5
30 input "r = "; r
40 x = 0.02
50 print x
60 pitch = 220*4^x
70 sound pitch,duration,volume
80 x = r*x*(1–x)
90 goto 50
```

   a. Explain the purpose of each step of this program.

   b. Enter this program, or an equivalent program, into a computer. Run the program using the values 2.7, 3.2, 3.5, and 3.83 for r. Describe the results. Explain how the patterns in sound generated by the computer program compare to the numerical patterns you found in Activity 7 of Investigation 1.

Reflecting

1. In this unit, you have studied recursion in several contexts: recursion equations, recursive formulas for sequences, and function iteration. Recursion is sometimes described as a "self-referral" process. Explain why this is a reasonable description of recursion.

2. Explain why the fixed points for a function $f(x)$ correspond to the points of intersection of the graphs of $y = f(x)$ and $y = x$.

3. Why do you think it is sometimes said that you can never "see" a repelling fixed point?

4. In this lesson, you briefly explored a famous equation in mathematics and science: the logistic equation, $f(x) = rx(1 - x)$. This equation was first studied extensively in the 1970s. Some of the first discoveries about the behavior of the iterated equation came from trying to apply it as a model in biology and ecology. Its behavior turned out to be surprisingly complex and profound, giving rise to what is sometimes called the science of *chaos*.

   a. Review what you found out about the iterated behavior of the logistic equation in Activity 7 of Investigation 1, page 532. Why do you think the term *chaos* has been used to describe certain long-term behavior of the logistic equation?

   b. One of the first investigators of the logistic equation was an Australian biologist named Robert May. May argued that the world would be a better place if every student were given a pocket calculator and encouraged to play with the logistic equation. What do you think May meant?

   c. *Optional:* Obtain a copy of the book *Chaos: Making a New Science* by James Gleick (New York: Viking, 1987) and read Chapter 3, entitled "Life's Ups and Downs." This chapter is an entertaining account of some of the history of the logistic equation. Write a two-page report summarizing the chapter.

5. The idea of chaos in mathematics comes from a new area of mathematics that is sometimes called *chaos theory*. Chaos theory is related to certain long-term behavior of the logistic equation, which you examined in Activity 7 of Investigation 1, page 532. Read the article on the next page, which attempts to apply chaos theory to politics. Summarize the description of chaos given in the article. How does this description relate to the long-term behavior of the logistic equation? Do you think the conclusions in the article are valid? Why or why not?

Counting on Chaos to Save Day for Dole
by Al Kamen

It's come to this. Robert J. Dole's poll numbers are so bad that Rich Galen, director of political communications for House Speaker Newt Gingrich (R-Ga.), is touting "Chaos Theory" to inspire the GOP faithful.

"Stay with me, here," Galen began in a memo written last week "For Distribution to Talk Show Hosts," a regular salvo he sends out to about 100 or so conservative radio folks.

"There is a relatively new branch of science which is called Chaos Theory," he explained. It talks about a "butterfly fluttering its wings in Argentina which ultimately leads to a thunderstorm in New Jersey."

But "you will not be able to predict, with any degree of precision, when lightning will form and strike ... One second there is no lightning, and the next second the sky is bright. Chaos."

He went on: "Take another example. Suppose you take a wineglass and begin to squeeze it at its upper rim. If you continue to apply pressure, at some point the glass will break. The system will collapse entirely and instantaneously. Until the moment it breaks, it will be a perfectly usable glass. After the glass breaks, it will be nothing but a pile of shards."

"What does this have to do with the presidential campaign?" Galen asked, which seems like a pretty good question.

"My strong impression is there will come a time ... when the Clinton campaign, like the glass, will entirely and instantaneously collapse. One moment it will be a campaign, the next moment it will be unrecognizable."

"That's why we don't have to be frightened by the current Dole-Clinton polling numbers," he said. Chaos theory will save the day, or at least win New Jersey.

"What we must do, however, is to continue to keep the pressure on. If we get discouraged [and] stop squeezing the rim of the glass, then the glass will never break."

Now we know why the Republicans are infinitely more interesting than the Democrats. The Republicans look to science. All the Democrats can say is: "It's the economy, stupid."

Source: *The Washington Post*, September 16, 1996.

Extending

1. The recursive formula for a geometric sequence looks like the combined recursion equation $A_n = rA_{n-1} + b$ without the added b. This connection can be used to find a function formula for combined recursion equations. The strategy involves building from a function formula for a geometric sequence.

   a. What is the function formula for a geometric sequence with recursive formula $A_n = rA_{n-1}$ and initial value A_0?

   b. As the next step, think about the long-term behavior of $A_n = r^n A_0$ and compare it to the long-term behavior of $A_n = rA_{n-1} + b$. Consider the situation when $|r| < 1$.

   ■ Explain why the long-term behavior of $A_n = rA_{n-1} + b$ is attracted to its fixed point.

   ■ What is the long-term behavior of $A_n = r^n A_0$?

c. Now modify the formula $A_n = r^n A_0$ so that it has the same long-term behavior as $A_n = rA_{n-1} + b$: Begin by adding the fixed point, denoted *FIX*, to the function formula $A_n = r^n A_0$ so that the new function will have the same long-term behavior as $A_n = rA_{n-1} + b$. Explain why $A_n = r^n A_0 + FIX$ has long-term behavior converging to *FIX*, if $|r| < 1$.

d. Finally, modify the formula $A_n = r^n A_0 + FIX$ so that it has the same initial value A_0 as $A_n = rA_{n-1} + b$:

■ Explain why the initial value of $A_n = r^n A_0 + FIX$ is equal to $A_0 + FIX$.

■ Explain why the initial value of $A_n = r^n(A_0 - FIX) + FIX$ is equal to A_0.

e. The function formula $A_n = r^n(A_0 - FIX) + FIX$ has the same long-term behavior and the same initial value as the combined recursion equation $A_n = rA_{n-1} + b$. Use this formula to find A_5 for the recursion equation $A_n = 2A_{n-1} + 1$, with $A_0 = 3$. Then compute A_5 by successively evaluating $A_n = 2A_{n-1} + 1$; compare your result to what you calculated with the function formula.

f. Compare the function formula in Part e to the function formula you derived in Organizing Task 5 of Lesson 2, page 523. Resolve any apparent differences.

2. In Organizing Task 1, page 539, you investigated the method of function iteration to solve linear equations. Investigate if this method will work for quadratic equations. Consider the quadratic equation $2x^2 + 5x = 3$.

a. Which function should you iterate in order to use the method of function iteration to solve this equation? Iterate with several different initial values and describe the results in each case.

b. Solve this equation using another method. How many solutions are there?

c. What properties of fixed points allow you to either find or not find a solution when using the method of function iteration?

d. Use your calculator or computer software to help you sketch graphs of the iterated function and $y = x$ on the same set of axes. Locate the fixed points on this graph. At each of the fixed points, visualize a line drawn tangent to the graph of the iterated function at the fixed point. Estimate the slope of each of these tangent lines. For which fixed point is the absolute value of the slope of the tangent line greater than 1? For which tangent line is the absolute value of the slope less than 1?

e. Recall the connection between iterating linear functions and slope. For this task, explain how the slope of the tangent line at a fixed point tells you if the fixed point is attracting or repelling. Explain what attracting or repelling fixed points have to do with solving nonlinear equations using the method of function iteration.

3. Although it is relatively easy to iterate linear functions graphically with a fair degree of accuracy, it is quite difficult to iterate nonlinear functions graphically. This is because, as you have seen, the shape of a graphical iteration is determined by the slope of the graph of the iterated function. And while lines have constant slopes, graphs of nonlinear functions have changing slopes. Thus, it is usually necessary to use a computer or graphing calculator to accurately iterate nonlinear functions graphically. A graphical iteration tool is built into many calculators and computer graphing packages, or such a tool can be quickly programmed.

a. Consult a manual, if necessary, to find how to use your calculator or computer to iterate graphically. Practice by graphically iterating $f(x) = -0.8x + 6$. You should get a graph that looks like the one below.

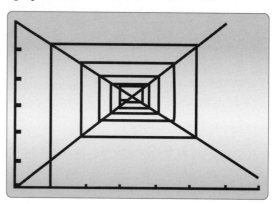

b. In Modeling Task 3, page 538, you were asked to iterate the function $h(x) = 3.2x - 0.8x^2$. Use a graphing calculator or computer to iterate $h(x)$ graphically, starting with $x = 2.6$. Compare the graphical iteration pattern to the numerical iteration results.

c. In Modeling Task 1, page 537, you were asked to iterate the function $f(x) = x^3 - x^2 + 1$. Graphically iterate $f(x)$ to illustrate each of your results in Modeling Task 1.

4. In this lesson, you iterated algebraic functions. It is also possible to iterate geometric transformations. As an example, play the following Chaos Game.

a. On a clean sheet of paper, draw the vertices of a large triangle. Any type of triangle will work, but for your first time playing the game, use an isosceles triangle. Label the vertices with the numbers 1, 2, and 3.

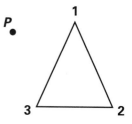

b. Start with a point anywhere on the sheet of paper. This is your initial input. Randomly choose one of the vertices (for example, use a random number generator to choose one of the numbers 1, 2, or 3), and mark a new point one-half of the distance between your input and that vertex. This is your first output and also your new input. Then randomly choose another vertex and mark the next point, half the distance from the new input to that vertex. Repeat this process until you have plotted six points.

c. The goal of the Chaos Game is to see what happens in the long term. What do you think the pattern of plotted points will look like if you plot 300 points? Make a conjecture.

d. Program a calculator or computer to play the Chaos Game and then carry out several hundred iterations. Since you are interested only in the long-term behavior, you might carry out the first 10 iterations without plotting the resulting points and then plot all points thereafter.

e. Repeat the game for several other initial points. Do you think you will always get the same resulting figure? Try it.

f. The figure that results from the Chaos Game is an example of a familiar *fractal*. One of the most important characteristics of fractals is that they are *self-similar*, which means that if you zoom in, you keep seeing figures just like the original figure. What is the scale factor of successively smaller triangles in the fractal you produced?

g. Give a geometrical explanation for why the Chaos Game will always generate a Sierpinski triangle. (For more about Sierpinski triangles, see Modeling Task 5, page 520.)

Looking Back

In this unit, you have investigated sequential change in a variety of contexts using the tools of recursion and iteration. You have extended the idea of using *NOW* and *NEXT* to model sequential change; you have studied recursion equations, function iteration, and sequences; and you have made connections to previous work with linear, exponential, and polynomial models. In this final lesson, you will pull together and review all the ideas in the unit.

1. In Lesson 1, you modeled a variety of situations with combined recursion equations, that is, recursion equations of the form $A_n = rA_{n-1} + b$. In Lesson 3, you iterated linear functions. These two topics are closely connected. In this activity, you will summarize key features of that connection.

By using different values for r and b in the combined recursion equation $A_n = rA_{n-1} + b$, you can build models for different situations. Four different possibilities are indicated by the table below. One recursion equation has already been entered into the table.

Four Different Versions of the Recursion Equation $A_n = rA_{n-1} + b$		
	$0 < r < 1$	$r > 1$
$b < 0$		
$b > 0$	$A_n = 0.8A_{n-1} + 1{,}000$	

Choose *two* of the empty table entries. For each entry, write an appropriate recursion equation and prepare two reports. Title each report with the particular recursion equation on which you are reporting. Each report should include the following analysis of the chosen recursion equation and its use as a mathematical model.

a. Briefly describe a real-world situation that can be modeled by the recursion equation along with a chosen initial value.

b. Rewrite the recursion equation as an equation using *NOW* and *NEXT*.

c. Write a linear function that can be iterated to yield the same sequence as the successive values of the recursion equation. Choose an initial value.

- Iterate the function and describe the long-term behavior.

- Find the fixed point and decide whether it is attracting, repelling, or neither. Explain in terms of slope.

- Sketch a graph showing graphical iteration of the function for the initial value previously chosen.

d. Sketch a graph of n versus A_n, using the same initial value you chose in Part c.

e. Describe the long-term behavior of the real-world situation being modeled, for different initial values. Refer to the fixed point and its properties, but keep your description in the context of the particular situation being modeled.

2. Many irregular shapes found in the natural world can be modeled by fractals. Study the first few stages of the fractal tree shown below.

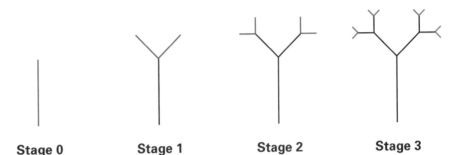

Stage 0   Stage 1   Stage 2   Stage 3

a. Write the number of new branches at each stage for the first several stages. Then write recursive and function formulas that describe this sequence. Use one of the formulas to predict the number of new branches at Stage 12. Check your prediction using the other formula.

b. Find the total number of branches at Stage 12.

c. Suppose that the length of the initial branch is 1 unit and that the branches at each successive stage of the fractal tree are half the length of the branches at the previous stage.

   ■ Write the total length of all the branches at each stage for the first several stages.

   ■ Find the total length of all the branches at Stage 15.

3. When you attend a movie, concert, or theater production, you may notice that the number of seats in a row increases as you move from the front of the theater to the back. This permits the seats in consecutive rows to be offset from one another so that you have a less obstructed view of the stage.

The center section of the orchestra level of Laser Auditorium is arranged so that there are 42 seats in the first row, 44 seats in the second row, 46 seats in the third row, and so on for a total of 25 rows.

  a. Determine the number of seats in the last row in two different ways. Compare your result and your methods to those of another group and resolve any differences.

  b. Determine the total number of seats in the center section of the orchestra level in at least two different ways. One method should involve using a rule showing the total number of seats as a function of number of rows n.

4. Nicole was investigating the maximum number of regions into which a plane is separated by n lines, no two of which are parallel and no three of which intersect at a point. For example, the diagram below shows the maximum number of regions for 3 lines.

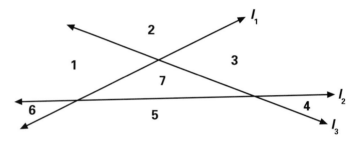

Nicole gathered the data shown in the table below.

Number of Lines	0	1	2	3	4
Number of Regions	1	2	4	7	11

  a. Verify the entries in the table.

  b. Find a function formula for the maximum number of regions formed by n lines using the method of finite differences.

  c. Write a recursion equation for this relationship.

5. Find recursive and function formulas for each of the sequences below. Then find the sum of the terms up through the term with subscript 15.

  a.

n	0	1	2	3	4	5	6	...	15	...
P_n	−3	2	7	12	17			...		...

  b.

n	0	1	2	3	4	5	6	...	15	...
L_n	600	300	150	75	37.5			...		...

When asked to make a list of topics covered in this unit, Shrita produced the following list:

- Recursion equations
- Population growth
- Compound interest
- Arithmetic sequences and sums
- Geometric sequences and sums
- Finite differences

- Linear functions
- Exponential functions
- Polynomial functions
- Function iteration
- Fixed points

a Examine each topic to see if you agree that it should be on the list. Discuss any questions you have about what a particular topic is or why it is on the list. Add any other topics that you can think of.

b Ray's list had just one item on it: combined recursion equations. Explain why Ray's list provides a reasonable summary of the unit. Which of the topics on Shrita's list are connected in some way to recursion equations of this form?

Be prepared to share your group's thinking with the entire class.

Looking Back at Course 3

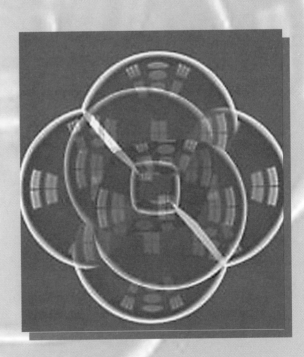

Making the Best of It: Optimal Forms and Strategies

In this course, you have studied important and broadly useful mathematics, including linear programming, election theory, surveys and confidence intervals, families of functions, similarity and congruence, normal distributions, control charts, iteration and recursion, and proof. You have used mathematical modeling and formal algebraic and geometric reasoning to solve problems in many different settings. In this Capstone, you will focus on a very important class of problems: *optimization problems*. To optimize means to find the "best." Think about optimization in the context of contemporary society and the units in this course. The units are listed below.

1. *Multiple-Variable Models*

2. *Modeling Public Opinion*

3. *Symbol Sense and Algebraic Reasoning*

4. *Shapes and Geometric Reasoning*

5. *Patterns in Variation*

6. *Families of Functions*

7. *Discrete Models of Change*

Think About This Situation

Most people want to make the best choices they can. That's why understanding optimization problems and strategies is so important. As a group, brainstorm possible responses to these questions and then be prepared to share your ideas with the entire class.

a What are some examples of optimization in the following contexts?
  - Business and industry
  - Education
  - Your daily life

b Describe at least one optimization situation from the Course 3 algebra and functions strand (Units 1, 3, and 6) and explain how you optimized it. Do the same for each of the other stands: geometry and trigonometry (Unit 4), statistics and probability (Units 2 and 5), and discrete mathematics (Units 2 and 7).

c Leonhard Euler, an 18th-century mathematician, said, "... nothing in all of the world will occur in which maximum or minimum rule is not somehow shining forth." Do you agree or disagree? Explain.

You will now pull together much of the mathematics you have been learning to analyze several new optimization situations. Each group should complete Investigation 1 and any two of Investigations 2 through 5. You will prepare a report on one of the investigations that you choose. Guidelines for the report are given on page 567. Verify your choices with your teacher before you begin.

Investigations 1 through 4 include optional "On Your Own" tasks. Individually, each group member should select and complete one of these tasks.

INVESTIGATION 1 ▶ Do Bees Build It Best?

As you brainstormed about possible examples of optimization in your daily life, you may not have considered optimal forms and strategies in nature. Consider, for example, the honeycombs that bees make for storing honey. They appear to be three-dimensional tilings of regular hexagonal prisms.

1. In Course 1, you experimented with regular polygon shapes and discovered that equilateral triangles, squares, and regular hexagons will tile a plane. Portions of these tilings are shown below. You will investigate why bees build hexagonal tilings.

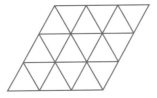 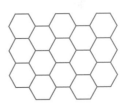

   a. What must be true of the measure of each angle of a regular polygon if the polygon is to tile a plane? Verify that the shapes above satisfy this criterion.

   b. Now suppose the perimeter of one cell of a honeycomb is 24 mm. Find the cross-sectional area of a cell, assuming the cell has the following shapes.

   ■ An equilateral triangle

   ■ A square

   ■ A regular hexagon

   c. Which cell has the greatest cross-sectional area for a fixed perimeter of 24 mm? As the number of sides of a regular polygon with fixed perimeter increases, how does the corresponding area change?

   d. Suppose the height of each cell is about 20 mm. Determine which of the three shapes in Part b produces the cell with the greatest volume.

e. Explain why the *lateral surface area* (the surface area not including the area of the bases) is fixed, regardless of the shape of the base, if the height *h* and perimeter *P* of a base of a regular polygonal prism are fixed.

2. Now that you have determined which of the three shapes in Activity 1 with fixed perimeter has the greatest area, investigate whether there are other regular polygonal shapes that will tile a plane and have a greater area measure.

a. Complete a copy of the table below, which relates the measure of each angle of a regular *n*-gon to the number of sides *n*.

Regular Polygons

Number of Sides, *n*	3	4	5	6	7	8
Measure of One Angle	60°	90°	108°	120°	?	?

b. Examine the sequence of angle measures in your completed table. Is the sequence an arithmetic sequence, a geometric sequence, or neither? Explain.

c. Formulate an algebraic rule to predict the measure of one angle of a regular polygon. Compare your rule and strategy for discovering it to those of another group. Resolve any differences.

d. Use your rule to predict the measure of one angle of a regular 20-gon. Could a bee form a honeycomb of regular 20-gons? Explain your reasoning.

e. Prove that the only regular polygons that will tile a plane have 3, 4, or 6 sides.

3. In what sense are honeycombs an optimal form?

4. Make a neat copy of your work on this investigation and file it at the location designated by your teacher. Examine the work filed by other groups and compare their work to what you did. Write a question to at least one group asking its members to explain something about their work that you found interesting or that you did not understand. Answer any questions your group receives.

▶ **On Your Own**

The cells of a complete honeycomb are hexagonal prisms arranged in two layers so that the cell openings for the two layers face in opposite directions. This arrangement compresses the base of the cells into trihedral pyramids, as shown in the vertical cross section at the right.

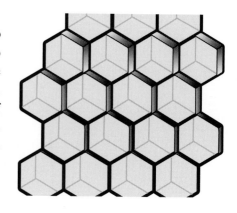

Using visualization and a combination of algebraic, geometric, and trigonometric reasoning, one can prove that the surface area of a cell is given by

$$SA = 6sh + 1.5s^2\left(\frac{\sqrt{3} - \cos\theta}{\sin\theta}\right),$$

where s is the side length of the hexagon, h is the height of a cell, and θ (the Greek letter "theta") is the angle made by a line parallel to the faces of the prism through the vertex of the pyramid and one of the edges of the pyramid.

a. What value of θ will give the minimal surface area?

b. For what value of θ will the surface area be maximal?

c. Rewrite the above formula in expanded form. Is it easier or more difficult to answer Parts a and b using this equivalent symbolic form? Explain your reasoning.

INVESTIGATION 2 From Bees to IQs

In Investigation 1, you verified that when building a honeycomb, bees use the best form possible. Among all regular polygons with fixed perimeter, the regular hexagon is the one which both tessellates and encloses the largest area. Thus, when the height of the prism is fixed, the hexagonal honeycomb cell encloses the maximum volume.

In this investigation, you will further investigate shapes with fixed perimeter but without the restriction that the shapes be regular polygons.

1. In *The Aeneid* by the Roman poet Vergil, a story is told about Queen Dido of Carthage. When Dido was a princess in the city of Tyre (now in Lebanon), her brother, King Pygmalion, killed her husband in order to capture her possessions. She fled by ship to a place in Africa that later became Carthage. She wanted to buy land from the local ruler, King Jarbas of Numidia. The king granted her only as much land as she could enclose in the hide of an ox. Dido was very clever in her interpretation of this decree. She had her people cut the hide into very thin strips and tie them together to form a cord of great length. She used the cord to surround the largest possible region of land. For Parts a and b that follow, suppose the length of the cord was 900 yards.

a. Suppose the shape of the region that Dido enclosed was a rectangle.

- Do all rectangles with a perimeter of 900 yards have the same area? Defend your answer by sketching a few such rectangles and computing their areas.

- What are the dimensions of the rectangular region that has maximum area? Explain your answer using symbolic rules, graphs, and tables. What type of rectangle is this?

b. What if the region Dido enclosed was not rectangular? Experiment with some nonrectangular shapes. Compare the areas of those shapes to the maximum area of a rectangular region you found in Part a. Make a conjecture about what shape with a perimeter of 900 yards has the maximum area. Compare and discuss your conjecture with other groups. (To provide evidence for your conjecture, you should determine the area of at least two nonrectangular shapes that have perimeters of 900 yards.)

2. A useful ratio for comparing shapes with respect to area and perimeter is $\frac{4\pi A}{P^2}$, where A represents the area of a given shape and P represents the perimeter of the shape. This ratio is called the **Isoperimetric Quotient (IQ)**.

   a. Compute the IQ for an equilateral triangle that has a perimeter of 900 yards. Compute the IQ for several other equilateral triangles with different perimeters. What do you notice?

   b. Determine the IQ for several circles. What pattern do you notice? Prove what you have discovered by using algebraic reasoning with the general formulas for area and circumference of a circle.

   c. Prove that similar figures have the same IQ.

   d. You found the IQ for equilateral triangles and circles in Parts a and b. Now determine the IQ for squares.

   e. The IQ for regular pentagons is 0.865. Determine the IQs for regular hexagons and regular octagons.

   f. Organize all your IQ data in a table. Describe any patterns in the data. Compare those patterns to visual patterns in the following diagram.

3. A famous theorem, called the **Isoperimetric Theorem**, states that for a fixed perimeter, the shape with maximum area is a circle.

   a. Does this match your conjecture in Part b of Activity 1? If not, go back and reexamine that activity.

   b. Why do you suppose bees don't use cylinders in building their honeycombs?

   c. Another statement of the Isoperimetric Theorem, using the IQ, is given here:

   For every region with area A and perimeter P, the following are true.
   - $\frac{4\pi A}{P^2} \leq 1$
   - $\frac{4\pi A}{P^2} = 1$ if and only if the region is circular.

   Does this statement agree with your IQ data in Activity 2? If not, go back and reexamine that activity.

In the Isoperimetric Theorem in Activity 3, you fix the perimeter, and the theorem tells you the shape with maximum area. Suppose you reverse this perspective. That is, fix the area and look for the shape with minimum perimeter. Now the problem is to find the shortest curve enclosing a given area in a plane.

4. Suppose you want to build a dog pen that has an area of 9 square meters. You want to use the least amount of fence to enclose the pen. How should you lay out the pen? Experiment with a few different regions and make a conjecture about the region with the smallest perimeter for a given area. Compare and discuss your conjecture with other groups. Resolve any differences.

5. Consider what happens in three dimensions. The IQ for three-dimensional shapes is $\frac{36\pi V^2}{S^3}$, where V represents volume and S represents surface area.

   a. Determine the IQ for cubes.

   b. Prove that the IQ for every sphere is 1. (Recall that the volume of a sphere is given by $V = \frac{4}{3}\pi r^3$ and the surface area of a sphere is given by $S = 4\pi r^2$.)

   c. For a fixed volume, what enclosing shape do you think will have minimum surface area? Explain your reasoning.

6. Make a neat copy of your work on this investigation and file it at the location designated by your teacher. Examine the work filed by other groups and compare their work to what you did. Write a question to at least one group asking its members to explain something about their work that you found interesting or that you did not understand. Answer any questions your group receives.

On Your Own

Choose one of the following tasks to complete.

a. In Activity 2, you found the Isoperimetric Quotients of several regular polygons. Express the IQ of a regular n-gon as a function of n only. Use your function to describe what happens to the IQ as n gets very large. Give a geometric interpretation of this situation. You may find it helpful to read or ask your teacher about what's called the *apothem* of a regular polygon.

b. In Activity 3, you were given two statements of the Isoperimetric Theorem. Prove that the statement in Part c is equivalent to the statement given at the beginning of Activity 3.

c. The optimal property of spheres from Part c of Activity 5 applies to soap bubbles. A single soap bubble has the shape of a sphere and uses the least surface area to enclose a given volume of air. This could be called the Single-Bubble Theorem. A double bubble exists when two bubbles are hooked together. Do you think a double bubble uses the least possible surface area to enclose two given volumes of air? Make a conjecture. Then do some research on what is currently known about the so-called Double-Bubble Conjecture, which is still unproven, and write a one-page report.

INVESTIGATION 3 ▶ Minimizing Distance

Many situations involve minimizing distance. For example, a manufacturer may want to find the shortest route for shipping products, a robotics engineer may want to minimize the distance traveled by a robot on a computerized assembly line, or a student may wish to find the shortest route to school. In this investigation, you will consider some other situations involving minimizing distance.

1. Many large oil fields lie under the ocean. Huge offshore oil rigs are used to drill for this oil. Underwater pipelines are built to transport the oil from the rigs to refineries on shore. Suppose that two offshore oil rigs are located as shown in the following diagram. (Units are in miles.) One refinery will be built along the shoreline to process the oil from both rigs.

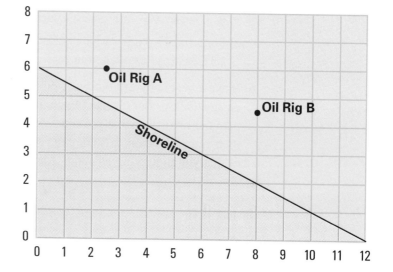

a. Under what conditions might it be best to locate the refinery as close to Oil Rig A as possible? Assuming those conditions, determine the coordinates of the optimal refinery location and the total length of underwater pipeline needed. Explain your method.

Now suppose there are no special conditions that might suggest locating the refinery closer to one oil rig than the other. Again, assume the refinery must be connected to both oil rigs via underwater pipelines. Since it is very expensive to build underwater pipelines, the oil company would like to build the fewest number of miles of pipeline. In Parts b through e that follow, consider the following question:

Where along the shore is the optimum location of the refinery?

b. State precisely what it means for the location of the refinery to be optimum. Then brainstorm with your group about some strategies that might work to find the optimum location. Try the strategies that seem most promising. Where should the refinery be located?

There is a variety of methods that can be used to find the optimum refinery location, some of which you may have used in Part b. In Parts c through e, you will investigate three possible methods, using ideas from statistics, algebra, and geometry. If you have previously used a method, go on to the next part.

c. Statistical Regression Method: Choose several points along the shore where the refinery could be located. Find the sum of the distances from each of these possible refinery locations to the two oil rigs. Make a scatterplot of the (*x-coordinate of potential refinery location, sum of distances*) data. Use the scatterplot and the statistical regression capabilities of your calculator or computer software to estimate the optimum location of the refinery. Explain your reasoning.

d. Algebraic Reasoning Method: Choose an arbitrary refinery location (x, y) on the shore. Write an expression showing the sum of the distances from (x, y) to each of the oil rigs. Find the equation of the line representing the shoreline, and use it to write the sum of distances in terms of x only. Use a table or graph to find the minimum value of this function. What is the optimum location of the refinery?

e. Geometric Transformation Method: Consider the shoreline as a line of reflection. Find the reflection image across this line of the point representing Oil Rig B. Think about paths from Oil Rig A to the shoreline to the *reflection image* of Oil Rig B, and compare those to paths from Oil Rig A to the shoreline to Oil Rig B. Using this strategy, describe a procedure for finding the optimum refinery location.

- Illustrate the procedure on a copy of the oil-rigs diagram.

- Find the coordinates of the optimum refinery location.

- Find the minimum total distance to the two oil rigs.

2. A fundamental idea related to minimizing distance is that the shortest distance between two unobstructed points on a flat surface is a straight line. This idea is captured in a famous theorem called the Triangle Inequality Theorem. Along with the Pythagorean Theorem, the Triangle Inequality Theorem is one of the most widely used geometry theorems. You may have investigated this theorem previously in Extending Task 1 (page 323) of Unit 4, "Shapes and Geometric Reasoning."

Triangle Inequality Theorem

The sum of the lengths of two sides of a triangle is greater than the length of the third side.

a. Use the Law of Cosines and what you know about the range of the cosine function to prove that in $\triangle ABC$, $b + c > a$.

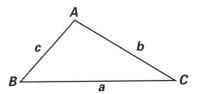

b. The Triangle Inequality Theorem was used in the transformation method for finding the optimum refinery location in Activity 1, although you may not have noticed it. Go back and examine the transformation method in Part e of Activity 1 and explain how the Triangle Inequality Theorem was used.

c. Oil fields are found inland as well as under the ocean. Suppose the locations of four inland oil wells are represented on a coordinate system as shown below. (Units are in miles.)

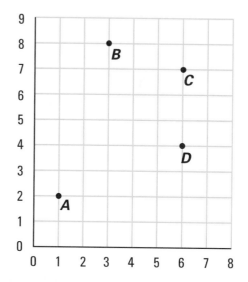

Because of mountainous surrounding territory, one refinery is to be built to process the oil from all four oil wells. Again, the goal is to minimize the total number of miles of pipeline needed to connect the refinery to each of the four oil wells. Find the optimum location of the refinery. Explain how you used, or could have used, the Triangle Inequality Theorem in your solution.

3. Make a neat copy of your work on this investigation and file it at the location designated by your teacher. Examine the work filed by other groups and compare their work to what you did. Write a question to at least one group asking its members to explain something about their work that you found interesting or that you did not understand. Answer any questions your group receives.

▶**On Your Own**

Choose one of the following tasks to complete.

a. In Activity 1, you used several methods to find the optimum refinery location. Model the oil-refinery problem using a geometry drawing program that allows you to construct, measure, and move geometric figures. Demonstrate how to use the software to estimate the optimum location of the refinery.

b. Consider a situation similar to the one in Activity 2, except with three oil wells. The three oil wells are located on a coordinate system as shown in the following diagram. (Units are in miles.)

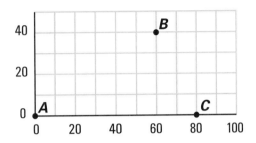

The problem, as before, is to find the optimum location of a refinery that will service all the oil wells. That is, you must find a point R such that the sum of the distances from R to each of the three points A, B, and C is minimum. This problem is sometimes called a *Steiner tree problem* or *Fermat's problem*. Research to find out how to solve this problem. Write a brief report on what you find.

INVESTIGATION 4 Best-Fitting Data Models

In Course 3 and in previous courses, when trying to make sense of data you often looked for the "best-fitting" model. This strategy capitalizes on the statistical regression capabilities of graphing calculators or computer software. As you have previously seen, the effectiveness of this method depends on first examining a scatterplot of the data for patterns or overall trends.

1. Information about the number of births in a country is very useful for making governmental policy decisions. For example, funding decisions for health care and education programs are influenced by birth data.

   Examine the table below, which shows the number of births in Bangladesh. The entries from 1955 to 1990 are actual measurements; the entries from 1995 to 2025 are projections.

Bangladesh: Births			
Year	Births	Year	Births
1955	2,137,842	1995	5,368,091
1960	2,406,409	2000	5,752,499
1965	2,723,170	2005	5,971,843
1970	3,166,872	2010	5,532,962
1975	3,714,227	2015	5,074,848
1980	4,163,936	2020	4,842,618
1985	4,531,385	2025	4,699,740
1990	4,878,024		

Source: World Resources Institute Database

a. Write a brief description of these data, including the following.

- At least one scatterplot
- Descriptions of patterns, trends, or unusual features
- Description of the entire data set, as well as interesting parts of the data

b. Does it seem reasonable that the data for 1995 to 2025 are projected from the trend in the actual data? What are some possible reasons or assumptions that could explain the trend in the projected data?

c. When fitting models to data, it is sometimes reasonable to fit different models to different parts of the data. Where would you "break" the data in order to find two "best-fitting" models? Explain your reasoning.

d. Find a model that is a good fit for the data from 1955 to 2000.

e. Plot separately the projected data from 2005 to 2025.

- Use the statistical regression capability of your calculator or computer software to fit an exponential function to these data.
- At what birth level does the graph of the exponential model level off?
- In the data table, it looks like the data level off at about 4,000,000 births. So the graph of the calculator- or computer-based exponential model levels off at a different place from the data. Refine your exponential model so that it has an asymptote at $y = 4,000,000$.

2. The table below shows data on infant mortality and adult female literacy in 1990 in 16 countries around the world.

Literacy-Mortality Data

Country	Percent Adult Female Literacy	Percent Infant Mortality
Nepal	13.2	12.8
Somalia	14.0	13.2
Pakistan	21.1	10.9
Angola	28.5	13.7
Egypt	33.8	6.5
Papua New Guinea	37.8	5.9
Morocco	38.0	8.2
Cameroon	42.6	9.4
Iran	43.3	5.2
Guatemala	47.1	5.9
Zimbabwe	60.3	6.6
Kuwait	66.7	1.8
Malaysia	70.4	2.4
Madagascar	72.9	12.0
Lebanon	73.1	4.8
Sri Lanka	83.5	2.8

Source: World Resources Institute Database

a. Make a scatterplot of the (*percent adult female literacy*, *percent infant mortality*) data. Describe any patterns, trends, or unusual features of the data.

b. Does there appear to be a linear association between percent adult female literacy and percent infant mortality? Graph the least squares regression line along with the scatterplot for these data. What is the correlation coefficient, and what does it tell you?

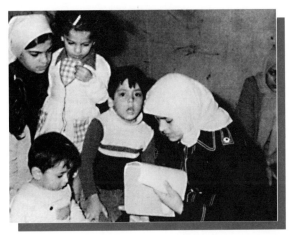

c. Recall that the least squares regression line is the line that gives the smallest sum of squared errors for a set of points. The general idea of the *sum of squared differences* is important and widely used in mathematics. Explain how each of the following can be interpreted in terms of the sum of squared differences.

■ The standard deviation of a distribution

■ The distance formula for the distance between two points

Try to think of another topic you have studied that involves the sum of squared differences.

d. Another application of the sum-of-squared-differences idea is found in a measure of error called the **root mean squared error (RMS)**. The RMS can help you analyze the literacy-mortality data. Examine this formula for computing the RMS.

$$\text{RMS} = \sqrt{\frac{\Sigma(y - \hat{y})^2}{n}}$$

where y is the actual y value and $\hat{y}$ is the corresponding value predicted from the regression equation. In this activity, y is *percent infant mortality*.

■ Give a verbal description of how to compute the RMS.

■ Based on the above formula, describe the meaning of the RMS.

■ How is the RMS different from and similar to the standard deviation?

■ Use your calculator or computer software to help you compute the RMS for the literacy-mortality data.

e. In some ways, the RMS is to the least squares regression line as the standard deviation is to the mean in a normal distribution. For example, about 68% of the data will typically be within one RMS of the least squares regression line, and about 95% will be within two RMSs. Let $y = f(x)$ represent the regression line. Graph the following on the same set of axes:

- Scatterplot of literacy-mortality data, with *literacy* on the horizontal axis
- $y = f(x)$
- $y = f(x) + \text{RMS}$
- $y = f(x) + 2(\text{RMS})$
- $y = f(x) - \text{RMS}$
- $y = f(x) - 2(\text{RMS})$

f. Identify any data points that lie outside the range of $y = f(x) \pm 2(\text{RMS})$. It is reasonable to consider such data points as outliers. Describe how the "RMS-plot" in Part e is like the *control charts* you studied in Unit 5, "Patterns in Variation."

g. Remove any outliers you found in Part f and recompute the regression line and the correlation coefficient. Is the fit better for the remaining data?

h. Can you conclude from your analysis so far that there is a cause-and-effect relationship between percent adult female literacy and percent infant mortality? Explain your reasoning and include a reasonable argument for why a country, such as Madagascar, could have a relatively high adult female literacy rate and yet also have a surprisingly high infant mortality rate.

i. The World Resources Institute Database contains literacy-mortality data for 1970 and 1990 on 86 countries, not just the 16 you have been analyzing. The table below shows some of the statistics computed for all 86 countries.

Literacy-Mortality Data for 86 Countries

	1970	1990
Correlation Coefficient (r)	0.853	0.847
RMS	2.479	2.340
Least Squares Regression Line	$y = -0.13x + 17.03$	$y = -0.13x + 15.23$

A separate analysis shows that there was a general increase in the literacy level of women from 1970 to 1990. As the literacy of adult women increased, did the association between adult female literacy and infant mortality get stronger? Explain your answer using the information in the table.

3. Make a neat copy of your work on this investigation and file it at the location designated by your teacher. Examine the work filed by other groups and compare their work to what you did. Write a question to at least one group asking its members to explain something about their work that you found interesting or that you did not understand. Answer any questions your group receives.

Find recent data on the annual number of births in Bangladesh.

- Do the projections given in Activity 1 match the actual recent data?

- Find a good model for this actual recent data. Make new projections based on your model and compare to the original projections. Explain.

INVESTIGATION 5 ▶ The Best Concert

Suppose your class is planning to put on a benefit concert to raise money for recent flood victims. You want the concert to be the best possible. In this situation, there are many factors to optimize.

1. What is the best type of music to feature at the concert? There are lots of choices, including, rock, country, blues, alternative, folk, R & B, classical, hip-hop, jazz, and easy listening. You want to appeal to as many people as possible, including yourselves!

   a. What are some mathematical methods you could use to determine the optimal choice of music for the concert?

   b. Suppose you decide to carry out a two-step procedure. First, you vote within your class to narrow the options down to just two choices; then you do a sample survey within the community to decide which of the two to choose. Suppose your class vote is summarized in the following preference table.

Musical Preferences

	Rankings			
Classical	1	1	5	5
Country	3	2	1	2
Jazz	4	5	3	1
Folk	5	4	4	4
Rock	2	3	2	3
Number of Voters	**5**	**7**	**8**	**9**

What are the top two music choices? Explain which vote-analysis method you used, how the method works, and why you used it.

2. Now you have two choices for the type of music to play at the concert. Suppose that you next conduct a sample survey of 40 people within the community to decide whether Choice 1 or Choice 2 should be played at the concert.

   a. Describe a good way to select the sample of 40 people. Then give an example of a poor sampling plan and explain why the plan is poor.

   b. Write a good survey question. Then give an example of a poorly worded question and explain why it is poor.

   c. Suppose 26 out of the 40 people in the sample prefer Choice 1. Construct a 90% confidence interval for the actual population percent. Write the interval using the margin of error.

   d. Think about how you would explain the results of the survey and its limitations. Which of the two types of music will you announce as the winner? Can you claim that, without doubt, a majority of people in the community prefer the winning choice? List several other key points you should include in your explanation.

3. Now that you've decided on the best music, it's time to advertise the concert. As usual, you want to optimize your strategy. In addition to placing posters around town, you will advertise on local television and radio. Donations from community businesses to pay for air time total $10,500.  You want to maximize your air time, whether from TV or radio, but you have to take into account the following facts and assumptions.

   ■ A 15-second radio ad costs $50.

   ■ A 30-second TV ad costs $750.

   ■ You want to have at least 8 TV ads, but you will take as many TV ads as you can get.

   ■ You have no minimum on radio ads, but you don't want more than 30 of them.

   a. Since you want as many TV ads as possible, suppose you spend all your money on TV ads. How many TV ads can you buy? What is your total air time using this strategy?

   b. Return to the original plan, maximizing air time from radio ads, TV ads, or both. Set up a linear programming problem that models this situation. How many radio and TV ads should you buy in order to maximize your total air time within the given constraints?

4. Of course, the most important factor to optimize regarding this benefit concert is profit. Since everyone is donating time and the school is providing facilities and equipment, there are no expenses and all income from ticket sales will be profit. Although the community has not had much experience with benefit concerts, there have been many community concerts in the past. Based on data from these past concerts, the chamber of commerce estimates that income from ticket sales $I(x)$ is a function of the price x, in dollars charged per ticket, according to the following rule: $I(x) = 2,000x - 50x^2$.

  a. According to this rule, what price would you have to charge per ticket in order to make $15,000?

  b. What is the most you could charge per ticket and still make money?

  c. What price should you charge per ticket in order to maximize income? What is the maximum income?

5. Make a neat copy of your work on this investigation and file it at the location designated by your teacher. Examine the work filed by other groups and compare their work to what you did. Write a question to at least one group asking its members to explain something about their work that you found interesting or that you did not understand. Answer any questions your group receives.

REPORTS: Putting It All Together

Finish this Capstone by preparing two reports, one group oral report and one individual written report as described below.

1. Your group should prepare a brief oral report that meets the following guidelines:

  ■ Choose one investigation from this Capstone. Confirm your choice with your teacher before beginning to prepare your report.

  ■ Examine the work that other groups have filed on your investigation. Compare your work to theirs, discuss any differences with the other groups, and modify your solutions, if you think you should.

  ■ Begin your presentation with a brief summary of your work in the investigation. Then explain your solutions to the various activities.

  ■ Be prepared to discuss alternative solutions, particularly those proposed by other groups that worked on the same investigation.

  ■ Be prepared to answer any questions.

2. Individually, write a two-page report summarizing how the mathematics you have learned can be used to model and solve optimization problems.

Checkpoint

In this course, you have learned important mathematical concepts and methods, and you have gained valuable experience in thinking mathematically. Look back over the investigations you completed in this Capstone and consider some of the mathematical thinking you have done. For each of the following habits of mind, describe, if possible, an example for which you found the habit to be helpful.

ⓐ Search for patterns

ⓑ Formulate or find a mathematical model

ⓒ Collect, analyze, and interpret data

ⓓ Make and check conjectures

ⓔ Describe and use an algorithm

ⓕ Visualize

ⓖ Simulate a situation

ⓗ Predict

ⓘ Experiment

ⓙ Prove

ⓚ Make connections—between mathematics and the real world and within mathematics itself

ⓛ Use a variety of representations—like tables, graphs, equations, words, and physical models

Be prepared to share your examples and thinking with the entire class.

Index of Mathematical Topics

Equations
    algebraic, rewriting in
        equivalent forms, *15*
    of circles with center not
        at origin, *252, 475*
    equivalent, *228*
    linked, *46–62*
    multiple-variable, solv-
        ing, *13*
    quadratic, *229–234*
    reasoning to solve,
        225–239
    recursion, *492–494, 498*
    systems of, *48, 60*
Equivalent expressions,
    192–197
Equivalent function rules, *189*
Euler circuit, *266*
Euler's formula, *19*
Explicit formula for a sequence,
    525
Exponential functions, *176,*
    432, 499
    decay, *425*
    discrete view, *505–529*
    growth, *425*
    half-life, *425*
    interpreting patterns in
        tables and graphs, *176*
    rate of change, *425*
    vertical translation, *445*

F

Factor, *275*
Factorial, *110, 415*
    notation, *110*
Factoring
    difference of two
        squares, *212–213*
    the quadratic, *209*
Fairness conditions, *103–104*
    consistent, *103*
    decisive, *103*
    nondictatorship, *103*
    ordered, *103*
    relevant, *103*
    unanimous, *103*
False alarms, *402–405*
    probability of, *403*
Feasible
    combinations, *67*
    points, *65, 69*
    set, *70, 72*
Fermat's problem, *561*
Fibonacci sequence, *527*
Finite differences, *515–518*
    table relation to function
        formula, *516*
Fixed points, *535*
    attracting, *536*
    of linear function, formula,
        539
    numerical iteration to
        find, *538*
    repelling, *536*
Floor function, *185*
Formulating definitions, *294*
Fractional rules
    finding zeroes of, *221*
    undefined, finding input
        values for, *221*
Fractions, *215–218*
    combining two by multi-
        plication or addition,
        216
    common errors in rewrit-
        ing algebraic, *217*

    and inverse variation
        rules, *215*
    rewriting as a product or
        sum of terms, *216*
Frequency distribution
    standard deviation, *370*
Function, *170–186*
    absolute value, *442*
    ceiling, *185*
    composition, *186*
    decreasing, *439*
    definition, *171*
    exponential, *176, 425,*
        432
    families, *431–433, 522*
    floor, *185*
    graphs and notation, *172*
    horizontal transformation,
        462–479
    increasing, *439*
    interpreting graphs,
        173, 439
    inverse power, *179*
    iteration, *530–545*
    linear, *175, 424, 432*
    notation, *171–172*
    periodic, *429, 432, 444*
    piecewise-defined, *186*
    quadratic, *176, 444*
    reflections, *441, 446–449*
    versus relationships, *182*
    square root, *433*
    with symbolic rules,
        175–179
    trigonometric, *177, 183*
    vertical transformation,
        441–446, 449–461
Function formula, *507*
    combined recursion equa-
        tions, *523, 542*
    relation to finite differ-
        ences table, *516*
    using regression methods
        to find, *522*
Function iteration, *530–545*
    and long-term behavior,
        532
    and *NOW-NEXT* equa-
        tions, *531*
    and recursion equations,
        531
    to solve linear equations,
        539
    to solve quadratic
        equations, *543*
    using computer or graph-
        ing calculator, *544*
Function notation
    advantages and disad-
        vantages of, *185*
    using, *171–172, 175*
Functions toolkit, *431–433*
    exponential functions,
        432
    linear functions, *432*
    periodic functions, *432*
    power functions, *432*
    square root function, *433*

G

Geometric construction
    angle bisector, *320*
    congruent angle, *320*
    congruent triangle, *320,*
        321
    perpendicular bisector,
        321

Geometric growth, *508*
Geometric reasoning,
    259–344
    reasoned arguments,
        260–296
Geometric sequences, *508, 515*
    interpreting recursive and
        function formulas, *509*
    sum of the terms formula,
        513
    writing recursive and
        function formulas, *509*
Geometric series, sum of infi-
    nite, *528*
Geometric transformations
    iterating, *544–545*
    method to minimize dis-
        tance, *559*
Geometry, *25–45*
    algebraic reasoning in,
        243–247
Golden rectangle, *131*
Graphical iteration, *534–535,*
    544
Graphing
    connected mode, *500*
    dot mode, *500*
Graphs
    complete, *516–518*
    transformations, *459*
    zeroes, *459*

H

Half-plane regions, *78*
Horizontal shifts
    of absolute value func-
        tions, *463*
    graphs, *463*
    of periodic functions, *464*
    of quadratic functions,
        464
    relation to quadratic for-
        mula, *477–479*
    relation to zeroes of qua-
        dratics, *477–479*
    symbolic rules, *463, 464*
    tables of values, *463*
Horizontal transformations,
    462–479
    horizontal shifts,
        463–466
    horizontal stretching and
        compressing, *466–469*
Horizontal translations, *463*
Hypothesis, *267*
    affirming the, *276*

I

"If and only if" form, *336*
If-then statement, *265, 266*
    symbolic representation
        of, *267*
    and Venn diagrams, *274*
Independent events
    Multiplication Rule, *404,*
        405, 410
    versus mutually exclusive
        events, *414*
Inductive reasoning, *267, 271*
    versus deductive, *275*
Inequalities
    constraint, *69*
    equivalent, *228*
    quadratic, *233*

    reasoning to solve,
        225–239
    writing and solving, *47,*
        48, 54
Inequality, properties of, *62*
Integers, theorems about,
    262, 264, 270, 271,
    273, 275
Interquartile range (IQR) of a
    distribution, *347*
    effect of adding constant
        to data values, *351*
    effect of multiplying data
        values by a constant, *351*
    versus standard deviation,
        350
Intersect option, *70*
Inverse, *277*
Inverse functions
    and asymptotes, *440*
    reflection across the
        x-axis, *446*
Inverse operations, *37, 62*
    to solve equations, *37*
    to solve proportions, *39*
Inverse power functions, inter-
    preting patterns in
        tables and graphs, *179*
Inverse variation models, *50*
Isoperimetric
    Quotient (IQ), *556*
    Theorem, *556*
Iterating functions, *530–545*

K

Kite, *330*
Koch snowflake, *521*

L

Lateral surface area, *554*
Lattice point, *65*
LCL. See *Lower control limit.*
Least squares regression, *291*
Like terms, combining, *205*
Likely populations, *154–159*
Linear association, *563*
Linear combinations, *11*
Linear equalities, graphing,
    70
Linear equations, *78–79*
    calculator-based meth-
        ods versus symbolic
        reasoning to solve, *238*
    graphing, *48*
    solving system of, by
        substitution, *83*
    solving system of two,
        70
    symbolic reasoning to
        solve, *226–229*
    using matrices to solve,
        517
    writing and solving, *47*
Linear factors, *209*
    multiplication of, using
        the distributive property,
        210
Linear function iteration,
    534–537
    and combined recursion
        equation, *546–547*
    to find fixed points, *535*

Linear functions, 432
  graphs, 424
  interpreting patterns in
    tables and graphs, *175*
  and long-term behavior
    of
      function iteration,
      535–536
  rate of change, 424
  reflection across the
    x-axis, 446
  symbolic expressions,
    424
  tables of values, 424
  vertical translation, 445
Linear inequalities, *78–79*
  calculator-based methods
    versus symbolic reason-
    ing to solve, *238*
  graphs of, *78*
  solving systems of, by
    graphing, *79*
Linear models
  and arithmetic growth,
    507
  discrete view, 505–529
  interpreting, *53*
  and patterns in table of
    values and shape of
    graph, *50*
Linear Pair Property, *280*
Linear programming, *63–85*
  finding best feasible
    points, *74–77*
  linear equations and
    inequalities, *78–79*
  using an algebraic
    model, *68–73*
Lines, intersecting
  reasoning about, *279–282*
  theorems about, *295*
Lines in 3-dimensional space,
  293
Linked equations, *46–62*
Linked variables, *2–24*
  patterns in indirect and
    inverse variation situa-
    tions, *3–5*
  patterns in tables of val-
    ues of direct/inverse
    combined variation,
    14–16
  rates and times, combin-
    ing, *11–14*
Logistic equations and long-
    term behavior, 532, 541
Long-term behavior
  additional amount
    added/subtracted, 490
  and function iteration,
    532
  increase/decrease rate,
    490
  influence on, by initial
    conditions, 489–490
  initial population, 489
  and logistic equations,
    532
Lower control limit (LCL), 389

M

Majority winner vote-analysis
  method, *97*
Margin of error, *135, 156,*
  160, 161

Matrices
  to model sequential
    change, 499–500
  to solve a system of three
    linear equations, 517
Matrix addition, properties of,
  205
Maximums and transformations,
  458
Mean
  effect of adding constant
    to data values, 352–353
  effect of multiplying data
    values by constant, 352
Mean absolute deviation
  (MAD), 348
  effect of adding constant
    to data values, 351
  effect of multiplying data
    values by constant, 351
  versus standard deviation,
    350
Mean of population symbol
  (μ), *19,* 363
Mean of sample ($\bar{x}$), 363
Median-fit procedure, *291*
Median-median line, *291*
  using calculator to find,
    293
Midline of the graph, 438
Midpoint Connector Theorems,
  332
Midpoint formula, *19*
Midrange, properties of, *249*
Minimums and transformations,
  458
Modified box plot, *137*
Modified runoff vote-analysis
  method, *106*
Modus ponens, 276
Multiple variable equations,
  solving, *13*
Multiple-variable models, *1–90*
  algebra, *25–45*
  geometry, *25–45*
  linear programming,
    63–85
  linked equations, *46–62*
  linked variables, *2–24*
  trigonometry, *25–45*
Multiplication Rule for
  independent events,
  404, 405
Mutually exclusive events
  Addition Rule, 404,
    405–415
  definition, 409
  versus independent
    events, 414

N

Negation of a simple statement,
  276
n-gon, formula for sum of
  measures of exterior
  angles, *295*
90% box plot, *137*
  for different sample sizes,
    144–145
  to find confidence inter-
    vals, *155, 156*
  finding the width of,
    150
  interval of likely out-
    comes, *142*

  patterns in, *142*
  and sample size, *146*
  using simulation and
    technology to construct,
    140
90% confidence interval, *156*
  interpreting, *157*
90% confidence level,formula
  to estimate margin of
  error for, *161*
Nondictatorship fairness condition, *103*
Nonlinear systems of equations, solving, *51, 54*
Normal distribution, 362–383
  characteristics, 363–371
  equation of a curve, 381
  overall shape, 367–368
  and percentile rank, 369
  relation to distribution of
    its standardized values,
    378
  relation to standard
    devia-
    tion, 363–371
  standardizing scores,
    371–383
  using sums to create, 399
Normally distributed, 363
NOW-NEXT equations, 438
  function iteration, 531
  for sequential change,
    489–491
  subscript notation, 492
  and transformations,
    460–461
Number theory, 275
Numerical iteration to find
  fixed points, 538

O

Objective function, *69*
Opinion poll, *116*
Opposite of a difference, *199*
Opposite of a sum, *199*
Optimization problems, 552
Ordered fairness condition,
  103
Outcomes, sample
  likely versus unlikely,
    140–143, 147
  as proportions, *146*
  as totals, *146*
Outlier, 347
  effect on standard devia-
    tion, 353, 357
Out-of-control processes,
  394–395
Out-of-control signals, 385–393
  due to mean changing,
    385
  due to standard deviation
    changing, 385
  false alarms, 402–405
  tests, 390–392
Output, *177*

P

Pairwise-comparison vote-
  analysis method, *97–98,*
  110–111
Parabola, finding vertex of,
  211
Parallel lines, *282–287*

  theorems, *283, 285,*
    290
Parallel Lines Property, *285*
Parallelograms, *325–339*
  definition, *326, 336*
  properties of, *244*
  reasoning about,
    326–330
  rhombus, *330*
  theorems, *317, 327, 328*
Parameters and patterns in
  tables and graphs, 431
Patterns
  in direct and inverse
    variation situations, *3–5*
  in values of direct,
    inverse, and combined
    variation, *15*
Percentile rank and normal distribution, 369–375
  interpreting *z*-score to
    find, 374
  table, 373
Perimeter, minimizing, 557
Period, 429
Periodic change, 428–430
Periodic functions, *43*, 432
  changing amplitude, 450
  from function rule, 467
  from graph, 466
  horizontal shifts, 464
  reflection across the
    x-axis, 446
  symbolic rules, 429, 464
  and vertical translation,
    444
Permutations, *110,* 415
Perpendicular Bisector
  Algorithm, *321*
Piecewise-defined function,
  186
Plane, tiling the, 553
Plot over time, 384, 387
Plurality winner vote-analysis
  method, *97*
  compared to sequential-
    elimination method, *114*
Point of inflection, 382
Point-slope equation of a line,
  19
Points-for-preferences vote-
  analysis method, *98*
Polygon
  angle measures of regular,
    554
  area/perimeter of regular,
    553
  formula for sum of mea-
    sures of angles, *295*
  rigid, *297*
Polynomial
  higher-degree, 212
  perfect cube, factoring,
    220
  quadratic, 212
  standard form, 196
Polynomial functions,
  discrete view, 505–529
  writing rules for given
    zeroes, 210
Population, *117*
Power functions, 432
Preference table, *94*
Preferential voting, *93–96*
Present value, 502
Prime number, 268

Probabilities
    adding, 410
    multiplying, 410
    using simulation to find,
        411–412
Probability of *A* and *B*, 266
Proof
    algebraic, 240–246
    analytic, *328*
    synthetic, *312, 328*
    using coordinates, *313,*
        328
Proof presentation
    if-then statements, *265,*
        266, 274
    paragraph form, *265*
    pictorally, *265*
Properties of equality, *15, 37,*
        62
    to solve equations, *37*
    to solve proportions, *39*
Proportions, *322*
Pythagorean Theorem, *26, 28*
    proof of, *244–245*

Q

Quadratic equations
    calculator-based meth-
        ods versus symbolic
        reasoning to solve, *238*
    completing the square, *224*
    factoring difference of
        two squares, 212–213
    and function iteration,
        543
    perfect square, *213, 223*
    possible roots of, *232*
    reasoning to solve,
        229–234
    roots and quadratic for-
        mula, *237*
    solving using factoring,
        231
    solving using the qua-
        dratic formula, *231*
Quadratic formula
    proof of, *242*, 479
    relation to horizontal
        shifts, 477–479
Quadratic functions, *208*
    factored form, 458
    finding maximum/mini-
        mum point, *209*
    finding vertex by sym-
        bolic reasoning, *232*
    graph, relation to formula
        calculations, *231*
    horizontal shifts, 464
    interpreting patterns in
        tables and graphs, *176,*
        426
    reflection across the
        x-axis, 446
    rules and tables, 444
    standard polynomial
        form, 458
    using zeroes to write
        symbolic rules, *232,* 464
    vertical stretching and
        shrinking, 451
    and vertical translation,
        444
Quadratic inequalities
    calculator-based meth-
        ods versus symbolic
        reasoning to solve, *238*

reasoning to solve,
    229–234
solving without calcula-
    tor or graph, *239*
Quadratic polynomials, *212*
Quadrilateral, *336*
    equilic, *338*
    theorems about, *328, 332*
    tree, *336*

R

Random sample, *126*
Randomized response tech-
    nique, *133–134*
Range, *177,* 438
    practical, *177*
    versus standard deviation,
        350
    theoretical, *177*
Rates and times, combining,
    11–14
    rate-time-amount rela-
        tions, *12*
Reasoned arguments,
    260–296
Reasoning, *225–239*
    algebraic, *240–252*
    about angles, *279–282*
    with congruence condi-
        tions, *316–319*
    about congruent trian-
        gles, *297–324*
    deductive, *269, 270, 271*
    inductive, *267, 271*
    inductive versus deduc-
        tive, *275*
    about intersecting lines,
        279–282
    about linear equations,
        226–229
    about linear inequalities,
        226–229
    about quadratic equa-
        tions, *229–234*
    about quadratic inequali-
        ties, *229–234*
    about similar triangles,
        297–324
    with similarity condi-
        tions, *316–319*
    symbolic, *226, 232, 241*
Rectangle
    definition, *329, 335*
    golden, *131*
    properties, *247*
    theorems about, *316,*
        328, 333, 335
Recurrence relations. *See
    Recursion equations.*
Recursion, 488–504
    mode on calculator/com-
        puter, 492
Recursion equations
    combined, 510
    and function interaction,
        531–533
    and functions, 530
    general form, 494
    interpreting, 493
    long-term trends, 498
    spreadsheets, 501
    using patterns in a table,
        503
Recursive formula, 506
    versus function formula,
        507

Reflections, 441, 446–449
    across the *x*-axis,
        446–449
    symbolic rules and data
        patterns, 446
Regression equations, using
    calculator to get, 459
Regression line, 564
    effect of outliers, 564
Relevant fairness condition,
    103
Rhombus, *330*
Right triangles, theorems
    about, *290, 312, 315,*
    342
RMS-plot, 563
Root mean squared error
    (RMS), 563
Roots of a quadratic equation,
    232, 237
Run chart. *See Plot over time.*
Runoff vote-analysis method, *97*
    compared to sequential-
        elimination method, *114*

S

s (standard deviation), 364
Sample, *115–134*
    outcomes, *146, 147*
    random, *126*
    selecting, *124–128*
    simple random, *126*
Sample size
    importance of consider-
        ing, *146*
    and 90% box plots, *146*
    relative width of box plot
        versus, *150*
    and width of confidence
        intervals, *159*
Sampling distributions,
    135–152
    definition, *136*
    intervals of likely sample
        outcomes, *140–143*
    likely outcomes versus
        unlikely outcomes,
        136–137
    modified box plot, *137*
    90% box plot, *137, 140,*
        142, 144–145
    simulation using ran-
        dom number generator
        or table, *136*
    standard box plot charts,
        144–146
Scale factor, *298*
Segments
    congruent, *305*
    perpendicular bisectors
        of, *321*
Sequences
    arithmetic, 506
    determining type, 509
    Fibonacci, 527
    geometric, 508
Sequential change
    and direct variation,
        503–504
    discrete dynamical sys-
        tems, 491
    mathematical models,
        489
    matrices, 499–500
    NOW-NEXT equations,
        489–491

using recursion, 488–504
    using subscript notation,
        491–494, 498
Sequential-elimination vote-
    analysis method, *114*
    compared to plurality
        method, *114*
    compared to runoff
        method, *114*
Series, 515
Side, included, *313*
Sierpinski
    carpet, 509
    triangle, 520
Sigma (Σ) notation, 525
Similar figures
    properties of, *298–304*
    theorems, *300–302, 304*
Simple random sample, *126*
Sine ratios, *27*
Sines, Law of, *28–31, 298*
    ambiguous case for, *306*
    to find angle measures, *30*
    to find length, *30*
    proof of, *245, 251*
    when to use, *35*
Size transformation, *267*
Skew lines, *293*
Slope and *y*-intercept of a line,
    formula, *242*
Sphere
    circumference formula,
        426
    surface area formula, 426
    volume formula, 426
Spreadsheets, 501
Square root function, 433
Squares
    definition, *335*
    length of a diagonal of,
        248
    theorem about, *335*
Standard box plot charts, *144*
    reading and using, *146*
    using software to con-
        struct, *152*
Standard deviation
    as average distance from
        the mean, 349–350
    computing and interpret-
        ing, 347–350
    effect of adding constant
        to data values, 352–353
    effect of inserting a new
        value, 353
    effect of multiplying data
        values by a constant,
        352
    effect of outlier, 353
    of a frequency distribu-
        tion, 370
    versus interquartile range
        (IQR), 350
    versus mean absolute
        deviation (MAD),
        348–350
    measuring variation,
        346–361
    population (σ), 364
    properties of, 351
    versus range, 350
    relation to normal distrib-
        ution, 363
    sample (*s*), 364
    using calculator to find,
        349
    and variability, 349

Standardized scores, 360,
371–383
comparisons, *28*
table, 373
Standardized values (*z*-scores),
372
formula for computing,
372
mean of, 378
standard deviation of, 378
Statistical process control,
346, 384–415
out-of-control signals,
385–393
Statistical regression capability
of calculator, 501
Statistical regression methods,
522
for distance, 559
Statistics
algebraic reasoning in,
243–247
Steiner tree problem, 561
Straightedges, 319
Subscript notation, 491–494
NOW-NEXT equations,
492–493
sequential change,
491–494, 498
Substitution, solving system of
linear equations by, *83*
Subtraction
multiplication distribut-
ing over, *198*
and negative numbers,
common mistakes in
rewriting expressions,
200
neither commutative nor
associative, *198*
in predicting profit, *197*
Sum of squared differences, 563
Surface area, minimizing, 557
Surveys, *115–134*
bias in, *121–124*
to estimate information
about a population, *122*
factual information ver-
sus opinion, *121*
judging validity of
results, *117*
randomized response
technique, *133–134*
response rate, *117*
unbiased, *122*
voting methods and, *121*
when to take, *117*
Symbolic logic, *278*
Symbolic reasoning
to find fixed points, 535
to find vertex of qua-
dratic function, *232*
to solve linear equa-
tions, *226–227*
to solve linear inequali-
ties, *226–227*
using for proof, *241*
Symbolic rules
and reflection of graphs,
440
and translation of graphs,
440
Synthetic proofs, *312, 328*
Systems of equations, *48, 60*

T

Tangent ratios, *27*
Theorems
AA Similarity Theorem,
302, 304
AAS Congruence
Theorem, *306, 309*
ASA Congruence
Theorem, *306, 309*
circles, chords and cen-
tral angles in, *322*
integer, product of an
even and an odd, *271*
integer, sum of an even
and an odd, *270*
integers, factors of sums
of, *275*
integers, product of two
odd, *273*
integers, sum of two
even, *264*
integers, sum of two
odd, *262*
about lines perpendicular
to a third line, *295*
Midpoint Connector
quadrilaterals, *332*
triangles, *332*
about parallel lines, *290*
parallel lines, conse-
quences of, *283*
parallel lines and corre-
sponding angles, *283*
parallel lines and exteri-
or angles, *283*
parallel lines and interi-
or angles, *283*
parallelograms, *317*
parallelograms, proper-
ties of, *327, 328*
quadrilateral, necessary
conditions to be a
parallelogram, *328*
rectangle, sufficient
conditions for, *333, 335*
rectangles, *317*
rectangles, properties of,
335
relations that guarantee
two lines are parallel,
285
rhombus, conditions
ensuring that a par-
allelogram is, *331*
rhombus, properties of
any, *331*
right triangle, sum of
measures of acute
angles, *290*
right triangles, *342*
right triangles, proving
congruence of, *312, 315*
SAS Congruence
Theorem, *306, 309*
SAS Similarity Theorem,
300–301, 304
segment, perpendicular
bisector of, *323*
square, properties of, *335*
SSS Congruence
Theorem, *306, 309*
SSS Similarity Theorem,
301, 304
trapezoid, angles of, *291*
triangle, angle measures
of equiangular, *290*
triangle, proof that sum
of angles is 180°, *287*

triangle, sum of mea-
sures of exterior
angles of, *295*
Triangle Inequality
Theorem, *323*, 559
triangles, conditions that
ensure two are similar
(SAS), *300–301*
triangles, isosceles, *324*
triangles, midpoint con-
nector for, *312–313*
triangles, relationship
between congruent and
similar, *305*
vertex-edge graph, degree
of a vertex in, *268*
Vertical Angle Theorem,
280, 294
Transformations
of graphs, 459
horizontal, 462–479
maximums, 458
minimums, 458
and *NOW-NEXT* equa-
tions, 460
regression equations, 459
zeroes, 458
Transformed data
mean absolute deviation
(MAD), *266*
mean of, *246, 266*
range of, *247*
Translation symmetry, 438
Transversal, *282–287*
exterior angles on same
side of, *283*
interior angles on same
side of, *283*
Trapezoid
area of, *203, 263–264*
theorem about, *291*
Trends, detecting over time in
data, 401
Triangle Inequality Theorem,
323, 559
Triangles
area of, finding, *44*
congruent, *297–324*
exterior angle of, *295*
isosceles, *324*
similar, *42, 297–324*
theorems, *287, 290,
295, 300–306, 309,
312–313, 315, 323,
324, 332, 342*
Triangulation, *26–27*
Trigonometric functions, *183*
interpreting patterns in
tables and graphs, *177*
Trigonometric identities, *44,
246*
Trigonometry, *25–45*
spherical, *45*

U

UCL. *See Upper control limit.*
Unanimous fairness condition,
103
Upper control limit (UCL), 389

V

Variables
linked, *2–24*
periodic, *428*

Variance, properties, 361
Variation, combined, *10*, 427
Venn diagrams, *274*
Vertical shrinking, 449–453
Vertical stretching, 449–453
Vertical transformation,
441–446, 449–461
Vertical translation, 442–446
and absolute value func-
tion rules and tables,
442–443
of exponential functions,
445
of linear functions, 445
and periodic function
rules, 444
and quadratic function
rules and tables, 444
Volume *V*, 553
of a cylinder, 435
of a sphere, 426
Vote-analysis methods, *96–102*
advantages and disad-
vantages of, *101*
Borda count method, *98*
choosing based on situa-
tion, *105*
Condorcet method, *97–98*
majority winner, *97*
modified runoff method,
106
pairwise-comparison
method, *97–98,
110–111*
plurality winner, *97*
points-for-preferences
method, *98*
runoff method, *97*
sequential-elimination
method, *114*
using software to carry
out, *99–100*
Voting, *116–120*
approval, *100–101*
fairness conditions,
103–104
insincere, *108*
models, *92–114*
preferential, *93–96*
strategic, *108*

W

Waiting-time distribution,
412–413, 524

X

$\bar{x}$ (mean), 363

Z

Zero property of multiplication, *209, 222*
Zeroes
effect of transformation
on, 458
of a function, *20*
of graphs, 459
and horizontal shift,
477–479
z-score, 372
and percentile rank in
normal distributions, 374

Index of Contexts

Restaurant
eating out, *123*
preference table, *94, 98*
Retail rental space, *253–255*
Retirement, 496
Rock tossing, 515–516
Roller coaster, *170*
Roof supports, *297*

S

St. Louis Gateway Arch, *238*
Sales commission, 520
Sampling calculator software, *140, 152, 158, 161*
Sanitary landfill, *167*
SAT scores, 371, 375, 376, 379
Satellite communication systems, *45*
Savings account, *16–17, 58–59,* 497
interest, *215,* 496, 497
School award certificate design, 347
School board election, *162*
Schools, 272
awards, *273*
uniforms, *273*
Science courses, 407
Sea levels, 426, 428, 437
Seat belts, *156–157*
Security guard, 250
Selling space, *68*
Shadow length, *311*
Shewhart, Walter A., 393
Shipping costs, *185*
Shoe, 460
company, *182*
store, 515
Shoulder width, 376
SIMBOX option of the *Sampling* calculator software, *140*
Site map, *33*
Skateboards, *81*
Skydiving, 505, 511–512, 522
Small business help, *132*
Small car survey, 408
personality type, 408
Sneakers buyers, *138*
Soap bubble, 557
Softball, *218*
Soft drinks
bottling, *10*
cooling, 441, 454
Sounds, *86–87, 179*
pitch, *86*
Speed limits, *118*
Spirals, 527
Sport, favorite, *166*
Sporting goods manufacturer, *81*
Spring water, bottling, *11*
Square, *274*
Stanford-Binet intelligence test, 375
STDBOX option of the *Sampling* calculator software, *152, 158*
Stereo system, *179*
Storage containers, 435
Student survey, *165*
Summer
Northern versus Southern Hemisphere, 474

Sunlight hours, 469
Havana, Cuba, 471
Melbourne, Australia, 472
Oslo, Norway, 472
Rio de Janeiro, Brazil, 472
Southern Hemisphere, 472
Stockholm, Sweden, 472
Washington, D.C., 471
Sunrise, 436, 469, 471
Sunset, 436, 469, 471
Supply and demand, *49–52*
Supreme Court, 272
Surveyor, *27, 33, 36*
Surveys, *115–134*
Suspension bridge, *181,* 470, 475
Swimming pools, 496–497
Swings, *326*

T

Talent show, *105*
Taxes, raising, *123*
Teen survey, *130*
Telephone
advertisement, *120*
calling cards, 507
cellular, *49, 160, 186, 229*
long distance call, *185*
Television, *23*
cable, *141*
viewing, *115, 139*
Temperature
apartment, 396
Celsius, *202*
Des Moines, 467
Earth, *422–428*
Fahrenheit, *202*
Phoenix, 470
pizza oven, 456
10-gram weight, 362
Test scores, 358
Textbook shortages, *118*
Theater seats, 547–548
Thermal conductivity, *8, 9*
Thermostat, 396
Ticket sales, *14, 52–55*
basketball game, *57–58*
projected income from, *53*
and ticket price, *52–55, 61*
Tides, *180,* 428, 429, 437, 438, 451, 469
Time, *215*
of a trip, *215*
Tipping, *203–204*
Tire pump, *18*
Tomato sauce, *159*
Toothpaste, *260*
Towers of Hanoi, 502–503
Trampoline, *176, 178, 208–209*
Transit, surveyor's, *33, 36*
Travel, *12–13, 22, 40, 88*
Troubleshooting chart, 277
Trout population, 488, 489–492, 499, 501, 537
Truck
bed, variable height, *279*
speed, *89*
T-shirts, *190,* 436
Tuition, college, 519

U

Unemployment, *129*
Used cars, 356
payments, 492–493

V

Varignon, Pierre, *337*
VCR, *143*
Vehicle, renting or leasing, *46, 61, 219, 226*
payment plans, *47–48, 492–493*
Video games, *63–66, 68–70, 72*
assembly time, *69*
production feasibility, *74–75, 78*
token production, 398
Voltage, *7,* 468
Volume of a cylinder, *215*
Voting
favorite songs, *113*
models, *92–114*
national and state elections, *113*
and social decision-making, *112*

W

Wages, hourly, 351–353
Wallpaper, *262*
Water slides, *6*
Water sports, *6, 24*
Wechsler Intelligence Scale for Children, 374
Weight
of baby boys, 369
of nickles, 368
Whales
Alaskan bowhead, 495, 538–539
Wildlife population, 493
Windchill, *20*
Window design
modern, *87–88*
traditional, *87–88*
Windshield wipers, *326*
Winter
Northern versus Southern Hemisphere, 474
Women, working, *119, 149, 163*
and golf, *163*
Woodcutting, decorative, *236*

Photo Credits